THE ONE YEAR BOOK OF
Bible Readings

THE
ONE YEAR®
BOOK OF
Bible Readings

Inspirational readings from
The Living Bible
for each day of the year

Tyndale House Publishers, Inc.
WHEATON, ILLINOIS

The One Year is a registered trademark of Tyndale House
Publishers, Inc.

The readings in the *One Year Book of Bible Readings* are
taken from *In Touch,* a compilation created by Edythe
Draper.

Library of Congress Cataloging-in-Publication Data

Bible. English. Living Bible. Selections. 1992.
    The one year book of Bible readings : inspirational
readings from The Living Bible for each day of the year.
        p.   cm.
    ISBN 0-8423-4590-6 (hardcover)
    ISBN 0-8423-4591-4 (softcover)
    1. Devotional calendars.   I. Tyndale House Publishers.
II. Title.
BS390.   1992   92-11331
220.5′208—dc20

Printed in the United States of America

98   97   96   95   94   93   92
8   7   6   5   4   3   2   1

PUBLISHER'S NOTE

The One Year Book of Bible Readings has been prepared to help you in the discipline of daily devotional Bible reading. Each day's reading is a short compilation composed of a number of topically related Scriptures. The passages included are referenced at the bottom of each page so favorite verses can be easily located in your own Bible.

Each day's reading is introduced by a special thought that speaks to pressing needs and concerns everyone has experienced. This thought is followed by Scripture passages that speak to these issues, bringing God's perspective and power into the problems, fears, and joys of everyday life.

This book will help you get in touch with God, who is able to bring solutions to even the deepest of problems. Each reading is filled with the hope, comfort, and wisdom that God offers to all who are willing to look to him for guidance and help. May this year and every year be enriched as you enjoy these daily portions from God's holy Word.

And now just as you trusted Christ to save you, trust him, too, for each day's problems; live in vital union with him. Let your roots grow down into him and draw up nourishment from him. See that you go on growing in the Lord, and become strong and vigorous in the truth you were taught. Let your lives over- flow with joy and thanksgiving for all he has done. Colossians 2:6, 7

Don't be afraid, for the Lord will go before you and will be with you; he will not fail nor forsake you.

O Lord, I know it is not within the power of man to map his life and plan his course. □ If you aren't going with us, don't let us move a step from this place.

The steps of good men are directed by the Lord. He delights in each step they take. If they fall it isn't fatal, for the Lord holds them with his hand.

You love me! You are holding my right hand! You will keep on guiding me all my life with your wisdom and counsel; and afterwards receive me into the glories of heaven! □ For I am convinced that nothing can ever separate us from his love. Death can't, and life can't. The angels won't, and all the powers of hell itself cannot keep God's love away. Our fears for today, our worries about tomorrow, or where we are—high above the sky, or in the deepest ocean—nothing will ever be able to separate us from the love of God demonstrated by our Lord Jesus Christ when he died for us.

Deut. 31:8.   Jer. 10:23.   Ex. 33:15.   Ps. 37:23, 24.   Ps. 73:23, 24. Rom. 8:38, 39.

Sing a new song to the Lord.

The Lord makes us strong! Sing praises. Sing to Israel's God. Sing, accompanied by drums: pluck the sweet lyre and harp. □ He has given me a new song to sing, of praises to our God. Many will hear of the glorious things he did for me, and stand in awe before the Lord, and put their trust in him.

Be bold and strong. Banish fear and doubt. For remember, the Lord your God is with you wherever you go. □ The joy of the Lord is your strength. □ Paul . . . thanked God and took courage.

The night is far gone, the day of his return will soon be here. So quit the evil deeds of darkness and put on the armor of right living, as we who live in the daylight should. Be decent and true in everything you do so that all can approve your behavior. Don't spend your time in wild parties and getting drunk or in adultery and lust, or fighting, or jealousy. But ask the Lord Jesus Christ to help you live as you should, and don't make plans to enjoy evil.

Is. 42:10. Ps. 81:1, 2. Ps. 40:3. Josh. 1:9. Neh. 8:10. Acts 28:15. Rom. 13:12–14.

I will not abandon you or fail to help you.

Every good thing the Lord had promised them came true.

God is not a man, that he should lie. He doesn't change his mind like humans do. Has he ever promised without doing what he said?

Understand, therefore, that the Lord your God is the faithful God who for a thousand generations keeps his promises and constantly loves those who love him and who obey his commands. □ He never forgets his promises. □ So don't be anxious about tomorrow. God will take care of your tomorrow too. Live one day at a time.

Can a mother forget her little child and not have love for her own son? Yet even if that should be, I will not forget you. See, I have tattooed your name upon my palm.

For the Lord your God has arrived to live among you. He is a mighty Savior. He will give you victory. He will rejoice over you in great gladness; he will love you and not accuse you. Is that a joyous choir I hear? No, it is the Lord himself exulting over you in happy song.

Josh. 1:5. Josh. 21:45. Num. 23:19. Deut. 7:9. Ps. 111:5. Mt. 6:34. Is. 49:15, 16. Zeph. 3:17.

He will keep in perfect peace all those who trust in him, whose thoughts turn often to the Lord!

Give your burdens to the Lord. He will carry them. He will not permit the godly to slip or fall. □ I will trust and not be afraid, for the Lord is my strength and song; he is my salvation.

O you men of little faith! Why are you so frightened? □ Don't worry about anything; instead, pray about everything; tell God your needs and don't forget to thank him for his answers. If you do this you will experience God's peace, which is far more wonderful than the human mind can understand. His peace will keep your thoughts and your hearts quiet and at rest as you trust in Christ Jesus. □ In quietness and confidence is your strength.

Out of justice . . . quietness and confidence will reign forever more. □ I am leaving you with a gift—peace of mind and heart! And the peace I give isn't fragile like the peace the world gives. So don't be troubled or afraid. □ Grace and peace from God who is, and was, and is to come!

Is. 26:3. Ps. 55:22. Is. 12:2. Mt. 8:26. Phil. 4:6, 7. Is. 30:15. Is. 32:17. Jn. 14:27. Rev. 1:4.

Jesus asked the man, What do you want?
Lord, he pleaded, I want to see.

Open my eyes to see wonderful things in your Word.

Then he opened their minds to understand at last these many Scriptures. □ But when the Father sends the Comforter instead of me—and by the Comforter I mean the Holy Spirit—he will teach you much, as well as remind you of everything I myself have told you. □ But whatever is good and perfect comes to us from God, the Creator of all light, and he shines forever without change or shadow.

God, the glorious Father of our Lord Jesus Christ . . . give you wisdom to see clearly and really understand who Christ is and all that he has done for you. I pray that your hearts will be flooded with light so that you can see something of the future he has called you to share. I want you to realize that God has been made rich because we who are Christ's have been given to him! I pray that you will begin to understand how incredibly great his power is to help those who believe him. It is that same mighty power that raised Christ from the dead and seated him in the place of honor at God's right hand in heaven.

Lk. 18:41. Ps. 119:18. Lk. 24:45. Jn. 14:26. Jas. 1:17. Eph. 1:17–20.

*Help me, Lord, to keep my mouth shut and
my lips sealed.*

Lord, if you keep in mind our sins then who
can ever get an answer to his prayers?

You aren't made unholy by eating non-kosher
food! It is what you *say* and *think* that makes you
unclean.

Gossip separates the best of friends. □ Some
people like to make cutting remarks, but the words
of the wise soothe and heal. Truth stands the test
of time; lies are soon exposed. □ No human being can tame the tongue. It is always ready to
pour out its deadly poison. And so blessing and
cursing come pouring out of the same mouth.
Dear brothers, surely this is not right!

Now is the time to cast off and throw away all
these rotten garments of anger, hatred, cursing,
and dirty language. Don't tell lies to each other;
it was your old life with all its wickedness that
did that sort of thing; now it is dead and gone. □
God wants you to be holy and pure.

Gentle words cause life and health.

*Ps. 141:3. Ps. 130:3. Mt. 15:11. Prov. 16:28. Prov. 12:18, 19.
Jas. 3:8, 10. Col. 3:8, 9. 1 Thess. 4:3. Prov. 15:4.*

You have given us a banner to rally to; all who love truth will rally to it.

Jehovah-nissi (Jehovah is my flag). □ They will reverence and glorify the name of God from west to east. For he will come like a flood-tide driven by Jehovah's breath.

May there be shouts of joy when we hear the news of your victory, flags flying with praise to God for all that he has done for you. □ The Lord has vindicated us. Come, let us declare in Jerusalem all the Lord our God has done. □ Overwhelming victory is ours through Christ who loved us enough to die for us. □ How we thank God for all of this! It is he who makes us victorious through Jesus Christ our Lord! □ Jesus, a perfect Leader.

I want to remind you that your strength must come from the Lord's mighty power within you. □ Prove yourself to be a real soldier by fighting the Lord's battles. □ Take courage and work, for I am with you, says the Lord of Hosts. Don't be afraid. □ Look around you! Vast fields of human souls are ripening all around us, and are ready now for reaping.

Ps. 60:4. Ex. 17:15. Is. 59:19. Ps. 20:5. Jer. 51:10. Rom. 8:37. 1 Cor. 15:57. Hebr. 2:10. Eph. 6:10. 1 Sam. 18:17. Hag. 2:4, 5. Jn. 4:35.

Only one thing worth being concerned about.

Many say that God will never help us. Prove them wrong, O Lord, by letting the light of your face shine down upon us. Yes, the gladness you have given me is far greater than their joys at harvest time as they gaze at their bountiful crops.

As the deer pants for water, so I long for you, O God. I thirst for God, the living God. □ O God, my God! How I search for you! How I thirst for you in this parched and weary land where there is no water.

"I am the Bread of Life. No one coming to me will ever be hungry again. Those believing in me will never thirst." "Sir, give us that bread every day of our lives." □ Mary sat on the floor, listening to Jesus as he talked. □ The one thing I want from God, the thing I seek most of all, is the privilege of meditating in his Temple, living in his presence every day of my life, delighting in his incomparable perfections and glory. □ Your goodness and unfailing kindness shall be with me all of my life, and afterwards I will live with you forever in your home.

Lk. 10:42. Ps. 4:6, 7. Ps. 42:1, 2. Ps. 63:1. Jn. 6:35, 34. Lk. 10:39. Ps. 27:4. Ps. 23:6.

Oh, that you would burst forth from the skies and come down!

Come quickly, my beloved, and be like a gazelle or young deer upon the mountains of spices. □ Even we Christians . . . groan to be released from pain and suffering. We, too, wait anxiously for that day when God will give us our full rights as his children, including the new bodies he has promised us—bodies that will never be sick again and will never die. □ Bend down the heavens, Lord, and come. The mountains smoke beneath your touch.

Jesus has gone away to heaven, and some day, just as he went, he will return. □ He will come again, but not to deal again with our sins. This time he will come bringing salvation to all those who are eagerly and patiently waiting for him. □ In that day the people will proclaim, "This is our God, in whom we trust, for whom we waited. Now at last he is here." What a day of rejoicing!

He who has said all these things declares: "Yes, I am coming soon!" Amen! Come, Lord Jesus! □ Looking forward to that wonderful time we've been expecting, when his glory shall be seen— the glory of our great God and Savior Jesus Christ. □ Our homeland is in heaven.

Is. 64:1. Song 8:14. Rom. 8:23. Ps. 144:5. Acts 1:11. Hebr. 9:28. Is. 25:9. Rev. 22:20. Tit. 2:13. Phil. 3:20.

Don't let the sun go down with you still angry.

"If a brother sins against you, go to him privately and confront him with his fault. If he listens and confesses it, you have won back a brother. . . ." "Sir, how often should I forgive a brother who sins against me? Seven times?" "No," Jesus replied, "seventy times seven."

When you are praying, first forgive anyone you are holding a grudge against, so that your Father in heaven will forgive you your sins too.

Since you have been chosen by God who has given you this new kind of life, and because of his deep love and concern for you, you should practice tenderhearted mercy and kindness to others. Don't worry about making a good impression on them but be ready to suffer quietly and patiently. Be gentle and ready to forgive; never hold grudges. Remember, the Lord forgave you, so you must forgive others. □ Be kind to each other, tenderhearted, forgiving one another, just as God has forgiven you because you belong to Christ.

Eph. 4:26. Mt. 18:15, 21, 22. Mk. 11:25. Col. 3:12, 13. Eph. 4:32.

*I am completely discouraged—I lie in the
dust. Revive me by your Word.*

Since you became alive again, so to speak, when
Christ arose from the dead, now set your sights
on the rich treasures and joys of heaven. Let
heaven fill your thoughts; don't spend your time
worrying about things down here. Your real life
is in heaven with Christ and God. □ Our homeland is in heaven, where our Savior the Lord
Jesus Christ is; and we are looking forward to his
return from there. When he comes back he will
take these dying bodies of ours and change them
into glorious bodies like his own, using the same
mighty power that he will use to conquer all else
everywhere.

We naturally love to do evil things that are
just the opposite from the things that the Holy
Spirit tells us to do. □ Dear brothers, you have
no obligations whatever to your old sinful nature
to do what it begs you to do. For if you keep on
following it you are lost and will perish, but if
through the power of the Holy Spirit you crush it
and its evil deeds, you shall live. □ You are only
visitors here. Since your real home is in heaven
I beg you to keep away from the evil pleasures of
this world; they are not for you, for they fight
against your very souls.

*Ps. 119:25. Col. 3:1–3. Phil. 3:20, 21. Gal. 5:17. Rom. 8:12, 13.
1 Pet. 2:11.*

The faith God has given you.

His faith is weak. □ His faith and trust grew ever stronger, and he praised God.

O man of little faith. Why did you doubt? □ Your faith is large, and your request is granted.

"Do you believe I can make you see?" "Yes, Lord," they told him, "we do." "Because of your faith it will happen."

We need more faith. □ Build up your lives ever more strongly upon the foundation of our holy faith. □ Let your roots grow down into him and draw up nourishment from him. See that you go on growing in the Lord, and become strong and vigorous in the truth. □ It is this God who has made you and me into faithful Christians. □ After you have suffered a little while, our God, who is full of kindness through Christ, will give you his eternal glory. He personally will come and pick you up, and set you firmly in place, and make you stronger than ever.

We must bear the burden of being considerate of the doubts and fears of others. Let's please the other fellow, not ourselves. □ Don't criticize each other. . . . Try instead to live in such a way that you will never make your brother stumble by letting him see you doing something he thinks is wrong.

Rom. 12:3. Rom. 14:1. Rom. 4:20. Mt. 14:31. Mt. 15:28. Mt. 9:28, 29. Lk. 17:5. Jude 20. Col. 2:7. 2 Cor. 1:21. 1 Pet. 5:10. Rom. 15:1. Rom. 14:13.

*You have lovingly delivered me from death;
you have forgiven all my sins.*

God showed how much he loved us by sending his only Son into this wicked world to bring to us eternal life through his death. In this act we see what real love is: it is not our love for God, but his love for us when he sent his Son to satisfy God's anger against our sins.

Where is another God like you, who pardons the sins of the survivors among his people? You cannot stay angry with your people, for you love to be merciful. Once again you will have compassion on us. You will tread our sins beneath your feet; you will throw them into the depths of the ocean. □ O Lord my God, I pleaded with you, and you gave me my health again. You brought me back from the brink of the grave, from death itself, and here I am alive! □ When I had lost all hope, I turned my thoughts once more to the Lord. And my earnest prayer went to you in your holy Temple. □ I waited patiently for God to help me; then he listened and heard my cry. He lifted me out of the pit of despair, out from the bog and the mire, and set my feet on a hard, firm path and steadied me as I walked along.

*Is. 38:17. 1 Jn. 4:9, 10. Mic. 7:18, 19. Ps. 30:2, 3. Jon. 2:7.
Ps. 40:1, 2.*

All that I know is hazy and blurred.

We can see and understand only a little about God now, as if we were peering at his reflection in a poor mirror; but someday we are going to see him in his completeness, face to face.

We have seen and proved that what the prophets said came true. You will do well to pay close attention to everything they have written, for, like lights shining into dark corners, their words help us to understand many things that otherwise would be dark and difficult. When you consider the wonderful truth of the prophets' words, then the light will dawn in your souls and Christ the Morning Star will shine in your hearts. □ Your words are a flashlight to light the path ahead of me, and keep me from stumbling.

Dear friends, remember what the apostles of our Lord Jesus Christ told you, that in the last times there would come . . . scoffers. □ The Holy Spirit tells us clearly that in the last times some in the church will turn away from Christ and become eager followers of teachers with devil-inspired ideas.

Dear children, this world's last hour has come. □ The night is far gone, the day of his return will soon be here. Put on the armor of right living.

1 Cor. 13:12. 1 Cor. 13:12. 2 Pet. 1:19. Ps. 119:105. Jude 17, 18. 1 Tim. 4:1. 1 Jn. 2:18. Rom. 13:12.

Serve each other with humble spirits.

Anyone wanting to be a leader among you must be your servant. And if you want to be right at the top, you must serve like a slave. Your attitude must be like my own, for I, the Messiah, did not come to be served, but to serve, and to give my life as a ransom for many.

If anyone thinks he is too great to stoop to this, he is fooling himself. He is really a nobody. □ As God's messenger I give each of you God's warning: Be honest in your estimate of yourselves, measuring your value by how much faith God has given you. □ If you merely obey me; you should not consider yourselves worthy of praise. For you have simply done your duty!

We are in deep trouble for bringing you God's comfort and salvation. But in our trouble God had comforted us—and this, too, to help you: to show you from our personal experience how God will tenderly comfort you when you undergo these same sufferings. He will give you the strength to endure. □ This precious treasure—this light and power that now shine within us—is held in a perishable container, that is, in our weak bodies. Everyone can see that the glorious power within must be from God and is not our own.

1 Pet. 5:5. Mt. 20:26–28. Gal. 6:3. Rom. 12:3. Lk. 17:10. 2 Cor. 1:6, 7. 2 Cor. 4:7.

God's own personal possession.

You belong to Christ, and Christ is God's. □ I am my beloved's and I am the one he desires. □ I am his. □ The Son of God . . . loved me and gave himself for me.

Your own body does not belong to you. For God has bought you with a great price. So use every part of your body to give glory back to God, because he owns it. □ The Lord has rescued you from prison . . . to be his special people, his own inheritance; this is what you are today.

You are *God's* garden . . . you are *God's* building. □ But Christ, God's faithful Son, is in complete charge of God's house. And we Christians are God's house—he lives in us—if we keep up our courage firm to the end, and our joy and our trust in the Lord. □ Living building-stones . . . his holy priests.

"They shall be mine," says the Lord of Hosts, "in that day when I make up my jewels." □ And all of them, since they are mine, belong to you; and you have given them back to me with everything else of yours, and so *they are my glory*.

Deut. 32:9. 1 Cor. 3:23. Song 7:10. Song 2:16. Gal. 2:20. 1 Cor. 6:19, 20. Deut. 4:20. 1 Cor. 3:9. Hebr. 3:6. 1 Pet. 2:5. Mal. 3:17. Jn. 17:10.

He prunes those branches that bear fruit for even larger crops.

He is like a blazing fire refining precious metal and he can bleach the dirtiest garments! Like a refiner of silver he will sit and closely watch as the dross is burned away.

We can rejoice . . . when we run into problems and trials for we know that they are good for us—they help us learn to be patient. And patience develops strength of character in us and helps us trust God more each time we use it until finally our hope and faith are strong and steady. Then, when that happens, we are able to hold our heads high no matter what happens and know that all is well, for we know how dearly God loves us, and we feel this warm love everywhere within us because God has given us the Holy Spirit to fill our hearts with his love. □ Let God train you, for he is doing what any loving father does for his children. Whoever heard of a son who was never corrected? If God doesn't punish you when you need it, as other fathers punish their sons, then it means that you aren't really God's son at all—that you don't really belong in his family. Being punished isn't enjoyable while it is happening—it hurts! But afterwards we can see the result, a quiet growth in grace and character. So take a new grip with your tired hands, stand firm on your shaky legs.

Jn. 15:2. Mal. 3:2, 3. Rom. 5:3–5. Hebr. 12:7, 8, 11, 12.

*For this great God is our God forever and
ever. He will be our guide until we die.*

O Lord, I will honor and praise your name, for
you are my God; you do such wonderful things!
You planned them long ago, and now you have
accomplished them just as you said! □ The Lord
himself is my inheritance, my prize. He is my
food and drink, my highest joy!

He helps me do what honors him the most.
Even when walking through the dark valley of
death I will not be afraid, for you are close beside
me, guarding, guiding all the way. □ You are
holding my right hand! You will keep on guiding
me all my life with your wisdom and counsel; and
afterwards receive me into the glories of heaven!
Whom have I in heaven but you? And I desire no
one on earth as much as you! My health fails; my
spirits droop, yet God remains! He is the strength
of my heart; he is mine forever! □ No wonder we
are happy in the Lord! For we are trusting him.
We trust his holy name. □ The Lord will work
out his plans for my life—for your lovingkindness,
Lord, continues forever. Don't abandon me—you
made me.

*Ps. 48:14. Is. 25:1. Ps. 16:5. Ps. 23:3, 4. Ps. 73:23–26. Ps. 33:21.
Ps. 138:8.*

Lord, when doubts fill my mind, when my heart is in turmoil, quiet me and give me re-newed hope and cheer.

When my heart is faint and overwhelmed, lead me to the mighty, towering Rock of safety.

"O God," I cried, "I am in trouble—help me." □ Give your burdens to the Lord. He will carry them. He will not permit the godly to slip or fall.

I am as a little child who doesn't know his way around. □ If you want to know what God wants you to do, ask him, and he will gladly tell you.

Who is adequate for such a task? □ I am rotten through and through so far as my old sinful nature is concerned. □ I am with you; that is all you need. My power shows up best in weak people.

Cheer up, son! For I have forgiven your sins! Daughter . . . all is well! Your faith has healed you.

I shall be fully satisfied; I will praise you with great joy . . . I lie awake at night thinking of you—of how much you have helped me—and how I rejoice through the night beneath the pro-tecting shadow of your wings. I follow close be-hind you, protected by your strong right arm.

Ps. 94:19. Ps. 61:2. Is. 38:14. Ps. 55:22. 1 Kgs. 3:7. Jas. 1:5. 2 Cor. 2:16. Rom. 7:18. 2 Cor. 12:9. Mt. 9:2, 22. Ps. 63:5–8.

*Persecuted . . . preaching salvation through
faith in the cross of Christ alone.*

If anyone wants to be a follower of mine, let
him deny himself and take up his cross and follow me.

Don't you realize that making friends with
God's enemies—the evil pleasures of this world—
makes you an enemy of God? I say it again, that
if your aim is to enjoy the evil pleasure of the
unsaved world, you cannot also be a friend of
God. □ (We) must enter into the Kingdom of
God through many tribulations.

Those who believe in him will never be dis-
appointed. □ He is very precious to you who believe.

God forbid that I should boast about anything
except the cross of our Lord Jesus Christ. Because
of that cross my interest in all the attractive things
of the world was killed long ago, and the world's
interest in me is also long dead. □ I have been
crucified with Christ. □ Those who belong to
Christ have nailed their natural evil desires to his
cross and crucified them there.

If we think that our present service for him is
hard, just remember that some day we are going
to sit with him and rule with him. But if we give
up when we suffer, and turn against Christ, then
he must turn against us.

*Gal. 5:11. Mt. 16:24. Jas. 4:4. Acts 14:22. Rom. 9:33. 1 Pet. 2:7.
Gal. 6:14. Gal. 2:20. Gal. 5:24. 2 Tim. 2:12.*

The Lord is coming soon.

The Lord himself will come down from heaven with a mighty shout and with the soul-stirring cry of the archangel and the great trumpet-call of God. And the believers who are dead will be the first to rise to meet the Lord. Then we who are still alive and remain on the earth will be caught up with them in the clouds to meet the Lord in the air and remain with him forever. So comfort and encourage each other with this news. □ He who has said all these things declares: "Yes, I am coming soon!" Amen! Come, Lord Jesus!

Dear friends, while you are waiting for these things to happen and for him to come, try hard to live without sinning; and be at peace with everyone so that he will be pleased with you when he returns. □ Keep away from every kind of evil. May the God of peace himself make you entirely pure and devoted to God; and may your spirit and soul and body be kept strong and blameless until that day when our Lord Jesus Christ comes back again. God, who called you to become his child, will do all this for you, just as he promised.

Be patient. And take courage, for the coming of the Lord is near.

Phil. 4:5. 1 Thess. 4:16–18. Rev. 22:20. 2 Pet. 3:14. 1 Thess. 5:22–24. Jas. 5:8.

The choicest vine.

My Beloved has a vineyard on a very fertile hill. He plowed it and took out all the rocks and planted his vineyard with the choicest vines. . . . He waited for the harvest, but the grapes that grew were wild and sour and not at all the sweet ones he expected. □ How could this happen? How could this be? For when I planted you, I chose my seed so carefully—the very best. Why have you become this degenerate race of evil men?

When you follow your own wrong inclinations your lives will produce these evil results: impure thoughts, eagerness for lustful pleasure . . . envy, murder, drunkenness, wild parties, and all that sort of thing. But when the Holy Spirit controls our lives he will produce this kind of fruit in us: love, joy, peace, patience, kindness, goodness, faithfulness, gentleness and self-control.

I am the true vine and my Father is the Gardener. He lops off every branch that doesn't produce. And he prunes those branches that bear fruit for even larger crops. Take care to live in me, and let me live in you. My true disciples produce bountiful harvests. This brings great glory to my Father.

Gen. 49:11. Is. 5:1, 2. Jer. 2:21. Gal. 5:19, 21–23. Jn. 15:1, 2, 4, 8.

*God says he will accept and acquit us . . .
if we trust Jesus Christ to take away our
sins.*

God took the sinless Christ and poured into
him our sins. Then, in exchange, he poured God's
goodness into us! □ Christ . . . taking the curse
for our wrongdoing upon himself. □ It is from
God alone that you have your life through Christ
Jesus. He showed us God's plan of salvation; he
was the one who made us acceptable to God; he
made us pure and holy and gave himself to purchase our salvation. □ He saved us—not because
we were good enough to be saved, but because of
his kindness and pity—by washing away our sins
and giving us the new joy of the indwelling Holy
Spirit whom he poured out upon us with wonderful fullness—and all because of what Jesus Christ
our Savior did.

Everything else is worthless when compared
with the priceless gain of knowing Christ Jesus
my Lord. I have put aside all else, counting it
worth less than nothing, in order that I can have
Christ, and become one with him, no longer
counting on being saved by being good enough or
by obeying God's laws, but by trusting Christ to
save me; for God's way of making us right with
himself depends on faith—counting on Christ
alone.

*Rom. 3:22. 2 Cor. 5:21. Gal. 3:13. 1 Cor. 1:30. Tit. 3:5, 6.
Phil. 3:8, 9.*

Adopted into the bosom of his family, and calling to him, Father, Father.

Jesus . . . looked up to heaven and said, "Father . . . Holy Father . . . O righteous Father." □ Because we are his sons God has sent the Spirit of his Son into our hearts, so now we can rightly speak of God as our dear Father. □ All of us, whether Jews or Gentiles, may come to God the Father with the Holy Spirit's help because of what Christ has done for us. Now you are no longer strangers to God and foreigners to heaven, but you are members of God's very own family, citizens of God's country, and you belong in God's household with every other Christian.

I will go home to my father and say, "Father, I have sinned against both heaven and you, and am no longer worthy of being called your son. Please take me on as a hired man." So he returned home to his father. And while he was still a long distance away, his father saw him coming, and was filled with loving pity and ran and embraced him and kissed him.

Surely you are still our Father! Our Redeemer from ages past.

Rom. 8:15. Jn. 17:1, 11, 25. Gal. 4:6. Eph. 2:18, 19. Lk. 15:18–20. Is. 63:16.

*So let us go out to him beyond the city walls
[that is, outside the interests of this world,
being willing to be despised] to suffer with
him there, bearing his shame.*

Dear friends, don't be bewildered or surprised when you go through the fiery trials ahead, for this is no strange, unusual thing that is going to happen to you. Instead, be really glad because these trials will make you partners with Christ in his suffering, and afterwards you will have the wonderful joy of sharing his glory in that coming day when it will be displayed. □ God will tenderly comfort you when you undergo these same sufferings. He will give you the strength to endure.

Be happy if you are cursed and insulted for being a Christian, for when that happens the Spirit of God will come upon you with great glory.

They left the Council chamber rejoicing that God had counted them worthy to suffer dishonor for his name. □ Moses . . . chose to share ill-treatment with God's people instead of enjoying the fleeting pleasures of sin. He thought that it was better to suffer for the promised Christ than to own all the treasures of Egypt, for he was looking forward to the great reward that God would give him.

Hebr. 13:13, 14. 1 Pet. 4:12, 13. 2 Cor. 1:7. 1 Pet. 4:14. Acts 5:41. Hebr. 11:25, 26.

May your strength match the length of your days.

When you are arrested and stand trial, don't worry about what to say in your defense. Just say what God tells you to. Then you will not be speaking, but the Holy Spirit will. ☐ So don't be anxious about tomorrow. God will take care of your tomorrow too. Live one day at a time.

The God of Israel gives strength and mighty power to his people. Blessed be God! ☐ He gives power to the tired and worn out, and strength to the weak.

I am with you; that is all you need. My power shows up best in weak people. Now I am glad to boast about how weak I am; I am glad to be a living demonstration of Christ's power, instead of showing off my own power and abilities. Since I know it is all for Christ's good, I am quite happy about "the thorn" and about insults and hardships, persecutions and difficulties; for when I am weak, then I am strong—the less I have, the more I depend on him. ☐ I can do everything God asks me to with the help of Christ who gives me the strength and power. ☐ March on, my soul, with strength!

Deut. 33:25. Mk. 13:11. Mt. 6:34. Ps. 68:35. Is. 40:29. 2 Cor. 12:9, 10. Phil. 4:13. Judg. 5:21.

Do not resent it when God chastens and corrects you.

Being punished isn't enjoyable while it is happening—it hurts! But afterwards we can see the result, a quiet growth in grace and character. □ The Holy Spirit . . . will produce this kind of fruit.

He is like a father to us, tender and sympathetic to those who reverence him.

Though our bodies are dying, our inner strength in the Lord is growing every day. These troubles and sufferings of ours are, after all, quite small and won't last very long. Yet this short time of distress will result in God's richest blessing upon us forever and ever! So we do not look at what we can see right now, the troubles all around us, but we look forward to the joys in heaven which we have not yet seen. The troubles will soon be over, but the joys to come will last forever.

Even though Jesus was God's Son, he had to learn from experience what it was like to obey, when obeying meant suffering. □ He had the same temptations we do, though he never once gave way to them and sinned.

Prov. 3:11. Hebr. 12:11. Gal. 5:22. Ps. 103:13. 2 Cor. 4:16–18.
Hebr. 5:8. Hebr. 4:15.

The God who looked upon me.

O Lord, you have examined my heart and know everything about me. You know when I sit or stand. When far away you know my every thought. You chart the path ahead of me, and tell me where to stop and rest. Every moment, you know where I am. This is too glorious, too wonderful to believe! I can *never* be lost to your Spirit! I can *never* get away from my God!

The Lord is watching everywhere and keeps his eye on both the evil and the good. □ For God is closely watching you and he weighs carefully everything you do. □ God knows your evil hearts. Your pretense brings you honor from the people, but it is an abomination in the sight of God. □ The eyes of the Lord search back and forth across the whole earth, looking for people whose hearts are perfect toward him, so that he can show his great power in helping them.

Jesus . . . knew mankind to the core. No one needed to tell him how changeable human nature is. □ Lord, you know my heart. □ You know I am your friend.

Gen. 16:13. Ps. 139:1–4, 6, 7. Prov. 15:3. Prov. 5:21. Lk. 16:15. 2 Chron. 16:9. Jn. 2:24, 25. Jn. 21:17. Jn. 21:16.

With all my heart I will praise you. I will give glory to your name forever.

True praise is a worthy sacrifice; this really honors me. ☐ It is good to say thank you to the Lord, to sing praises to the God who is above all gods. Every morning tell him, "Thank you for your kindness," and every evening rejoice in all his faithfulness.

Let everything alive give praises to the Lord.

Dear brothers, I plead with you to give your bodies to God. Let them be a living sacrifice, holy —the kind he can accept. When you think of what he has done for you, is this too much to ask? ☐ As a sacrifice for sin . . . Jesus suffered and died outside the city, where his blood washed our sins away. With Jesus' help we will continually offer our sacrifice of praise to God by telling others of the glory of his name. ☐ Always give thanks for everything to our God and Father in the name of our Lord Jesus Christ.

The Lamb is worthy . . . the Lamb who was slain. He is worthy to receive the power, and the riches, and the wisdom, and the strength, and the honor, and the glory, and the blessing.

Ps. 86:12. Ps. 50:23. Ps. 92:1, 2. Ps. 150:6. Rom. 12:1. Hebr. 13:11, 12, 15. Eph. 5:20. Rev. 5:12.

*Let us run with patience the particular race
that God has set before us. Keep your eyes
on Jesus, our leader and instructor.*

Anyone who wants to follow me must put aside
his own desires and conveniences and carry his
cross with him every day and keep close to me! □
No one can become my disciple unless he first sits
down and counts his blessings—and then re-
nounces them all for me. □ Quit the evil deeds of
darkness.

To win the contest you must deny yourselves
many things that would keep you from doing your
best. I run straight to the goal with purpose in
every step. I fight to win. I'm not just shadow-
boxing or playing around. Like an athlete I punish my body, treating it roughly, training it to do
what it should, not what it wants to. □ I am still
not all I should be but I am bringing all my energies to bear on this one thing: Forgetting the
past and looking forward to what lies ahead, I
strain to reach the end of the race and receive
the prize for which God is calling us up to heaven
because of what Christ Jesus did for us. □ Oh,
that we might know the Lord! Let us press on to
know him, and he will respond to us as surely as
the coming of dawn or the rain of early spring.

*Hebr. 12:1, 2. Lk. 9:23. Lk. 14:33. Rom. 13:12. 1 Cor. 9:25, 27.
Phil. 3:13, 14. Hos. 6:3.*

It is good for a young man to be under discipline.

Teach a child to choose the right path, and when he is older he will remain upon it.

Since we respect our fathers here on earth, though they punish us, should we not all the more cheerfully submit to God's training so that we can begin really to live? Our earthly fathers trained us for a few brief years, doing the best for us that they knew how, but God's correction is always right and for our best good, that we may share his holiness.

Lord, in their distress they sought for you. When your punishment was on them, they poured forth a whispered prayer. □ I used to wander off until you punished me; now I closely follow all you say. The punishment you gave me was the best thing that could have happened to me, for it taught me to pay attention to your laws.

I know the plans I have for you, says the Lord. They are plans for good and not for evil, to give you a future and a hope. □ Humble yourselves under the mighty hand of God, in his good time he will lift you up.

Lam. 3:27. Prov. 22:6. Hebr. 12:9, 10. Is. 26:16. Ps. 119:67, 71. Jer. 29:11. 1 Pet. 5:6.

*If you refuse to drive out the people living
there, those who remain will be as cinders in
your eyes and thorns in your sides.*

Fight on for God. □ I use God's mighty weapons, not those made by men, to knock down the devil's strongholds. With these weapons I can capture rebels and bring them back to God, and change them into men whose hearts' desire is obedience to Christ.

Dear brothers, you have no obligations whatever to your old sinful nature to do what it begs you to do. For if you keep on following it you are lost and will perish, but if through the power of the Holy Spirit you crush it and its evil deeds, you shall live.

For we naturally love to do evil things that are just the opposite from the things that the Holy Spirit tells us to do; and the good things we want to do when the Spirit has his way with us are just the opposite of our natural desires. These two forces within us are constantly fighting each other to win control over us, and our wishes are never free from their pressures. □ There is something else deep within me, in my lower nature, that is at war with my mind. □ Overwhelming victory is ours through Christ who loved us enough to die for us.

Num. 33:55. 1 Tim. 6:12. 2 Cor. 10:4, 5. Rom. 8:12, 13. Gal. 5:17. Rom. 7:23. Rom. 8:37.

Ordinary sin receives heavy punishment, but how much more this sin of yours which has been committed against the Lord?

If you sin, there is someone to plead for you before the Father. His name is Jesus Christ, the one who is all that is good and who pleases God completely. He is the one who took God's wrath against our sins upon himself, and brought us into fellowship with God. □ For God sent Christ Jesus to take the punishment for our sins and to end all God's anger against us. He used Christ's blood and our faith as the means of saving us from his wrath. And now in these days also he can receive sinners in this same way, because Jesus took away their sins. But isn't this unfair for God to let criminals go free and say they are innocent? No, for he does it on the basis of their trust in Jesus who took away their sins.

What can we ever say to such wonderful things as these? If God is on our side, who can ever be against us? Who dares accuse us whom God has chosen for his own? Will God? No! He is the one who has forgiven us and given us right standing with himself. Who then will condemn us? Will Christ? *No!* For he is the one who died for us and came back to life again for us and is sitting at the place of highest honor next to God, pleading for us there in heaven.

1 Sam. 2:25. 1 Jn. 2:1, 2. Rom. 3:25, 26. Rom. 8:31, 33, 34.

The stars differ from each other in their beauty and brightness.

They had been arguing about which of them was the greatest! He sat down and called them around him and said, "Anyone wanting to be the greatest must be the least—the servant of all!" □ Serve each other with humble spirits, for God gives special blessings to those who are humble, but sets himself against those who are proud. If you will humble yourselves under the mighty hand of God, in his good time he will lift you up.

Your attitude should be the kind that was shown us by Jesus Christ, who . . . laid aside his mighty power and glory, taking the disguise of a slave and becoming like men. It was because of this that God raised him up to the heights of heaven and gave him a name which is above every other name, that at the name of Jesus every knee shall bow in heaven and on earth and under the earth.

Those who are wise—the people of God—shall shine as brightly as the sun's brilliance, and those who turn many to righteousness will glitter like stars forever.

1 Cor. 15:41. Mk. 9:34. 35. 1 Pet. 5:5, 6. Phil. 2:5–7, 9, 10. Dan. 12:3.

Take courage and work, for I am with you,
says the Lord of Hosts.

I am the Vine; you are the branches. Whoever lives in me and I in him shall produce a large crop of fruit. For apart from me you can't do a thing. □ I can do everything God asks me to with the help of Christ who gives me the strength and power. □ Your strength must come from God's mighty power within you. □ The joy of the Lord is your strength.

The Lord of Hosts says, "Get on with the job and finish it! You have been listening long enough!" □ Bring cheer to all discouraged ones. Encourage those who are afraid. Tell them, "Be strong, fear not, for your God is coming to destroy your enemies. He is coming to save you." □ The Lord . . . said, "I will make you strong."

If God is on our side, who can ever be against us? □ It is God himself, in his mercy, who has given us this wonderful work [of telling his Good News to others] and so we never give up.

Let us not get tired of doing what is right, for after a while we will reap a harvest of blessing if we don't get discouraged and give up. □ We thank God for all of this! It is he who makes us victorious through Jesus Christ our Lord!

Hag. 2:4. Jn. 15:5. Phil. 4:13. Eph. 6:10. Neh. 8:10. Zech. 8:9. Is. 35:3, 4. Judg. 6:14. Rom. 8:31. 2 Cor. 4:1. Gal. 6:9. 1 Cor. 15:57.

Even darkness cannot hide from God.

God carefully watches the goings on of all mankind; he sees them all. No darkness is thick enough to hide evil men from his eyes. □ Can anyone hide from me? Am I not everywhere in all of heaven and earth?

You don't need to be afraid of the dark any more, nor fear the dangers of the day; nor dread the plagues of darkness, nor disasters in the morning. For Jehovah is my refuge! I choose the God above all gods to shelter me. How then can evil overtake me or any plague come near? □ He will never let me stumble, slip or fall. For he is always watching, never sleeping.

Jehovah himself is caring for you! He is your defender. He protects you day and night. He keeps you from all evil, and preserves your life.

Even when walking through the dark valley of death I will not be afraid, for you are close beside me, guarding, guiding all the way.

Ps. 139:12. Job 34:21, 22. Jer. 23:24. Ps. 91:5, 6, 9, 10. Ps. 121:3–7. Ps. 23:4.

Never return.

If they had wanted to, they could have gone back to the good things of this world. But they didn't want to. They were living for heaven. Moses . . . chose to share ill-treatment with God's people instead of enjoying the fleeting pleasures of sin. He thought that it was better to suffer for the promised Christ than to own all the treasures of Egypt. □ Those whose faith has made them good in God's sight must live by faith, trusting him in everything. Otherwise, if they shrink back, God will have no pleasure in them. □ Anyone who lets himself be distracted from the work I plan for him is not fit for the Kingdom of God.

God forbid that I should boast about anything except the cross of our Lord Jesus Christ. Because of that cross my interest in all the attractive things of the world was killed long ago, and the world's interest in me is also long dead. □ The Lord has said, "Leave them; separate yourselves from them; don't touch their filthy things, and I will welcome you."

God who began the good work within you will keep right on helping you grow in his grace until his task within you is finally finished on that day when Jesus Christ returns.

Deut. 17:16. Hebr. 11:15, 16, 25, 26. Hebr. 10:38. Lk. 9:62. Gal. 6:14. 2 Cor. 6:17. Phil. 1:6.

My purpose is to give life in all its fullness.

The wages of sin is death, but the free gift of God is eternal life through Jesus Christ our Lord. □ The sin of this one man, Adam, caused death to be king over all, but all who will take God's gift of forgiveness and acquittal are kings of life because of this one man, Jesus Christ. □ Death came into the world because of what one man (Adam) did, and it is because of what this other man (Christ) has done that now there is the resurrection from the dead. Everyone dies because all of us are related to Adam, being members of his sinful race, and wherever there is sin, death results. But all who are related to Christ will rise again. □ Our Savior Jesus Christ . . . broke the power of death and showed us the way of everlasting life through trusting him.

And what is it that God has said? That he has given us eternal life, and that this life is in his Son. So whoever has God's Son has life; whoever does not have his Son, does not have life. □ God did not send his Son into the world to condemn it, but to save it.

Jn. 10:10. Rom. 6:23. Rom. 5:17. 1 Cor. 15:21, 22. 2 Tim. 1:10. 1 Jn. 5:11, 12. Jn. 3:17.

*How kind our Lord was, for he showed me
how to trust him and become full of the love
of Christ Jesus.*

You know how full of love and kindness our
Lord Jesus was: though he was so very rich, yet
to help you he became so very poor, so that by
being poor he could make you rich. □ The more
we see our sinfulness, the more we see God's
abounding grace forgiving us.

Because of his kindness you have been saved
through trusting Christ. And even trusting is not
of yourselves; it too is a gift from God. Salvation
is not a reward for the good we have done, so
none of us can take any credit for it. □ We, too,
have trusted Jesus Christ, that we might be accepted by God because of faith—and not because
we have obeyed the Jewish laws. For no one will
ever be saved by obeying them. □ He saved us—
not because we were good enough to be saved, but
because of his kindness and pity—by washing away
our sins and giving us the new joy of the indwelling
Holy Spirit whom he poured out upon us with wonderful fullness—and all because of what Jesus
Christ our Savior did.

*1 Tim. 1:14. 2 Cor. 8:9. Rom. 5:20. Eph. 2:8, 9. Gal. 2:16. Tit.
3:5, 6.*

When you have eaten your fill, bless the Lord your God for the good land he has given you.

Beware that in your plenty you don't forget the Lord your God. □ One of them came back to Jesus, shouting, "Glory to God, I'm healed!" He fell flat on the ground in front of Jesus, face downward in the dust, thanking him for what he had done. This man was a despised Samaritan. Jesus asked, "Didn't I heal ten men? Where are the nine? Does only this foreigner return to give glory to God?"

For everything God made is good, and we may eat it gladly if we are thankful for it, and if we ask God to bless it, for it is made good by the Word of God and prayer. □ The Lord's blessing is our greatest wealth. All our work adds nothing to it!

I bless the holy name of God with all my heart. Yes, I will bless the Lord and not forget the glorious things he does for me. He forgives all my sins. He heals me. He ransoms me from hell. He surrounds me with lovingkindness and tender mercies. He fills my life with good things! My youth is renewed like the eagle's!

Deut. 8:10. Deut. 8:11. Lk. 17:15–18. 1 Tim. 4:4, 5. Prov. 10:22. Ps. 103:1–5.

Jesus . . . pitied them.

Jesus Christ is the same yesterday, today, and forever. □ Jesus the Son of God is our great High Priest who has gone to heaven itself to help us; therefore let us never stop trusting him. This High Priest of ours understands our weaknesses, since he had the same temptations we do, though he never once gave way to them and sinned. □ Because he is a man he can deal gently with other men, though they are foolish and ignorant, for he, too, is surrounded with the same temptations and understands their problems very well. □ Then he returned to the three disciples and found them asleep. "Simon," he said. "Asleep? Couldn't you watch with me even one hour? Watch with me and pray lest the Tempter overpower you. For though the spirit is willing enough, the body is weak."

He is like a father to us, tender and sympathetic to those who reverence him. For he knows we are but dust.

You are merciful and gentle, Lord, slow in getting angry, full of constant lovingkindness and of truth; so look down in pity and grant strength to your servant and save me.

Mt. 14:14. Hebr. 13:8. Hebr. 4:14, 15. Hebr. 5:2. Mk. 14:37, 38. Ps. 103:13, 14. Ps. 86:15, 16.

*Your eyes light up your inward being. A
pure eye lets sunshine into your soul.*

The man who isn't a Christian can't under-
stand and can't accept these thoughts from God,
which the Holy Spirit teaches us. They sound
foolish to him, because only those who have the
Holy Spirit within them can understand what the
Holy Spirit means. Others just can't take it in. □
Open my eyes to see wonderful things in your
Word.

I am the Light of the world. So if you follow
me, you won't be stumbling through the darkness,
for living light will flood your path. □ We Christians have no veil over our faces; we can be mirrors that brightly reflect the glory of the Lord.
And as the Spirit of the Lord works within us, we
become more and more like him. □ For God, who
said, "Let there be light in the darkness," has
made us understand that it is the brightness of
his glory that is seen in the face of Jesus Christ.

God, the glorious Father of our Lord Jesus
Christ . . . give you wisdom to see clearly and
really understand who Christ is and all that he has
done for you. . . . So that you can see something of the future he has called you to share.

*Lk. 11:34. 1 Cor. 2:14. Ps. 119:18. Jn. 8:12. 2 Cor. 3:18. 2 Cor.
4:6. Eph. 1:17, 18.*

Those who feared and loved the Lord spoke often of him to each other. And he had a Book of Remembrance drawn up in which he recorded the names of those who feared him and loved to think about him.

Suddenly Jesus himself came along and joined them and began walking beside them. □ Where two or three gather together because they are mine, I will be right there among them.

Remember what Christ taught and let his words enrich your lives and make you wise; teach them to each other and sing them out in psalms and hymns and spiritual songs, singing to the Lord with thankful hearts. □ Speak to each other about these things every day while there is still time, so that none of you will become hardened against God, being blinded by the glamor of sin. □ Talk about them when you are at home or out for a walk; at bedtime and the first thing in the morning.

I tell you this, that you must give account on Judgment Day for every idle word you speak. Your words now reflect your fate then: either you will be justified by them or you will be condemned.

I will talk to others all day long about your justice and your goodness.

Mal. 3:16. Lk. 24:15. Mt. 18:20. Col. 3:16. Hebr. 3:13. Deut. 6:7. Mt. 12:36, 37. Ps. 71:24.

I am all that you need.

Whom have I in heaven but you? And I desire no one on earth as much as you! My health fails; my spirits droop, yet God remains! He is the strength of my heart; he is mine forever! □ The Lord himself is my inheritance, my prize. He is my food and drink, my highest joy! He guards all that is mine. He sees that I am given pleasant brooks and meadows as my share. What a wonderful inheritance!

My soul claims the Lord as my inheritance; therefore I will hope in him.

Your laws are my joyous treasure forever.

O God, my God! How I search for you! How I thirst for you in this parched and weary land where there is no water. How I long to find you! I shall be fully satisfied; I will praise you with great joy. I lie awake at night thinking of you—of how much you have helped me—and how I rejoice through the night beneath the protecting shadow of your wings.

My beloved is mine and I am his.

Num. 18:20. Ps. 73:25, 26. Ps. 16:5, 6. Lam. 3:24. Ps. 119:111. Ps. 63:1, 5–7. Song. 2:16.

Who can ever say, I have cleansed my heart;
I am sinless.

The Lord looks down from heaven on all mankind to see if there are any who are wise, who want to please God. But no, all have strayed away; all are rotten with sin. □ Those who are . . . bent on following their old evil desires, can never please God.

I know I am rotten through and through so far as my old sinful nature is concerned. No matter which way I turn I can't make myself do right. I want to but I can't. □ We are all infected and impure with sin. When we put on our prized robes of righteousness we find they are but filthy rags.

If we could be saved by his laws, then God would not have had to give us a different way to get out of the grip of sin—for the Scriptures insist we are all its prisoners. The only way out is through faith in Jesus Christ; the way of escape is open to all who believe him. □ God was in Christ, restoring the world to himself, no longer counting men's sins against them but blotting them out.

If we say that we have no sin, we are only fooling ourselves, and refusing to accept the truth. But if we confess our sins to him, he can be depended on to forgive us and to cleanse us from every wrong.

Prov. 20:9. Ps. 14:2, 3. Rom. 8:8. Rom. 7:18. Is. 64:6. Gal. 3:22.
2 Cor. 5:19. 1 Jn. 1:8, 9.

The mighty oceans thunder your praise.

You are mightier than all the breakers pounding on the seashores of the world! □ O Jehovah, Commander of the heavenly armies, where is there any other Mighty One like you? Faithfulness is your very character. You rule the oceans when their waves arise in fearful storms; you speak, and they lie still.

"Have you no respect at all for me?" the Lord God asks. "How can it be that you don't even tremble in my presence? I set the shorelines of the world by perpetual decrees, so that the oceans, though they toss and roar, can never pass those bounds."

When you go through deep waters and great trouble, I will be with you. When you go through rivers of difficulty, you will not drown.

Peter went over the side of the boat and walked on the water toward Jesus. But when he looked around at the high waves, he was terrified and began to sink. "Save me, Lord," he shouted. Instantly Jesus reached out his hand and rescued him. "O man of little faith," Jesus said, "why did you doubt?"

When I am afraid, I will put my confidence in you.

Ps. 93:3. Ps. 93:4. Ps. 89:8, 9. Jer. 5:22. Is. 43:2. Mt. 14:29–31. Ps. 56:3.

How fragrant your cologne, and how great your name.

Christ . . . loved you and gave himself to God as a sacrifice to take away your sins. And God was pleased, for Christ's love for you was like sweet perfume to him. □ He is very precious to you who believe. □ God raised him up to the heights of heaven and gave him a name which is above every other name, that at the name of Jesus every knee shall bow in heaven and on earth and under the earth.□ For in Christ there is all of God in a human body.

If you love me, obey me. □ God loves us, and we feel this warm love everywhere within us because God has given us the Holy Spirit to fill our hearts with his love. □ As far as God is concerned there is a sweet, wholesome fragrance in our lives. It is the fragrance of Christ within us, an aroma to both the saved and the unsaved all around us.

O Lord our God, the majesty and glory of your name fills all the earth and overflows the heavens. □ Emmanuel . . . God with us. □ These will be his royal titles: Wonderful, Counselor, The Mighty God, The Everlasting Father, The Prince of Peace. □ The Lord is a strong fortress. The godly run to him and are safe.

Song 1:3. Eph. 5:2. 1 Pet. 2:7. Phil. 2:9, 10. Col. 2:9. Jn. 14:15. Rom. 5:5. 2 Cor. 2:15. Ps. 8:1. Mt. 1:23. Is. 9:6. Prov. 18:10.

Lord, don't desert me now! You alone are
my hope.

Many say that God will never help us. Prove
them wrong, O Lord, by letting the light of your
face shine down upon us. □ I will sing each
morning about your power and mercy. For you
have been my high tower of refuge, a place of
safety in the day of my distress.

In my prosperity I said, This is forever; nothing can stop me now! Then, Lord, you turned
your face away from me and cut off your river of
blessings. Suddenly my courage was gone; I was
terrified and panic-stricken. I cried to you, O Lord;
oh, how I pled: "What will you gain, O Lord,
from killing me? How can I praise you then to all
my friends? How can my dust in the grave speak
out and tell the world about your faithfulness?
Hear me, Lord; oh, have pity and help me."

For a brief moment I abandoned you. But with
great compassion I will gather you. In a moment
of anger I turned my face a little while; but with
everlasting love I will have pity on you, says the
Lord, your Redeemer. □ Your weeping shall suddenly be turned to wonderful joy. □ Weeping
may go on all night, but in the morning there is
joy.

Jer. 17:17. Ps. 4:6. Ps. 59:16. Ps. 30:6–10. Is. 54:7, 8. Jn. 16:20.
Ps. 30:5.

*The Ten Commandments were given so that
all could see the extent of their failure.*

How can you demand purity in one born impure? □ I was born a sinner, yes, from the moment
my mother conceived me.

Once you were under God's curse, doomed forever for your sins. We started out bad, being born
with evil natures, and were under God's anger just
like everyone else. □ I don't understand myself
at all, for I really want to do what is right, but I
can't. I do what I don't want to—what I hate. I
know I am rotten through and through so far as
my old sinful nature is concerned. No matter
which way I turn I can't make myself do right.

When Adam sinned, sin entered the entire
human race. His sin spread death throughout all
the world. What a contrast between Adam and
Christ. For this one man, Jesus Christ, brought
forgiveness to many through God's mercy. Adam
caused many to be sinners because he disobeyed
God, and Christ caused many to be made acceptable to God because he obeyed.

The power of the life-giving Spirit—and this
power is mine through Christ Jesus—has freed
me from the vicious circle of sin and death.

How we thank God for all of this! It is he who
makes us victorious through Jesus Christ our
Lord.

*Rom. 5:20. Job 14:4. Ps. 51:5. Eph. 2:1, 3. Rom. 7:15, 18.
Rom. 5:12, 14, 15, 19. Rom. 8:2. 1 Cor. 15:57.*

*The Lord grants wisdom! His every word is
a treasure of knowledge and understanding.*

Trust the Lord completely; don't ever trust
yourself. □ If you want to know what God wants
you to do, ask him, and he will gladly tell you,
for he is always ready to give a bountiful supply
of wisdom to all who ask him. □ God is far wiser
than . . . the wisest man, and God in his weakness—Christ dying on the cross—is far stronger
than any man. □ God has deliberately chosen to
use ideas the world considers foolish and of little
worth in order to shame those people considered
by the world as wise and great. So that no one
anywhere can ever brag in the presence of God.

As your plan unfolds, even the simple can understand it. □ I have thought much about your
words, and stored them in my heart so that they
would hold me back from sin.

All who were there spoke well of him and
were amazed by the beautiful words that fell
from his lips. □ "He says such wonderful things,"
they mumbled. "We've never heard anything like
it." □ It is from God alone that you have your life
through Christ Jesus.

*Prov. 2:6. Prov. 3:5. Jas. 1:5. 1 Cor. 1:25. 1 Cor. 1:27, 29. Ps.
119:130. Ps. 119:11. Lk. 4:22. Jn. 7:46. 1 Cor. 1:30.*

They steeled themselves against his love and complained against him in the desert while he was testing them.

They . . . demanded better food, testing God's patience to the breaking point.

Jesus, full of the Holy Spirit, left the Jordan River, being urged by the Spirit out into the barren wastelands of Judea, where Satan tempted him for forty days. He ate nothing all that time, and was very hungry. Satan said, "If you are God's Son, tell this stone to become a loaf of bread." But Jesus replied, ". . . other things in life are much more important than bread."

When someone wants to do wrong it is never God who is tempting him, for God never wants to do wrong and never tempts anyone else to do it. Temptation is the pull of man's own evil thoughts and wishes. These evil thoughts lead to evil actions and afterwards to the death penalty from God.

Since he himself has been through suffering and temptation, he knows what it is like when we suffer and are tempted, and he is wonderfully able to help us. □ Simon, Simon, Satan has asked to have you, to sift you like wheat, but I have pleaded in prayer for you that your faith should not completely fail.

Hebr. 3:8. Ps. 106:14. Lk. 4:1–4. Jas. 1:13–15. Hebr. 2:18. Lk. 22:31, 32.

Light is sown for the godly and joy for the good.

Those who sow tears shall reap joy. Yes, they go out weeping, carrying seed for sowing, and return singing, carrying their sheaves. □ Plant the good seeds of righteousness and you will reap a crop of my love.

All honor to God, the God and Father of our Lord Jesus Christ; for it is his boundless mercy that has given us the privilege of being born again, so that we are now members of God's own family. Now we live in the hope of eternal life because Christ rose again from the dead. So be truly glad! There is wonderful joy ahead, even though the going is rough for a while down here. These trials are only to test your faith, to see whether or not it is strong and pure. It is being tested as fire tests gold and purifies it—and your faith is far more precious to God than mere gold; so if your faith remains strong after being tried in the test tube of fiery trials, it will bring you much praise and glory and honor on the day of his return.

We will reap a harvest of blessing if we don't get discouraged and give up.

Ps. 97:11. Ps. 126:5, 6. Hos. 10:12. 1 Pet. 1:3, 6, 7. Gal. 6:9.

Where is the man who fears the Lord? God will teach him how to choose the best.

The Lord guided them by a pillar of cloud during the daytime, and by a pillar of fire at night.

Your words are a flashlight to light the path ahead of me, and keep me from stumbling. □ If you leave God's paths and go astray, you will hear a Voice behind you say, "No, this is the way; walk here." □ I will instruct you (says the Lord) and guide you along the best pathway for your life; I will advise you and watch your progress. Don't be like a senseless horse or mule that has to have a bit in its mouth to keep it in line! Many sorrows come to the wicked, but abiding love surrounds those who trust in the Lord. So rejoice in him, all those who are his, and shout for joy, all those who try to obey him. □ And when we obey him, every path he guides us on is fragrant with his lovingkindness and his truth.

O Lord, I know it is not within the power of man to map his life and plan his course. □ Show me the path where I should go, O Lord; point out the right road for me to walk.

Ps. 25:12. Ex. 13:21. Ps. 119:105. Is. 30:21. Ps. 32:8–11. Ps. 25:10. Jer. 10:23. Ps. 25:4.

You can sleep without fear; you need not be afraid of disaster . . . for the Lord is with you; he protects you.

Soon a terrible storm arose. High waves began to break into the boat until it was nearly full of water and about to sink. Jesus was asleep at the back of the boat with his head on a cushion.

Don't worry about anything; instead, pray about everything; tell God your needs and don't forget to thank him for his answers. If you do this you will experience God's peace, which is far more wonderful than the human mind can understand. His peace will keep your thoughts and your hearts quiet and at rest as you trust in Christ Jesus.

I will lie down in peace and sleep, for though I am alone, O Lord, you will keep me safe. □ God wants his loved ones to get their proper rest.

As the murderous stones came hurtling at him, Stephen prayed, "Lord Jesus, receive my spirit." And he fell to his knees, shouting, "Lord, don't charge them with this sin!" And with that, he died. □ We are not afraid, but are quite content to die, for then we will be at home with the Lord.

Prov. 3:24. Mk. 4:37, 38. Phil. 4:6, 7. Ps. 4:8. Ps. 127:2. Acts 7:59, 60. 2 Cor. 5:8.

Who can realize the terrors of your anger?

That afternoon, the whole earth was covered with darkness for three hours, from noon until three o'clock. About three o'clock, Jesus shouted, "Eli, Eli, lama sabachthani," which means, "My God, my God, why have you forsaken me?" □ God laid on him the guilt and sins of every one of us.

There is now no condemnation awaiting those who belong to Christ Jesus. □ Since we have been made right in God's sight by faith in his promises, we can have real peace with him because of what Jesus Christ our Lord has done for us. □ Christ has brought us out from under the doom of that impossible system by taking the curse for our wrongdoing upon himself.

God showed how much he loved us by sending his only Son into this wicked world to bring to us eternal life through his death. In this act we see what real love is: it is not our love for God, but his love for us when he sent his Son to satisfy God's anger against our sins. □ He can receive sinners . . . because Jesus took away their sins . . . He does it on the basis of their trust in Jesus.

Ps. 90:11. Mt. 27:45, 46. Is. 53:6. Rom. 8:1. Rom. 5:1. Gal. 3:13. 1 Jn. 4:9, 10. Rom. 3:26.

*The Lord God says, I am ready to hear
. . . and to grant them their requests. Let them
but ask.*

The reason you don't have what you want is
that you don't ask God for it.

Ask, and you will be given what you ask for.
Seek, and you will find. Knock, and the door will
be opened. For everyone who asks, receives. Anyone who seeks, finds. If only you will knock, the
door will open. □ And we are sure of this, that he
will listen to us whenever we ask him for anything
in line with his will. And if we really know he is
listening when we talk to him and make our requests, then we can be sure that he will answer
us. □ If you want to know what God wants you
to do, ask him, and he will gladly tell you, for he
is always ready to give a bountiful supply of wisdom to all who ask him.

The eyes of the Lord are intently watching all
who live good lives, and he gives attention when
they cry to him. Yes, the Lord hears the good
man when he calls to him for help.

Present your petitions over my signature! And
I won't need to ask the Father to grant you these
requests, for the Father himself loves you dearly
because you love me.

*Ezk. 36:37. Jas. 4:2. Mt. 7:7, 8. 1 Jn. 5:14, 15. Jas. 1:5. Ps.
34:15, 17. Jn. 16:26, 27.*

Shall we receive only pleasant things from the hand of God and never anything unpleasant?

I know, O Lord, that your decisions are right and that your punishment was right and did me good. □ O Lord, you are our Father. We are the clay and you are the Potter. We are all formed by your hand. □ It is the Lord's will . . . let him do what he thinks best.

Like a refiner of silver he will sit and closely watch as the dross is burned away. □ When he punishes you, it proves that he loves you. When he whips you it proves you are really his child. □ The student shares his teacher's fate. The servant shares his master's! □ And even though Jesus was God's Son, he had to learn from experience what it was like to obey, when obeying meant suffering.

Be really glad—because these trials will make you partners with Christ in his suffering, and afterwards you will have the wonderful joy of sharing his glory in that coming day when it will be displayed. □ "These are the ones coming out of the Great Tribulation," he said; "they washed their robes and whitened them by the blood of the Lamb."

Job 2:10. Ps. 119:75. Is. 64:8. 1 Sam. 3:18. Mal. 3:3. Hebr. 12:6. Mt. 10:25. Hebr. 5:8. 1 Pet. 4:13. Rev. 7:14.

Resist the devil and he will flee from you.

"Get out of here, Satan," Jesus told him. "The Scriptures say, Worship only the Lord God. Obey only him." Then Satan went away, and angels came and cared for Jesus.

Your strength must come from the Lord's mighty power within you. Put on all of God's armor so that you will be able to stand safe against all strategies and tricks of Satan. □ Take no part in the worthless pleasures of evil and darkness, but instead, rebuke and expose them. □ Keep from being outsmarted by Satan; for we know what he is trying to do. □ Be careful— watch out for attacks from Satan, your great enemy. He prowls around like a hungry, roaring lion, looking for some victim to tear apart. Stand firm when he attacks. Trust the Lord; and re- member that other Christians all around the world are going through these sufferings, too. □ Every child of God can obey him, defeating sin and evil pleasure by trusting Christ to help him.

For I am convinced that nothing can ever separate us from his love. Death can't, and life can't. The angels won't, and all the powers of hell itself cannot keep God's love away.

Jas. 4:7. Mt. 4:10, 11. Eph. 6:10, 11. Eph. 5:11. 2 Cor. 2:11. 1 Pet. 5:8, 9. 1 Jn. 5:4. Rom. 8:38.

A rainbow glowing like an emerald encircled his throne.

I seal this promise with this sign: I have placed my rainbow in the clouds as a sign of my promise until the end of time, to you and to all the earth. For I will see the rainbow in the cloud and remember my eternal promise to every living being on the earth. □ An everlasting covenant . . . eternal, final, sealed. □ He has given us both his promise and his oath, two things we can completely count on, for it is impossible for God to tell a lie. Now all those who flee to him to save them can take new courage when they hear such assurances from God; now they know without doubt that he will give them the salvation he has promised them. This certain hope of being saved is a strong and trustworthy anchor for our souls, connecting us with God himself behind the sacred curtains of heaven, where Christ has gone ahead to plead for us from his position as our High Priest, with the honor and rank of Melchizedek. □ In this man Jesus, there is forgiveness for your sins. Everyone who trusts in him is freed from all guilt and declared righteous.

Jesus Christ is the same yesterday, today, and forever.

Rev. 4:3. Gen. 9:12, 13, 16. 2 Sam. 23:5. Hebr. 6:18, 19. Acts 13:38, 39. Hebr. 13:8.

*God . . . will give . . . a bountiful sup-
ply . . . to all who ask him.*

Jesus . . . said to her, "Where are your ac-
cusers? Didn't even one of them condemn you?"
"No, sir," she said. And Jesus said, "Neither do I.
Go and sin no more."

What a difference between man's sin and God's
forgiveness! For this one man, Adam, brought
death to many through his *sin*. But this one man,
Jesus Christ, brought forgiveness to many through
God's *mercy*. Adam's *one* sin brought the penalty
of death to many, while Christ freely takes away
many sins and gives glorious life instead.

God is so rich in mercy; he loved us so much
that even though we were spiritually dead and
doomed by our sins, he gave us back our lives
again when he raised Christ from the dead—only
by his undeserved favor have we ever been saved
—and lifted us up from the grave into glory along
with Christ, where we sit with him in the heavenly
realms—all because of what Christ Jesus did.
And now God can always point to us as examples
of how very, very rich his kindness is, as shown
in all he has done for us through Jesus Christ.

Since he did not spare even his own Son for us
but gave him up for us all, won't he also surely
give us everything else?

Jas. 1:5. Jn. 8:10, 11. Rom. 5:15, 16. Eph. 2:4–7. Rom. 8:32.

A man's conscience is the Lord's search-light exposing his hidden motives.

"Hurl the stones at her until she dies. But only he who never sinned may throw the first!" And the Jewish leaders slipped away one by one, beginning with the eldest.

"Who told you you were naked?" the Lord God asked. "Have you eaten fruit from the tree I warned you about?"

Knowing what is right to do and then not doing it is sin. ☐ If we have bad consciences and feel that we have done wrong, the Lord will surely feel it even more, for he knows everything we do. But, dearly loved friends, if our consciences are clear, we can come to the Lord with perfect assurance and trust.

There is nothing wrong with meat, but it is wrong to eat it if it makes another stumble. Happy is the man who does not sin by doing what he knows is right.

Search me, O God, and know my heart; test my thoughts. Point out anything you find in me that makes you sad, and lead me along the path of everlasting life.

Prov. 20:27. Jn. 8:7, 9. Gen. 3:11. Jas. 4:17. 1 Jn. 3:20, 21. Rom. 14:20, 22. Ps. 139:23, 24.

*Don't brag about your plans for tomorrow—
wait and see what happens.*

Your cry came to me at a favorable time, when
the doors of welcome were wide open. I helped
you on a day when salvation was being offered.
□ My light will shine out for you just a little
while longer. Walk in it while you can, and go
where you want to go before the darkness falls,
for then it will be too late for you to find your
way. Make use of the Light while there is still
time; then you will become light bearers.

Whatever you do, do well, for in death, where
you are going, there is no working or planning, or
knowing, or understanding.

Friend, you have enough stored away for years
to come. Now take it easy! Wine, women and
song for you! Fool! Tonight you die. Then who
will get it all? Yes, every man is a fool who gets
rich on earth but not in heaven.

For the length of your lives is as uncertain as
the morning fog—now you see it; soon it is gone.
□ This world is fading away, and these evil, forbidden things will go with it, but whoever keeps
doing the will of God will live forever.

*Prov. 27:1. 2 Cor. 6:2. Jn. 12:35, 36. Eccl. 9:10. Lk. 12:19–21.
Jas. 4:14. 1 Jn. 2:17.*

You are forever, and your years never end.

Before the mountains were created, before the earth was formed, you are God without beginning or end.

I am the Lord—I do not change. That is why you are not already utterly destroyed. ☐ Jesus Christ is the same yesterday, today, and forever.

Whatever is good and perfect comes to us from God, the Creator of all light, and he shines forever without change or shadow. ☐ God's gifts and his call can never be withdrawn; he will never go back on his promises.

God is not a man, that he should lie. He doesn't change his mind like humans do. ☐ His compassion never ends. It is only the Lord's mercies that have kept us from complete destruction.

Jesus lives forever and continues to be a Priest so that no one else is needed. He is able to save completely all who come to God through him. Since he will live forever, he will always be there to remind God that he had paid for their sins with his blood. ☐ Don't be afraid! I am the First and the Last.

Ps. 102:27. Ps. 90:2. Mal. 3:6. Hebr. 13:8. Jas. 1:17. Rom. 11:29. Num. 23:19. Lam. 3:22. Hebr. 7:24, 25. Rev. 1:17.

Jehovah-nissi . . . Raise the banner of the Lord.

If God is on our side, who can ever be against us? ☐ He is for me. How can I be afraid? What can mere man do to me?

You have given us a banner to rally to; all who love truth will rally to it.

The Lord is my light and my salvation; whom shall I fear? Yes, though a mighty army marches against me, my heart shall know no fear. I am confident that God will save me.

God is with us; he is our leader. ☐ The commander of the armies of heaven is here among us. He, the God of Jacob, has come to rescue us.

They will wage war against the Lamb and the Lamb will conquer them.

What fools the nations are to rage against the Lord. How strange that men should try to outwit God. God in heaven merely laughs. He is amused by all their puny plans. ☐ Call your councils of war, develop your strategies, prepare your plans of attacking us and perish. For God is with us.

Ex. 17:15. Rom. 8:31. Ps. 118:6. Ps. 60:4. Ps. 27:1, 3. 2 Chron. 13:12. Ps. 46:7. Rev. 17:14. Ps. 2:1, 4. Is. 8:10.

Trust the Lord completely; don't ever trust yourself.

In everything you do, put God first, and he will direct you and crown your efforts with success. □ O my people, trust him all the time. Pour out your longings before him, for he can help!

I will instruct you (says the Lord) and guide you along the best pathway for your life; I will advise you and watch your progress. Don't be like a senseless horse or mule that has to have a bit in its mouth to keep it in line! Many sorrows come to the wicked, but abiding love surrounds those who trust in the Lord. □ If you leave God's paths and go astray, you will hear a Voice behind you say, "No, this is the way; walk here." □ And the Lord will guide you continually, and satisfy you with all good things, and keep you healthy too; and you will be like a well-watered garden, like an ever-flowing spring.

O Lord, I know it is not within the power of man to map his life and plan his course. □ If you aren't going with us, don't let us move a step from this place.

Prov. 3:5, 6. Ps. 62:8. Ps. 32:8–10. Is. 30:21. Is. 58:11. Jer. 10:23. Ex. 33:15.

The prize for which God is calling us up to heaven because of what Christ Jesus did for us.

You will have treasure in heaven . . . come, follow me. □ I will give you great blessings.

His master praised him for good work. You have been faithful in handling this small amount, he told him, so now I will give you many more responsibilities. Begin the joyous tasks I have assigned to you. □ They shall reign forever and ever.

Your reward will be a never-ending share in his glory and honor. □ The crown of life. □ A crown . . . waiting for me. □ A heavenly reward that never disappears.

Father, I want them with me—these you've given me—so that they can see my glory. You gave me the glory because you loved me before the world began. □ To . . . remain with him forever.

What we suffer now is nothing compared to the glory he will give us later.

No mere man has ever seen, heard or even imagined what wonderful things God has ready for those who love the Lord. But we know about these things because God has sent his Spirit to tell us.

Phil. 3:14. Mt. 19:21. Gen. 15:1. Mt. 25:21. Rev. 22:5. 1 Pet. 5:4. Jas. 1:12. 2 Tim. 4:8. 1 Cor. 9:25. Jn. 17:24. 1 Thess. 4:17. Rom. 8:18. 1 Cor. 2:9, 10.

He willingly bent his shoulder to the task.

For examples of patience in suffering, look at the Lord's prophets. □ All these things happened to them as examples—as object lessons to us—to warn us against doing the same things; they were written down so that we could read about them and learn from them in these last days as the world nears its end.

Shall we receive only pleasant things from the hand of God and never anything unpleasant? □ Job is an example of a man who continued to trust the Lord in sorrow; from his experiences we can see how the Lord's plan finally ended in good, for he is full of tenderness and mercy. □ It is the Lord's will . . . let him do what he thinks best.

Give your burdens to the Lord. He will carry them. He will not permit the godly to slip or fall. □ It was *our* grief he bore, *our* sorrows that weighed him down.

Come to me and I will give you rest—all of you who work so hard beneath a heavy yoke. Wear my yoke—for it fits perfectly—and let me teach you; for I am gentle and humble, and you shall find rest for your souls; for I give you only light burdens.

Gen. 49:15. Jas. 5:10. 1 Cor. 10:11. Job. 2:10. Jas. 5:11. 1 Sam. 3:18. Ps. 55:22. Is. 53:4. Mt. 11:28–30.

O God, I cried, I am in trouble—help me.

O God enthroned in heaven, I lift my eyes to you. We look to Jehovah our God for his mercy and kindness just as a servant keeps his eyes upon his master or a slave girl watches her mistress for the slightest signal. □ O God, listen to me! Hear my prayer! For wherever I am, though far away at the ends of the earth, I will cry to you for help. When my heart is faint and overwhelmed, lead me to the mighty, towering Rock of safety. For you are my refuge, a high tower where my enemies can never reach me. I shall live forever in your tabernacle; oh, to be safe beneath the shelter of your wings. □ To the poor, O Lord, you are a refuge from the storm, a shadow from the heat.

Christ, who suffered for you, is your example. Follow in his steps: he never sinned, never told a lie, never answered back when insulted; when he suffered he did not threaten to get even; he left his case in the hands of God who always judges fairly. □ This High Priest of ours understands our weaknesses, since he had the same temptations we do, though he never once gave way to them and sinned. So let us come boldly to the very throne of God and stay there to receive his mercy and to find grace to help us in our times of need.

Is. 38:14. Ps. 123:1, 2. Ps. 61:1–4. Is. 25:4. 1 Pet. 2:21–23. Hebr. 4:15, 16.

Fight on for God.

Trouble was on every hand and all around us; within us, our hearts were full of dread and fear. □ Don't be afraid . . . our army is bigger than theirs. □ Your strength must come from God's mighty power within you.

You come to me with a sword and a spear, but I come to you in the name of the Lord of the armies of heaven and of Israel—the very God whom you have defied. □ God is my strong fortress . . . he gives me skill in war and strength to bend a bow of bronze. □ Our . . . power and success comes from God.

The angel of the Lord guards and rescues all who reverence him. □ "Lord, open his eyes and let him see." And the Lord opened the young man's eyes so that he could see horses of fire and chariots of fire everywhere upon the mountain.

How much more do I need to say? It would take too long to recount the stories. . . . These people all trusted God and as a result won battles, overthrew kingdoms. . . . Some were made strong again after they had been weak or sick. Others were given great power in battle; they made whole armies turn and run away.

1 Tim. 6:12. 2 Cor. 7:5. 2 Kgs. 6:16. Eph. 6:10. 1 Sam. 17:45. 2 Sam. 22:33, 35. 2 Cor. 3:5. Ps. 34:7. 2 Kgs. 6:17. Hebr. 11:32–34.

He grants good sense to the godly—his saints. He is their shield, protecting them and guarding their pathway.

The Lord God . . . led them all the way, and had selected the best places for them to camp, and had guided them by a pillar of fire at night and a pillar of cloud during the day. □ He spreads his wings over them, even as an eagle overspreads her young. She carries them upon her wings—as does the Lord his people! . . . The Lord alone was leading them. □ The steps of good men are directed by the Lord. He delights in each step they take. If they fall it isn't fatal, for the Lord holds them with his hand. □ The good man does not escape all troubles—he has them too. But the Lord helps him in each and every one. □ For the Lord watches over all the plans and paths of godly men, but the paths of the godless lead to doom. □ And we know that all that happens to us is working for our good if we love God and are fitting into his plans. □ We have the Lord our God to fight our battles for us!

The Lord your God has arrived to live among you. He is a mighty Savior. He will give you victory. He will rejoice over you in great gladness.

Prov. 2:8. Deut. 1:32, 33. Deut. 32:11, 12. Ps. 37:23, 24. Ps. 34:19. Ps. 1:6. Rom. 8:28. 2 Chron. 32:8. Zeph. 3:17.

You have forgiven all my sins.

Where is another God like you, who pardons the sins of the survivors among his people? You cannot stay angry with your people, for you love to be merciful. Once again you will have compassion on us. You will tread our sins beneath your feet; you will throw them into the depths of the ocean!

"For a brief moment I abandoned you. But with great compassion I will gather you. In a moment of anger I turned my face a little while; but with everlasting love I will have pity on you," says the Lord, your Redeemer. □ I will forgive and forget their sins.

What happiness for those whose guilt has been forgiven! What joys when sins are covered over! What relief for those who have confessed their sins and God has cleared their record. □ The blood of Jesus his Son cleanses us from every sin. If we say that we have no sin, we are only fooling ourselves, and refusing to accept the truth. But if we confess our sins to him, he can be depended on to forgive us and to cleanse us from every wrong. [And it is perfectly proper for God to do this for us because Christ died to wash away our sins.]

Is. 38:17. Mic. 7:18, 19. Is. 54:7, 8. Jer. 31:34. Ps. 32:1, 2. 1 Jn. 1:7–9.

*I know the one in whom I trust, and I am
sure that he is able to safely guard all that I
have given him until the day of his return.*

Able to do far more than we would ever dare
to ask or even dream of.

Able to make it up to you by giving you everything you need and more, so that there will not
only be enough for your own needs, but plenty
left over to give joyfully to others.

Able to help us . . . when we suffer and are
tempted.

Able to save completely all who come to God
through him. Since he will live forever, he will
always be there to remind God that he has paid
for their sins with his blood.

Able to keep you from slipping and falling away,
and to bring you, sinless and perfect, into his
glorious presence with mighty shouts of everlasting
joy.

Able to safely guard all that I have given him
until the day of his return.

He will take these dying bodies of ours and
change them into glorious bodies like his own,
using the same mighty power that he will use to
conquer all else everywhere.

"Do you believe?" . . . "Yes, Lord," they told
him, "we do." "Because of your faith it will
happen!"

*2 Tim. 1:12. Eph. 3:20. 2 Cor. 9:8. Hebr. 2:18. Hebr. 7:25.
Jude 24. 2 Tim. 1:12. Phil. 3:21. Mt. 9:28, 29.*

Jehovah provides.

Don't fail me, Lord, for I am trusting you. Don't let my enemies succeed.

The Lord isn't too weak to save you. And he isn't getting deaf! He can hear you when you call! □ There shall come out of Zion a Deliverer.

Happy is the man who has the God of Jacob as his helper, whose hope is in the Lord his God. □ The eyes of the Lord are watching over those who fear him, who rely upon his steady love. He will keep them from death even in times of famine!

It is he who will supply all your needs from his riches in glory, because of what Christ Jesus has done for us. □ For God has said, I will never, *never* fail you nor forsake you. That is why we can say without any doubt or fear, The Lord is my Helper and I am not afraid of anything that mere man can do to me. □ He is my strength, my shield from every danger. I trusted in him, and he helped me. Joy rises in my heart until I burst out in songs of praise to him. The Lord protects his people.

Gen. 22:14. Ps. 25:2. Is. 59:1. Rom. 11:26. Ps. 146:5. Ps. 33:18, 19. Phil. 4:19. Hebr. 13:5, 6. Ps. 28:7, 8 .

The things that please him.

You can never please God without faith, without depending on him. □ Those who are still under the control of their old sinful selves, bent on following their old evil desires, can never please God. □ Jehovah enjoys his people; he will save the humble. Let his people rejoice in this honor.

Praise the Lord if you are punished for doing right! Of course, you get no credit for being patient if you are beaten for doing wrong; but if you do right and suffer for it, and are patient beneath the blows, God is well pleased. □ Be beautiful inside, in your hearts, with the lasting charm of a gentle and quiet spirit which is so precious to God.

True praise is a worthy sacrifice; this really honors me. Those who walk my paths will receive salvation from the Lord. □ Then I will praise God with my singing! My thanks will be his praise—that will please him more than sacrificing a bullock or an ox.

Dear brothers, I plead with you to give your bodies to God. Let them be a living sacrifice, holy —the kind he can accept. When you think of what he has done for you, is this too much to ask?

1 Jn. 3:22. Hebr. 11:6. Rom. 8:8. Ps. 149:4. 1 Pet. 2:19, 20.
1 Pet. 3:4. Ps. 50:23. Ps. 69:30, 31. Rom. 12:1.

I am standing here depressed and gloomy.

He will keep in perfect peace all those who trust in him, whose thoughts turn often to the Lord! Trust in the Lord God always, for in the Lord Jehovah is your everlasting strength.

Give your burdens to the Lord. He will carry them. He will not permit the godly to slip or fall. □ He has not despised my cries of deep despair; he has not turned and walked away. When I cried to him, he heard and came. □ Is any among you suffering? He should keep on praying about it.

Don't be troubled or afraid. □ Don't worry about *things*—food, drink and clothes. For you already have life and a body—and they are far more important than what to eat and wear. Look at the birds! They don't worry about what to eat —they don't need to sow or reap or store up food —for your heavenly Father feeds them. And you are far more valuable to him than they are. Will all your worries add a single moment to your life? And why worry about your clothes? Look at the field lilies! They don't worry about theirs. Yet King Solomon in all his glory was not clothed as beautifully as they. And if God cares so wonderfully for flowers that are here today and gone tomorrow, won't he more surely care for you? □ Don't be faithless any longer. Believe! □ I am with you always.

Ps. 42:6. Is. 26:3, 4. Ps. 55:22. Ps. 22:24. Jas. 5:13. Jn. 14:27. Mt. 6:25–30. Jn. 20:27. Mt. 28:20.

Don't hide your light! Let it shine for all;
let your good deeds glow for all to see, so that
they will praise your heavenly Father.

Live as Christians should. □ Keep away from every kind of evil. □ Be happy if you are cursed and insulted for being a Christian, for when that happens the Spirit of God will come upon you with great glory. Don't let me hear of your suffering for murdering or stealing or making trouble or being a busybody and prying into other people's affairs. □ In everything you do, stay away from complaining and arguing, so that no one can speak a word of blame against you. You are to live clean, innocent lives as children of God in a dark world full of people who are crooked and stubborn. Shine out among them like beacon lights. □ Make people want to believe in our Savior and God.

Never forget to be truthful and kind. Hold these virtues tightly. Write them deep within your heart. If you want favor with both God and man, and a reputation for good judgment and common sense, then trust the Lord completely; don't ever trust yourself. □ Fix your thoughts on what is true and good and right. Think about things that are pure and lovely, and dwell on the fine, good things in others. Think about all you can praise God for and be glad about.

Mt. 5:15, 16. Phil. 1:27. 1 Thess. 5:22. 1 Pet. 4:14, 15. Phil. 2:14, 15.
Tit. 2:10. Prov. 3:3, 4. Phil. 4:8.

The Lord our righteousness.

We are all infected and impure with sin. When we put on our prized robes of righteousness we find they are but filthy rags.

I walk in the strength of the Lord God. I tell everyone that you alone are just and good. □ How happy God has made me! For he has clothed me with garments of salvation and draped about me the robe of righteousness. I am like a bridegroom in his wedding suit or a bride with her jewels.

Bring the finest robe in the house and put it on. □ Wear the cleanest and whitest and finest of linens. Fine linen represents the good deeds done by the people of God.

Everything else is worthless when compared with the priceless gain of knowing Christ Jesus my Lord. I have put aside all else, counting it worth less than nothing, in order that I can have Christ, and become one with him, no longer counting on being saved by being good enough or by obeying God's laws, but by trusting Christ to save me; for God's way of making us right with himself depends on faith—counting on Christ alone.

Jer. 23:6. Is. 64:6. Ps. 71:16. Is. 61:10. Lk. 15:22. Rev. 19:8. Phil. 3:8, 9.

His suffering made Jesus a perfect Leader.

"My soul is crushed with horror and sadness to the point of death . . . stay here . . . stay awake with me." He went forward a little, and fell face downward on the ground, and prayed, "My Father! If it is possible, let this cup be taken away from me. But I want your will, not mine." □ He was in such agony of spirit that he broke into a sweat of blood, with great drops falling to the ground as he prayed more and more earnestly.

Death stared me in the face—I was frightened and sad. □ Their contempt has broken my heart; my spirit is heavy within me. If even one would show some pity, if even one would comfort me! □ No one gives me a passing thought. No one will help me; no one cares a bit what happens to me.

We despised him and rejected him—a man of sorrows, acquainted with bitterest grief. We turned our backs on him and looked the other way when he went by. He was despised and we didn't care. He was wounded and bruised for *our* sins. He was chastised that we might have peace; he was lashed—and we were healed! He was oppressed and he was afflicted, yet he never said a word.

Therefore, I will give him the honors of one who is mighty and great, because he has poured out his soul unto death.

Hebr. 2:10. Mt. 26:38, 39. Lk. 22:44. Ps. 116:3. Ps. 69:20. Ps. 142:4. Is. 53:3, 5, 7, 12.

The Lord made the heaven, earth, and sea,
and everything in them.

The heavens are telling the glory of God; they
are a marvelous display of his craftsmanship. □
He merely spoke, and the heavens were formed,
and all the galaxies of stars. He made the oceans,
pouring them into his vast reservoirs. When he
but spoke the world began! It appeared at his
command! □ All the peoples of the world are
nothing in comparison with him—they are but a
drop in the bucket, dust on the scales. He picks
up the islands as though they had no weight at all.

Who else has held the oceans in his hands and
measured off the heavens with his ruler? Who else
knows the weight of all the earth and weighs the
mountains and the hills?

By faith—by believing God—we know that the
world and the stars—in fact, all things—were
made at God's command; and that they were all
made from things that can't be seen.

When I look up into the night skies and see the
work of your fingers—the moon and the stars
you have made—I cannot understand how you
can bother with mere puny man, to pay any attention to him!

Ex. 20:11. Ps. 19:1. Ps. 33:6, 7, 9. Is. 40:15. Is. 40:12. Hebr. 11:3.
Ps. 8:3, 4.

*I will sing in unknown tongues and also in
ordinary language, so that I can understand
the praise I am giving.*

Be filled . . . with the Holy Spirit, and controlled
by him. Talk with each other much about the Lord,
quoting psalms and hymns and singing sacred
songs, making music in your hearts to the Lord.
□ Remember what Christ taught and let his words
enrich your lives and make you wise; teach them
to each other and sing them out in psalms and
hymns and spiritual songs, singing to the Lord
with thankful hearts.

I will praise the Lord and call on all men everywhere to bless his holy name forever and forever.

Praise the Lord! How good it is to sing his
praises! How delightful and how right! Sing out
your thanks to him; sing praises to our God, accompanied by harps.

And I heard a sound from heaven like the roaring of a great waterfall or the rolling of mighty
thunder. It was the singing of a choir accompanied
by harps. □ And I saw in heaven another mighty
pageant . . . all were holding harps of God, and
they were singing the song of Moses, the servant
of God, and the song of the Lamb: "Great and
marvelous are your doings, Lord God Almighty.
Just and true are your ways, O King of ages."

*1 Cor. 14:15. Eph. 5:18, 19. Col. 3:16. Ps. 145:21. Ps. 147:1, 7.
Rev. 14:2. Rev. 15:1–4.*

God wanted all of himself to be in his Son.

The Father loves . . . his Son, and God has given him everything there is. □ God raised him up to the heights of heaven and gave him a name which is above every other name, that at the name of Jesus every knee shall bow in heaven and on earth and under the earth, and every tongue shall confess that Jesus Christ is Lord, to the glory of God the Father. □ Far, far above any other king or ruler or dictator or leader. Yes, his honor is far more glorious than that of anyone else either in this world or in the world to come. □ Christ himself is the Creator who made everything in heaven and earth, the things we can see and the things we can't; the spirit world with its kings and kingdoms, its rulers and authorities; all were made by Christ for his own use and glory.

Christ died and rose again . . . so that he can be our Lord both while we live and when we die. □ You have everything when you have Christ, and you are filled with God through your union with Christ. He is the highest Ruler, with authority over every other power. □ We have all benefited from the rich blessings he brought to us—blessing upon blessing heaped upon us!

Col. 1:19. Jn. 3:35. Phil. 2:9–11. Eph. 1:21. Col. 1:16. Rom. 14:9.
Col. 2:10. Jn. 1:16.

*He had the same temptations we do, though
he never once gave way to them and sinned.*

How lovely and fresh looking it was! And it
would make her so wise! So she ate some of the
fruit and gave some to her husband, and he ate
it too. □ Stop loving this evil world and all that it
offers you, for when you love these things you
show that you do not really love God.

Then Satan tempted him to get food by changing stones into loaves of bread. But Jesus told
him, "No! For the Scriptures tell us that bread
won't feed men's souls: obedience to every word
of God is what we need." Next Satan took him to
the peak of a very high mountain and showed him
the nations of the world and all their glory. "I'll
give it all to you," he said, "if you will only kneel
and worship me." "Get out of here, Satan," Jesus
told him. □ Stop loving this evil world and all
that it offers you . . . these are not from God.

For since he himself has now been through
suffering and temptation, he knows what it is like
when we suffer and are tempted, and he is wonderfully able to help us.

Happy is the man who doesn't give in and do
wrong when he is tempted.

*Hebr. 4:15. Gen. 3:6. 1 Jn. 2:15. Mt. 4:3, 4, 8–10. 1 Jn. 2:15, 16.
Hebr. 2:18. Jas. 1:12.*

My eyes grew weary of looking up for help.

Pity me, O Lord, for I am weak. Heal me, for my body is sick, and I am upset and disturbed. My mind is filled with apprehension and with gloom. Oh, restore me soon. Come, O Lord, and make me well. In your kindness save me. □ My heart is in anguish within me. Stark fear overpowers me. Trembling and horror overwhelm me. Oh, for wings like a dove, to fly away and rest.

You need to keep on patiently doing God's will. □ And let us not get tired of doing what is right, for after a while we will reap a harvest of blessing if we don't get discouraged and give up.

As they were straining their eyes for another glimpse, suddenly two white-robed men were standing there among them, and said, "Men of Galilee, why are you standing here staring at the sky? Jesus has gone away to heaven, and some day, just as he went, he will return." □ Our homeland is in heaven, where our Savior the Lord Jesus Christ is; and we are looking forward to his return from there. □ Looking forward to that wonderful time we've been expecting, when his glory shall be seen—the glory of our great God and Savior Jesus Christ.

Is. 38:14. Ps. 6:2–4. Ps. 55:4–6. Hebr. 10:36. Gal. 6:9. Acts 1:10, 11. Phil. 3:20. Tit. 2:13.

*As soon as God had brought his servant to
life again, he sent him . . . to bless you by
turning you back from your sins.*

All honor to God, the God and Father of our
Lord Jesus Christ; for it is his boundless mercy
that has given us the privilege of being born again,
so that we are now members of God's own family.
Now we live in the hope of eternal life because
Christ rose again from the dead.

Our . . . Savior Jesus Christ . . . died under
God's judgment against our sins, so that he could
rescue us from constant falling into sin and make
us his very own people, with cleansed hearts and
real enthusiasm for doing kind things for others.
□ Be holy now in everything you do, just as the
Lord is holy, who invited you to be his child. He
himself has said, "You must be holy, for I am
holy."

God, the Father of our Lord Jesus Christ . . .
has blessed us with every blessing in heaven because we belong to Christ. □ For in Christ there
is all of God in a human body; *so you have everything when you have Christ.* □ We have all
benefited from the rich blessings he brought to us
—blessing upon blessing heaped upon us!

Since he did not spare even his own Son for us
but gave him up for us all, won't he also surely
give us everything else?

*Acts 3:26. 1 Pet. 1:3. Tit. 2:13, 14. 1 Pet. 1:15, 16. Eph. 1:3. Col.
2:9, 10. Jn. 1:16. Rom. 8:32.*

Encourage and cheer me with your words.

Never forget your promises to me your servant; for they are my only hope. □ O God, I cried, I am in trouble—help me.

All heaven and earth shall pass away, yet my words remain forever true. □ You know very well that God's promises to you have all come true.

Fear not, for I am with you. Do not be dismayed. I am your God. I will strengthen you; I will help you; I will uphold you with my victorious right hand. □ "Take courage and work, for I am with you," says the Lord of Hosts. □ "Not by might, nor by power, but by my Spirit," says the Lord of Hosts—"you will succeed because of my Spirit, though you are few and weak." □ Constantly remind the people about these laws, and you yourself must think about them every day and every night so that you will be sure to obey all of them. For only then will you succeed. Yes, be bold and strong. Banish fear and doubt. For remember, the Lord your God is with you wherever you go.

Your strength must come from the Lord's mighty power within you.

Ps. 119:28. Ps. 119:49. Is. 38:14. Lk. 21:33. Josh. 23:14. Is. 41:10. Hag. 2:4. Zech. 4:6. Josh. 1:8, 9. Eph. 6:10.

*Wake up! Strengthen what little remains—
for even what is left is at the point of death.*

The end of the world is coming soon. Therefore be earnest, thoughtful men of prayer. □ Be
careful—watch out for attacks from Satan, your
great enemy. He prowls around like a hungry,
roaring lion, looking for some victim to tear apart.
□ Watch out. Be very careful never to forget what
you have seen God doing for you. May his miracles have a deep and permanent effect upon your
lives. □ And those whose faith has made them
good in God's sight must live by faith, trusting
him in everything. Otherwise, if they shrink back,
God will have no pleasure in them. . . . Our
faith in him assures our souls' salvation.

Keep a sharp lookout! For you do not know
when I will come, at evening, at midnight, early
dawn or late daybreak. Don't let me find you
sleeping. *Watch for my return!*

Fear not, for I am with you. Do not be dismayed. I am your God. I will strengthen you; I
will help you; I will uphold you with my victorious right hand. I am holding you by your right
hand—I, the Lord your God—and I say to you,
"Don't be afraid; I am here to help you."

*Rev. 3:2. 1 Pet. 4:7. 1 Pet. 5:8. Deut. 4:9. Hebr. 10:38, 39. Mk.
13:35–37. Is. 41:10, 13.*

Is his lovingkindness gone forever?

He remembered our utter weakness, for his lovingkindness continues forever. □ Show the great power [of your patience] by forgiving our sins and showing us your steadfast love. □ Where is another God like you, who pardons the sins of the survivors among his people? You cannot stay angry with your people, for you love to be merciful. Once again you will have compassion on us. You will tread our sins beneath your feet; you will throw them into the depths of the ocean. □ He saved us—not because we were good enough to be saved, but because of his kindness and pity —by washing away our sins and giving us the new joy of the indwelling Holy Spirit.

What a wonderful God we have—he is the Father of our Lord Jesus Christ, the source of every mercy, and the one who so wonderfully comforts and strengthens us in our hardships and trials.

Our merciful and faithful High Priest before God, a Priest . . . both merciful to us and faithful to God in dealing with the sins of the people. For since he himself has now been through suffering and temptation, he knows what it is like when we suffer and are tempted, and he is wonderfully able to help us.

Ps. 77:8. Ps. 136:23. Num. 14:18. Mic. 7:18, 19. Tit. 3:5. 2 Cor. 1:3, 4. Hebr. 2:17, 18.

*Lot took a long look at the fertile plains of
the Jordan River, well watered everywhere
(this was before Jehovah destroyed Sodom
and Gomorrah); the whole section was like
the Garden of Eden. So that is what Lot
chose—the Jordan valley to the east of them.*

Lot . . . was a good man.

Don't be misled; remember that you can't ignore God and get away with it: a man will always
reap just the kind of crop he sows! □ Remember
what happened to Lot's wife!

Don't be teamed with those who do not love
the Lord, for what do the people of God have in
common with the people of sin? How can light
live with darkness? The Lord has said, Leave
them; separate yourselves from them; don't touch
their filthy things, and I will welcome you, and
be a Father to you, and you will be my sons and
daughters. □ Don't even associate with such people. For though once your heart was full of darkness, now it is full of light from the Lord, and
your behavior should show it! Learn as you go
along what pleases the Lord. Take no part in the
worthless pleasures of evil and darkness, but instead, rebuke and expose them. □ Learn to put
aside your own desires so that you will become
patient and godly, gladly letting God have his
way with you. The more you go on in this way,
the more you will grow strong spiritually and become fruitful and useful to our Lord Jesus Christ.

*Gen. 13:10, 11. 2 Pet. 2:7, 8. Gal. 6:7. Lk. 17:32. 2 Cor. 6:14, 17.
Eph. 5:7, 8, 10, 11. 2 Pet. 1:6, 8.*

Holy, holy, holy, Lord God Almighty.

The praises of our fathers surrounded your throne. ☐ "Don't come any closer," God told him. "Take off your shoes, for you are standing on holy ground. I am the God of your fathers—the God of Abraham, Isaac, and Jacob." (Moses covered his face with his hands, for he was afraid to look at God.) ☐ "With whom will you compare me? Who is my equal?" asks the Holy One. ☐ I am the Lord your God, your Savior, the Holy One of Israel. I am the Lord, and there is no other Savior.

Be holy now in everything you do, just as the Lord is holy, who invited you to be his child. He himself has said, "You must be holy, for I am holy." ☐ Haven't you yet learned that your body is the home of the Holy Spirit God gave you, and that he lives within you? Your own body does not belong to you.

And so . . . I plead with you to give your bodies to God. Let them be a living sacrifice, holy —the kind he can accept. When you think of what he has done for you, is this too much to ask?

Rev. 4:8. Ps. 22:3. Ex. 3:5, 6. Is. 40:25. Is. 43:3, 11. 1 Pet. 1:15, 16. 1 Cor. 6:19. Rom. 12:1.

I will never, never *fail you nor forsake you.*

That is why we can say without any doubt or
fear, The Lord is my Helper and I am not afraid
of anything that mere man can do to me.

I am with you, and will protect you wherever
you go, and will bring you back safely to this land;
I will be with you constantly until I have finished
giving you all I am promising. □ Be strong! Be
courageous! Do not be afraid of them! For the
Lord your God will be with you. He will neither
fail you nor forsake you.

Demas has left me. He loved the good things of
this life. The first time I was brought before the
judge no one was here to help me. Everyone had
run away. I hope that they will not be blamed
for it. But the Lord stood with me and gave me
the opportunity to boldly preach a whole sermon
for all the world to hear. □ If my father and
mother should abandon me, you would welcome
and comfort me.

I am with you always, even to the end of the
world. □ I am the First and Last, the Living One
who died, who is now alive forevermore. □ I will
not abandon you or leave you as orphans in the
storm—I will come to you. □ I am leaving you
with a gift—peace of mind and heart!

*Hebr. 13:5. Hebr. 13:6. Gen. 28:15. Deut. 31:6. 2 Tim. 4:10, 16,
17. Ps. 27:10. Mt. 28:20. Rev. 1:18. Jn. 14:18 Jn. 14:27.*

The Kingdom of Heaven can be illustrated by the story of a man going into another country, who called together his servants and loaned them money to invest for him . . . dividing it in proportion to their abilities.

Don't you realize that you can choose your own master? You can choose sin (with death) or else obedience (with acquittal). The one to whom you offer yourself—he will take you and be your master and you will be his slave.

It is the same and only Holy Spirit who gives all these gifts and powers, deciding which each one of us should have. The Holy Spirit displays God's power through each of us as a means of helping the entire church. □ God has given each of you some special abilities; be sure to use them to help each other, passing on to others God's many kinds of blessings. □ The most important thing about a servant is that he does just what his master tells him to. □ Much is required from those to whom much is given, for their responsibility is greater.

Who is adequate for such a task as this? □ I can do everything God asks me to with the help of Christ who gives me the strength and power.

Mt. 25:14, 15. Rom. 6:16. 1 Cor. 12:11, 7. 1 Pet. 4:10. 1 Cor. 4:2. Lk. 12:48. 2 Cor. 2:16. Phil. 4:13.

*When the Holy Spirit controls our lives he
will produce . . . love.*

God is love, and anyone who lives in love is
living with God and God is living in him. □ How
dearly God loves us, and we feel this warm love
everywhere within us because God has given us
the Holy Spirit to fill our hearts with his love. □
He is very precious to you who believe. □ Our
love for him comes as a result of his loving us
first. □ Whatever we do, it is certainly not for
our own profit, but because Christ's love controls
us now. Since we believe that Christ died for all
of us, we should also believe that we have died to
the old life we used to live. He died for all so that
all who live—having received eternal life from
him—might live no longer for themselves, to
please themselves, but to spend their lives pleasing Christ who died and rose again for them.

God himself is teaching you to love one another. □ I demand that you love each other as
much as I love you. □ Most important of all,
continue to show deep love for each other, for
love makes up for many of your faults. □ Be full
of love for others, following the example of Christ
who loved you and gave himself to God as a
sacrifice to take away your sins. And God was
pleased, for Christ's love for you was like sweet
perfume to him.

*Gal. 5:22. 1 Jn. 4:16. Rom. 5:5. 1 Pet. 2:7. 1 Jn. 4:19. 2 Cor.
5:14, 15. 1 Thess. 4:9. Jn. 15:12. 1 Pet. 4:8. Eph. 5:2.*

The good man's reward lasts forever.

After a long time their master returned from his trip and called them to him to account for his money. The man to whom he had entrusted the $5,000 brought him $10,000. His master praised him for good work. "You have been faithful in handling this small amount," he told him, "so now I will give you many more responsibilities. Begin the joyous tasks I have assigned to you."

We must all stand before Christ to be judged and have our lives laid bare—before him. Each of us will receive whatever he deserves for the good or bad things he has done in his earthly body.

I have fought long and hard for my Lord, and through it all I have kept true to him. And now the time has come for me to stop fighting and rest. In heaven a crown is waiting for me which the Lord, the righteous Judge, will give me on that great day of his return. And not just to me, but to all those whose lives show that they are eagerly looking forward to his coming back again.

I am coming soon! Hold tightly to the little strength you have—so that no one will take away your crown.

Prov. 11:18. Mt. 25:19–21. 2 Cor. 5:10. 2 Tim. 4:7, 8. Rev. 3:11.

God . . . will do what he says.

God is not a man, that he should lie; he doesn't change his mind like humans do. Has he ever promised, without doing what he said? □ The Lord has sworn and will never change his mind.

God also bound himself with an oath, so that those he promised to help would be perfectly sure and never need to wonder whether he might change his plans. He has given us both his promise and his oath, two things we can completely count on, for it is impossible for God to tell a lie. Now all those who flee to him to save them can take new courage when they hear such assurances from God; now they can know without doubt that he will give them the salvation he has promised them. □ So if you are suffering according to God's will, keep on doing what is right and trust yourself to the God who made you, for he will never fail you.

I know the one in whom I trust, and I am sure that he is able to safely guard all that I have given him until the day of his return. □ God, who called you to become his child, will do all this for you, just as he promised. □ He carries out and fulfills all of God's promises, no matter how many of them there are; and we have told everyone how faithful he is, giving glory to his name.

1 Cor. 10:13. Num. 23:19. Hebr. 7:21. Hebr. 6:17, 18. 1 Pet. 4:19. 2 Tim. 1:12. 1 Thess. 5:24. 2 Cor. 1:20.

Lead on with courage and strength.

The Lord is my light and my salvation; whom shall I fear? □ He gives power to the tired and worn out, and strength to the weak. Even the youths shall be exhausted, and the young men will all give up. But they that wait upon the Lord shall renew their strength. They shall mount up with wings like eagles; they shall walk and not faint. □ My health fails; my spirits droop, yet God remains! He is the strength of my heart; he is mine forever.

What can we ever say to such wonderful things as these? If God is on our side, who can ever be against us? Since he did not spare even his own Son for us but gave him up for us all, won't he also surely give us everything else? □ He is for me! How can I be afraid? What can mere man do to me? □ It is only by your power and through your name that we tread down our enemies. □ Overwhelming victory is ours through Christ who loved us enough to die for us.

So now, my son, may the Lord be with you and prosper you. Be strong and courageous, fearless and enthusiastic.

Josh. 1:18. Ps. 27:1. Is. 40:29–31. Ps. 73:26. Rom. 8:31, 32. Ps. 118:6. Ps. 44:5. Rom. 8:37. 1 Chron. 22:11, 13.

Riches can disappear fast. And the king's crown doesn't stay in his family forever.

Proud man! Frail as breath! A shadow! And all his busy rushing ends in nothing. He heaps up riches for someone else to spend. □ Let heaven fill your thoughts; don't spend your time worrying about things down here. □ Don't store up treasures here on earth where they can erode away or may be stolen. Store them in heaven where they will never lose their value, and are safe from thieves. If your profits are in heaven your heart will be there too.

Deny yourselves many things that would keep you from doing your best. An athlete goes to all this trouble just to win a blue ribbon or a silver cup, but we do it for a heavenly reward that never disappears. □ We do not look at what we can see right now, the troubles all around us, but we look forward to the joys in heaven which we have not yet seen. □ The good man's reward lasts forever. □ In heaven a crown is waiting for me which the Lord, the righteous Judge, will give me on that great day of his return. And not just to me, but to all those whose lives show that they are eagerly looking forward to his coming back again. □ Your reward will be a never-ending share in his glory and honor.

Prov. 27:23, 24. Ps. 39:6. Col. 3:2. Mt. 6:19–21. 1 Cor. 9:25. 2 Cor. 4:18. Prov. 11:18. 2 Tim. 4:8. 1 Pet. 5:4.

Isaac . . . was taking a walk out in the fields, meditating.

May my spoken words and unspoken thoughts be pleasing even to you, O Lord my Rock and my Redeemer.

When I look up into the night skies and see the work of your fingers—the moon and the stars you have made—I cannot understand how you can bother with mere puny man, to pay any attention to him! □ I want to express publicly before his people my heartfelt thanks to God for his mighty miracles. All who are thankful should ponder them with me.

Oh, the joys of those who do not follow evil men's advice, who do not hang around with sinners, scoffing at the things of God. But they delight in doing everything God wants them to, and day and night are always meditating on his laws and thinking about ways to follow him more closely. □ Constantly remind the people about these laws, and you yourself must think about them every day and every night. □ I will praise you with great joy. I lie awake at night thinking of you—of how much you have helped me—and how I rejoice through the night beneath the protecting shadow of your wings. I follow close behind you, protected by your strong right arm.

Gen. 24:62, 63. Ps. 19:14. Ps. 8:3, 4. Ps. 111:1, 2. Ps. 1:1, 2. Josh. 1:8. Ps. 63:5–8.

*How long will you forget me, Lord? For-
ever? How long will you look the other way
when I am in need?*

Whatever is good and perfect comes to us
from God, the Creator of all light, and he shines
forever without change or shadow. □ Yet they
say, "My Lord deserted us; he has forgotten us."
Never! Can a mother forget her little child and
not have love for her own son? Yet even if that
should be, I will not forget you.

I will not forget to help you. I've blotted out
your sins; they are gone like morning mist at
noon!

Although Jesus was very fond of Martha, Mary,
and Lazarus, he stayed where he was for the
next two days and made no move to go to them.
□ A woman . . . came to him, pleading, "Have
mercy on me, O Lord." But Jesus gave her no
reply—not even a word.

These trials are only to test your faith, to see
whether or not it is strong and pure. It is being
tested as fire tests gold and purifies it—and your
faith is far more precious to God than mere gold;
so if your faith remains strong after being tried in
the test tube of fiery trials, it will bring you much
praise and glory and honor on the day of his
return.

*Ps. 13:1. Jas. 1:17. Is. 49:14, 15. Is. 44:21, 22. Jn. 11:5, 6. Mt.
15:22, 23. 1 Pet. 1:7.*

He will supply all your needs from his riches in glory, because of what Christ Jesus has done for us.

Your heavenly Father already knows perfectly well that you need them, and he will give them to you if you give him first place in your life and live as he wants you to. □ Since he did not spare even his own Son for us but gave him up for us all, won't he also surely give us everything else? □ God has already given you everything you need. He has given you the whole world to use, and life and even death are your servants. He has given you all of the present and all of the future. All are yours, and you belong to Christ, and Christ is God's. □ We own nothing, and yet we enjoy everything.

Because the Lord is my Shepherd, I have everything I need! □ For Jehovah God is our Light and our Protector. He gives us grace and glory. No good thing will he withhold from those who walk along his paths. □ The living God . . . richly gives us all we need for our enjoyment. □ God is able to make it up to you by giving you everything you need and more, so that there will not only be enough for your own needs, but plently left over to give joyfully to others.

Phil. 4:19. Mt. 6:32, 33. Rom. 8:32. 1 Cor. 3:21–23. 2 Cor. 6:10. Ps. 23:1. Ps. 84:11. 1 Tim. 6:17. 2 Cor. 9:8.

*What do the people of God have in common
with the people of sin?*

They loved the darkness more than the Light,
for their deeds were evil. □ You are all children
of the light and of the day, and do not belong to
darkness and night.

Darkness had made him blind. □ Your words
are a flashlight to light the path ahead of me.

The land is full of darkness and cruel men. □
Love comes from God and those who are loving
and kind show that they are the children of God,
and that they are getting to know him better.
But if a person isn't loving and kind, it shows that
he doesn't know God—for God is love.

The evil man gropes and stumbles in the dark.
But the good man walks along in the ever-brightening light of God's favor; the dawn gives way to
morning splendor.

I have come as a Light to shine in this dark
world, so that all who put their trust in me will
no longer wander in the darkness. □ Though once
your heart was full of darkness, now it is full of
light from the Lord, and your behavior should
show it! Because of this light within you, you
should do only what is good and right and true.
Learn as you go along what pleases the Lord.

*2 Cor. 6:14. Jn. 3:19. 1 Thess. 5:5. 1 Jn. 2:11. Ps. 119:105.
Ps. 74:20. 1 Jn. 4:7, 8. Prov. 4:19, 18. Jn. 12:46. Eph. 5:8–10.*

If you are really serious about wanting to return to the Lord, get rid of your foreign gods and your Ashtaroth idols. Determine to obey only the Lord.

Dear children, keep away from anything that might take God's place in your hearts. □ The Lord has said, "Leave them; separate yourselves from them; don't touch their filthy things, and I will welcome you, and be a Father to you, and you will be my sons and daughters." □ You cannot serve two masters: God and money.

You must worship no other gods, but only Jehovah, for he is a God who claims absolute loyalty and exclusive devotion. □ Worship and serve him with a clean heart and a willing mind, for the Lord sees every heart and understands and knows every thought.

You deserve honesty from the heart; yes, utter sincerity and truthfulness. Oh, give me this wisdom. □ Men judge by outward appearance, but I look at a man's thoughts and intentions. □ Dearly loved friends, if our consciences are clear, we can come to the Lord with perfect assurance and trust. □ Cling tightly to your faith in Christ and always keep your conscience clear, doing what you know is right.

1 Sam. 7:3. 1 Jn. 5:21. 2 Cor. 6:17, 18. Mt. 6:24. Ex. 34:14. 1 Chron. 28:9. Ps. 51:6. 1 Sam. 16:7. 1 Jn. 3:21. 1 Tim. 1:19.

*Don't forget this, dear friends, that a day or
a thousand years from now is like tomorrow
to the Lord.*

This plan of mine is not what you would work
out, neither are my thoughts the same as yours!
For just as the heavens are higher than the earth,
so are my ways higher than yours, and my
thoughts than yours. As the rain and snow
come down from heaven and stay upon the
ground to water the earth . . . so also is my
Word. I send it out and it always produces fruit.
It shall accomplish all I want it to, and prosper
everywhere I send it.

For God has given them all up to sin so that
he could have mercy upon all alike. Oh, what a
wonderful God we have! How great are his wisdom and knowledge and riches! How impossible
it is for us to understand his decisions and his
methods! For who among us can know the mind
of the Lord? Who knows enough to be his counselor and guide? And who could ever offer to the
Lord enough to induce him to act? For everything
comes from God alone. Everything lives by his
power, and everything is for his glory. To him be
glory evermore.

So be on your guard, not asleep like the others.
Watch for his return. No matter what happens,
always be thankful, for this is God's will for you
who belong to Christ Jesus.

2 Pet. 3:8. Is. 55:8–11. Rom. 11:32–36. 1 Thess. 5:6, 18.

Lead me to the mighty, towering Rock of safety.

Don't worry about anything; instead, pray about everything; tell God your needs and don't forget to thank him for his answers. If you do this you will experience God's peace, which is far more wonderful than the human mind can understand. His peace will keep your thoughts and your hearts quiet and at rest as you trust in Christ Jesus.

I am overwhelmed and desperate, and you alone know which way I ought to turn. □ He knows every detail of what is happening to me; and when he has examined me, he will pronounce me completely innocent—as pure as solid gold! □ Lord, through all the generations you have been our home! □ To the poor, O Lord, you are a refuge from the storm, a shadow from the heat.

For who is God except our Lord? □ Who but he is as a rock? □ They shall never perish. No one shall snatch them away from me. □ Lord, you promised to let me live! Never let it be said that God failed me. □ This certain hope of being saved is a strong and trustworthy anchor for our souls, connecting us with God himself behind the sacred curtains of heaven.

Ps. 61:2. Phil. 4:6, 7. Ps. 142:3. Job 23:10. Ps. 90:1. Is. 25:4. Ps. 18:31. Jn. 10:28. Ps. 119:116. Hebr. 6:19.

My times are in your hands.

His holy ones are in his hands. □ Then the Lord said to Elijah, "Go to the east and hide by Cherith Brook at a place east of where it enters the Jordan River. Drink from the brook and eat what the ravens bring you, for I have commanded them to feed you." Then the Lord said to him, "Go and live in the village of Zarephath, near the city of Sidon. There is a widow there who will feed you. I have given her my instructions."

Don't worry about *things*—food, drink, money and clothes. For you already have life and a body —and they are far more important than what to eat and wear. Your heavenly Father already knows perfectly well that you need them, and he will give them to you if you give him first place in your life and live as he wants you to. So don't be anxious about tomorrow. God will take care of your tomorrow too. Live one day at a time.

Trust the Lord completely; don't ever trust yourself. In everything you do, put God first, and he will direct you and crown your efforts with success. □ Let him have all your worries and cares, for he is always thinking about you and watching everything that concerns you.

Ps. 31:15. Deut. 33:3. 1 Kgs. 17:2–4, 8, 9. Mt. 6:25, 32–34. Prov. 3:5, 6. 1 Pet. 5:7.

Since he will live forever, he will always be there to remind God that he has paid for their sins with his blood.

Who then will condemn us? Will Christ? *No!* For he is the one who died for us . . . and is sitting at the place of highest honor next to God, pleading for us there in heaven. □ Christ has entered into heaven itself, to appear now before God as our Friend.

If you sin, there is someone to plead for you before the Father. His name is Jesus Christ, the one who is all that is good and who pleases God completely. □ God is on one side and all the people on the other side, and Christ Jesus, himself man, is between them to bring them together.

Jesus the Son of God is our great High Priest who has gone to heaven itself to help us; therefore let us never stop trusting him. This High Priest of ours understands our weaknesses, since he had the same temptations we do, though he never once gave way to them and sinned. So let us come boldly to the very throne of God and stay there to receive his mercy and to find grace to help us in our times of need.

All of us . . . may come to God the Father with the Holy Spirit's help because of what Christ has done for us.

Hebr. 7:25. Rom. 8:34. Hebr. 9:24. 1 Jn. 2:1. 1 Tim. 2:5. Hebr. 4:14–16. Eph. 2:18.

All those who know your mercy, Lord, will count on you for help.

This is his name: The Lord Our Righteousness. □ I walk in the strength of the Lord God. I tell everyone that you alone are just and good.

His royal titles: Wonderful, Counselor. □ O Lord, I know it is not within the power of man to map his life and plan his course.

The Mighty God, The Everlasting Father. □ I know the one in whom I trust, and I am sure that he is able to safely guard all that I have given him until the day of his return.

The Prince of Peace. □ Christ himself is our way of peace. □ Since we have been made right in God's sight by faith in his promises, we can have real peace with him because of what Jesus Christ our Lord has done for us.

The Lord is a strong fortress. The godly run to him and are safe. □ Woe to those who run to Egypt for help, trusting their mighty cavalry and chariots instead of looking to the Holy One of Israel and consulting him. □ There is none like the God of Jerusalem—he descends from the heavens in majestic splendor to help you. The eternal God is your Refuge, and underneath are the everlasting arms.

Ps. 9:10. Jer. 23:6. Ps. 71:16. Is. 9:6. Jer. 10:23. Is. 9:6. 2 Tim. 1:12. Is. 9:6. Eph. 2:14. Rom. 5:1. Prov. 18:10. Is. 31:1. Deut. 33:26, 27.

Let us . . . purify ourselves, living in the wholesome fear of God.

Let us turn away from everything wrong, whether of body or spirit.

You deserve honesty from the heart; yes, utter sincerity and truthfulness. Oh, give me this wisdom. □ God wants us to turn from godless living and sinful pleasures and to live good, God-fearing lives day after day. □ Don't hide your light! Let it shine for all; let your good deeds glow for all to see, so that they will praise your heavenly Father. □ I don't mean to say I am perfect. I haven't learned all I should even yet.

When he comes we will be like him, as a result of seeing him as he really is. And everyone who really believes this will try to stay pure because Christ is pure.

This is what God has prepared for us and, as a guarantee, he has given us his Holy Spirit. □ Why is it that he gives . . . special abilities to do certain things best? It is that God's people will be equipped to do better work for him, building up the church, the body of Christ, to a position of strength and maturity; until finally we all believe alike about our salvation and about our Savior, God's Son, and all become full-grown in the Lord —yes, to the point of being filled full with Christ.

2 Cor. 7:1. Ps. 51:6. Tit. 2:12. Mt. 5:15, 16. Phil. 3:12. 1 Jn. 3:2, 3. 2 Cor. 5:5. Eph. 4:12, 13.

He has enriched your whole life.

When we were utterly helpless with no way of escape, Christ came at just the right time and died for us sinners who had no use for him. □ Since he did not spare even his own Son for us but gave him up for us all, won't he also surely give us everything else?

For in Christ there is all of God in a human body; *so you have everything when you have Christ,* and you are filled with God through your union with Christ. He is the highest Ruler, with authority over every other power.

Take care to live in me, and let me live in you. For a branch can't produce fruit when severed from the vine. Nor can you be fruitful apart from me. Yes, I am the Vine, you are the branches. Whoever lives in me and I in him shall produce a large crop of fruit. For apart from me you can't do a thing. □ Christ has given each of us special abilities—whatever he wants us to have out of his rich storehouse of gifts.

If you stay in me and obey my commands, you may ask any request you like, and it will be granted. □ Let his words enrich your lives and make you wise.

1 Cor. 1:5. Rom. 5:6. Rom. 8:32. Col. 2:9, 10. Jn. 15:4, 5. Eph. 4:7. Jn. 15:7. Col. 3:16.

I will tell of the lovingkindness of God. I will praise him for all he has done; I will rejoice in his great goodness.

He lifted me out of the pit of despair, out from the bog and the mire, and set my feet on a hard, firm path and steadied me as I walked along. □ The Son of God . . . loved me and gave himself for me. □ Since he did not spare even his own Son for us but gave him up for us all, won't he also surely give us everything else? □ God showed his great love for us by sending Christ to die for us while we were still sinners.

He has put his brand upon us—his mark of ownership—and given us his Holy Spirit in our hearts as guarantee that we belong to him. □ His presence within us is God's guarantee that he really will give us all that he promised; and the Spirit's seal upon us means that God has already purchased us and that he guarantees to bring us to himself.

God is so rich in mercy; he loved us so much that even though we were spiritually dead and doomed by our sins, he gave us back our lives again when he raised Christ from the dead—only by his undeserved favor have we ever been saved —and lifted us up from the grave into glory along with Christ, where we sit with him in the heavenly realms—all because of what Christ Jesus did.

Is. 63:7. Ps. 40:2. Gal. 2:20. Rom. 8:32. Rom. 5:8. 2 Cor. 1:22. Eph. 1:14. Eph. 2:4–6.

Don't talk so much. You keep putting your foot in your mouth. Be sensible and turn off the flow!

Dear brothers, don't ever forget that it is best to listen much, speak little, and not become angry. ☐ It is better to be slow-tempered than famous; it is better to have self-control than to control an army. ☐ If anyone can control his tongue, it proves that he has perfect control over himself in every other way. ☐ Your words . . . reflect your fate: either you will be justified by them or you will be condemned. ☐ Help me, Lord, to keep my mouth shut and my lips sealed.

Christ, who suffered for you, is your example. Follow in his steps. He never sinned, never told a lie, never answered back when insulted; when he suffered he did not threaten to get even; he left his case in the hands of God who always judges fairly. ☐ If you want to keep from becoming fainthearted and weary, think about his patience as sinful men did such terrible things to him. ☐ Gentle words cause life and health.

No falsehood can be charged against them; they are blameless.

Prov. 10:19. Jas. 1:19. Prov. 16:32. Jas. 3:2. Mt. 12:37. Ps. 141:3. 1 Pet. 2:21–23. Hebr. 12:3. Prov. 15:4 Rev. 14:5.

Tell me what to do, O Lord.

I will instruct you (says the Lord) and guide you along the best pathway for your life; I will advise you and watch your progress. □ The Lord is good and glad to teach the proper path to all who go astray; he will teach the ways that are right and best to those who humbly turn to him.

Yes, I am the Gate. Those who come in by way of the Gate will be saved and will go in and out and find green pastures.

Jesus told him, "I am the Way—yes, and the Truth and the Life. No one can get to the Father except by means of me." □ Now we may walk right into the very Holy of Holies where God is, because of the blood of Jesus. This is the fresh, new, life-giving way which Christ has opened up for us by tearing the curtain—his human body— to let us into the holy presence of God. And since this great High Priest of ours rules over God's household, let us go right in, to God himself, with true hearts fully trusting him to receive us.

Oh, that we might know the Lord! Let us press on to know him. □ And when we obey him, every path he guides us on is fragrant with his loving-kindness and his truth.

Ps. 27:11. Ps. 32:8. Ps. 25:8, 9. Jn. 10:9. Jn. 14:6. Hebr. 10:19– 22. Hos. 6:3. Ps. 25:10.

*When God's children are in need, you be the
one to help them out.*

One day David began wondering if any of
Saul's family was still living, for he wanted to be
kind to them, as he had promised Prince Jonathan.

Come, blessed of my Father, into the Kingdom prepared for you from the founding of the
world. For I was hungry and you fed me; I was
thirsty and you gave me water; I was a stranger
and you invited me into your homes; naked and
you clothed me; sick and in prison, and you
visited me. When you did it to these my brothers
you were doing it to me! □ And if, as my repre-
sentatives, you give even a cup of cold water to a
little child, you will surely be rewarded.

Don't forget to do good and to share what you
have with those in need, for such sacrifices are
very pleasing to him. □ For God is not unfair.
How can he forget your hard work for him, or
forget the way you used to show your love for
him—and still do—by helping his children. And
we are anxious that you keep right on loving
others as long as life lasts, so that you will get
your full reward.

*Rom. 12:13. 2 Sam. 9:1. Mt. 25:34–36, 40. Mt. 10:42. Hebr. 13:16.
Hebr. 6:10, 11.*

Are you seeking great things for yourself?
Don't do it.

Wear my yoke—for it fits perfectly—and let
me teach you; for I am gentle and humble, and
you shall find rest for your souls. □ Your attitude should be the kind that was shown us by
Jesus Christ, who, though he was God, did not
demand and cling to his rights as God, but laid
aside his mighty power and glory, taking the
disguise of a slave and becoming like men. And
he humbled himself even further, going so far as
actually to die a criminal's death on a cross.

If you refuse to take up your cross and follow
me, you are not worthy of being mine. □ Christ,
who suffered for you, is your example. Follow in
his steps. □ Many who are first now will be last
. . . and some who are last now will be first.

Do you want to be truly rich? You already are
if you are happy and good. After all, we didn't
bring any money with us when we came into the
world, and we can't carry away a single penny
when we die. So we should be well satisfied without money if we have enough food and clothing.
□ I have learned how to get along happily
whether I have much or little.

Jer. 45:5. Mt. 11:29. Phil. 2:5–8. Mt. 10:38. 1 Pet. 2:21. Mt.
19:30. 1 Tim. 6:6–8. Phil. 4:11.

Stay true to the Lord.

I have stayed in God's paths, following his steps. I have not turned aside. □ The Lord loves justice and fairness; he will never abandon his people. They will be kept safe forever. □ He keeps you from all evil, and preserves your life.

Those whose faith has made them good in God's sight must live by faith, trusting him in everything. Otherwise, if they shrink back, God will have no pleasure in them. But we have never turned our backs on God and sealed our fate. No, our faith in him assures our souls' salvation. □ These "against-Christ" people used to be members of our churches, but they never really belonged with us or else they would have stayed. When they left us it proved that they were not of us at all.

You are truly my disciples if you live as I tell you to. □ Those enduring to the end shall be saved. □ Keep your eyes open for spiritual danger; stand true to the Lord; act like men; be strong. □ Hold tightly to the little strength you have—so that no one will take away your crown. □ Everyone who conquers will be clothed in white, and I will not erase his name from the Book of Life, but I will announce before my Father and his angels that he is mine.

Phil. 4:1. Job 23:11. Ps. 37:28. Ps. 121:7. Hebr. 10:38, 39. 1 Jn. 2:19. Jn. 8:31. Mt. 24:13. 1 Cor. 16:13. Rev. 3:11. Rev. 3:5.

Our Lord Jesus . . . though he was so very rich, yet to help you . . . became so very poor, so that by being poor he could make you rich.

God wanted all of himself to be in his Son. □ God's Son shines out with God's glory and all that God's Son is and does marks him as God. He regulates the universe by the mighty power of his command. He is the one who died to cleanse us and clear our record of all sin, and then sat down in highest honor beside the great God of heaven. Thus he became far greater than the angels, as proved by the fact that his name, Son of God, which was passed on to him from his Father, is far greater than the names and titles of the angels. □ Who, though he was God, did not demand and cling to his rights as God, but laid aside his mighty power and glory, taking the disguise of a slave and becoming like men.

Foxes have dens and birds have nests, but I, the Messiah, have no home of my own—no place to lay my head.

God has already given you everything you need. . . . He has given you the whole world to use, and life and even death are your servants. He has given you all of the present and all of the future. All are yours, and you belong to Christ, and Christ is God's.

2 Cor. 8:9. Col. 1:19. Hebr. 1:3, 4. Phil. 2:6, 7. Mt. 8:20. 1 Cor. 3:21–23.

Our remaining time is very short.

How frail is man, how few his days, how full of trouble! He blossoms for a moment like a flower —and withers; as the shadow of a passing cloud, he quickly disappears. ☐ This world is fading away, and these evil, forbidden things will go with it, but whoever keeps doing the will of God will live forever. ☐ Everyone dies because all of us are related to Adam, being members of his sinful race, and wherever there is sin, death results. But all who are related to Christ will rise again. Death is swallowed up in victory. ☐ Living or dying we follow the Lord. Either way we are his.

Living means opportunities for Christ, and dying—well, that's better yet!

Do not let this happy trust in the Lord die away, no matter what happens. Remember your reward! You need to keep on patiently doing God's will if you want him to do for you all that he has promised. His coming will not be delayed much longer. ☐ The night is far gone, the day of his return will soon be here. So quit the evil deeds of darkness and put on the armor of right living. ☐ The end of the world is coming soon. Therefore be earnest, thoughtful men of prayer.

1 Cor. 7:29. Job 14:1, 2. 1 Jn. 2:17. 1 Cor. 15:22, 54. Rom. 14:8. Phil. 1:21. Hebr. 10:35–37. Rom. 13:12. 1 Pet. 4:7.

That time when his glory shall be seen—the glory of our great God and Savior Jesus Christ.

This certain hope of being saved is a strong and trustworthy anchor for our souls, connecting us with God himself behind the sacred curtains of heaven where Christ has gone ahead to plead for us. □ For he must remain in heaven until the final recovery of all things from sin. □ When he comes to receive praise and admiration because of all he has done for his people, his saints.

Even the things of nature, like animals and plants, suffer in sickness and death as they await this great event. And even we Christians . . . groan to be released from pain and suffering. We, too, wait anxiously for that day when God will give us our full rights as his children, including the new bodies he has promised us—bodies that will never be sick again and will never die. □ Dear friends, we are already God's children, right now, and we can't even imagine what it is going to be like later on. But we do know this, that when he comes we will be like him, as a result of seeing him as he really is. □ When Christ who is our real life comes back again, you will shine with him and share in all his glories.

"I am coming soon!" Amen! Come, Lord Jesus!

Tit. 2:13. Hebr. 6:19, 20. Acts 3:21. 2 Thess. 1:10. Rom. 8:22, 23. 1 Jn. 3:2. Col. 3:4. Rev. 22:20.

*Those who do what Christ tells them to will
learn to love God more and more.*

May the God of peace, who brought again
from the dead our Lord Jesus, equip you with all
you need for doing his will. May he who became
the great Shepherd of the sheep by an everlasting
agreement between God and you, signed with his
blood, produce in you through the power of Christ
all that is pleasing to him. To whom be glory forever and ever. Amen.

How can we be sure that we belong to him? By
looking within ourselves: are we really trying to
do what he wants us to? □ I will only reveal myself to those who love me and obey me. The
Father will love them too, and we will come to
them and live with them. □ If we stay close to
him, obedient to him, we won't be sinning either;
but as for those who keep on sinning, they should
realize this: They sin because they have never
really known him or become his. Oh, dear children, don't let anyone deceive you about this: if
you are constantly doing what is good, it is because you *are* good, even as he is.

As we live with Christ, our love grows more
perfect and complete; so we will not be ashamed
and embarrassed at the day of judgment, but can
face him with confidence and joy, because he
loves us and we love him too.

*1 Jn. 2:5. Hebr. 13:20, 21. 1 Jn. 2:3. Jn. 14:23. 1 Jn. 3:6, 7. 1 Jn.
4:17.*

A wise man controls his temper.

The Lord descended in the form of a pillar of cloud and stood there with him, and passed in front of him and announced the meaning of his name. "I am Jehovah, the merciful and gracious God," he said, "slow to anger and rich in steadfast love and truth."

Follow God's example in everything you do just as a much loved child imitates his father. □ When the Holy Spirit controls our lives he will produce this kind of fruit in us: love, joy, peace, patience, kindness, goodness, faithfulness, gentleness and self-control. □ Praise the Lord if you are punished for doing right! Of course, you get no credit for being patient if you are beaten for doing wrong; but if you do right and suffer for it, and are patient beneath the blows, God is well pleased. This suffering is all part of the work God has given you. Christ, who suffered for you, is your example. Follow in his steps: He never sinned, never told a lie, never answered back when insulted; when he suffered he did not threaten to get even; he left his case in the hands of God who always judges fairly.

Don't let the sun go down with you still angry —get over it quickly; for when you are angry you give a mighty foothold to the devil.

Prov. 14:29. Ex. 34:6. Eph. 5:1. Gal. 5:22, 23. 1 Pet. 2:19–23. Eph. 4:26.

God lives here.

Where two or three gather together because they are mine, I will be right there among them. □ I am with you always, even to the end of the world. □ I myself will go with you and give you success.

I can *never* be lost to your Spirit! I can *never* get away from God! If I go up to heaven, you are there; if I go down to the place of the dead, you are there. If I ride the morning winds to the farthest oceans, even there your hand will guide me, your strength will support me. If I try to hide in the darkness, the night becomes light around me. For even darkness cannot hide from God; to you the night shines as bright as day. □ Am I a God who is only in one place and cannot see what they are doing? Can anyone hide from me? Am I not everywhere in all of heaven and earth?

Is it possible that God would really live on earth? Why, even the skies and the highest heavens cannot contain you, much less this Temple. □ The high and lofty one who inhabits eternity, the Holy One, says this: I live in that high and holy place where those with contrite, humble spirits dwell; and I refresh the humble and give new courage to those with repentant hearts.

Gen. 28:16. Mt. 18:20. Mt. 28:20. Ex. 33:14. Ps. 139:7–12. Jer. 23: 23, 24. 1 Kgs. 8:27. Is. 57:15.

Keep away from anything that might take God's place in your hearts.

O my son, trust my advice. □ Let heaven fill your thoughts; don't spend your time worrying about things down here.

Son of dust, these men worship idols in their hearts—should I let them ask me anything? □ Away . . . with sinful, earthly things; deaden the evil desires lurking within you; have nothing to do with sexual sin, impurity, lust and shameful desires; don't worship the good things of life, for that is idolatry. □ People who long to be rich soon begin to do all kinds of wrong things to get money, things that hurt them and make them evil-minded and finally send them to hell itself. For the love of money is the first step toward all kinds of sin. Some people have even turned away from God because of their love for it, and as a result have pierced themselves with many sorrows. . . . You are God's man. Run from all these evil things and work instead at what is right and good, learning to trust him and love others, and to be patient and gentle. □ Don't become rich by extortion and robbery. □ My gifts are better than the purest gold or sterling silver!

If your profits are in heaven your heart will be there too. □ I [the Lord] look at a man's thoughts and intentions.

1 Jn. 5:21. Prov. 23:26. Col. 3:2. Ezk. 14:3. Col. 3:5. 1 Tim. 6:9–11. Ps. 62:10. Prov. 8:19. Mt. 6:21. 1 Sam. 16:7.

When the Holy Spirit controls our lives he will produce . . . joy.

Joy from the Holy Spirit. □ Inexpressible joy that comes from heaven itself.

Our hearts ache, but at the same time we have the joy of the Lord. □ Happy in spite of all my suffering. □ We . . . rejoice . . . when we run into problems and trials.

Jesus, our leader and instructor . . . willing to die a shameful death on the cross because of the joy he knew would be his afterwards. □ I have told you this so that you will be filled with my joy. Yes, your cup of joy will overflow! □ The more we undergo sufferings for Christ, the more he will shower us with his comfort and encouragement.

Always be full of joy in the Lord; I say it again, rejoice! □ The joy of the Lord is your strength.

You have let me experience the joys of life and the exquisite pleasures of your own eternal presence. □ For the Lamb standing in front of the throne will feed them and be their Shepherd and lead them to the springs of the Water of Life. And God will wipe their tears away. □ For them all sorrow and all sighing will be gone forever; only joy and gladness will be there.

Gal. 5:22. Rom. 14:17. 1 Pet. 1:8. 2 Cor. 6:10. 2 Cor. 7:4. Rom. 5:3. Hebr. 12:2. Jn. 15:11. 2 Cor. 1:5. Phil. 4:4 Neh. 8:10. Ps. 16:11. Rev. 7:17. Is. 35:10.

*You are to be perfect, even as your Father
in heaven is perfect.*

I am the Almighty; obey me and live as you
should. □ You shall be holy to me, for I the Lord
am holy, and I have set you apart from all other
peoples, to be mine.

God has bought you with a great price. So use
every part of your body to give glory back to God,
because he owns it.

So you have everything when you have Christ,
and you are filled with God through your union
with Christ. He is the highest Ruler, with authority over every other power. □ He died under
God's judgment against our sins, so that he could
rescue us from constant falling into sin. □ Try
hard to live without sinning; and be at peace with
everyone so that he will be pleased with you when
he returns.

Happy are all who perfectly follow the laws of
God. □ If anyone keeps looking steadily into
God's law for free men, he will not only remember it but he will do what it says, and God will
greatly bless him in everything he does. □ Search
me, O God, and know my heart; test my thoughts.
Point out anything you find in me that makes you
sad, and lead me along the path of everlasting
life.

*Mt. 5:48. Gen. 17:1. Lev. 20:26. 1 Cor. 6:20. Col. 2:10. Tit. 2:14.
2 Pet. 3:14. Ps. 119:1. Jas. 1:25. Ps. 139:23, 24.*

Keep none of the booty.

Leave them; separate yourselves from them; don't touch their filthy things. ☐ Dear brothers, you are only visitors here. Since your real home is in heaven I beg you to keep away from the evil pleasures of this world; they are not for you, for they fight against your very souls. ☐ Hate every trace of their sin.

We are already God's children, right now, and we can't even imagine what it is going to be like later on. But we do know this, that when he comes we will be like him, as a result of seeing him as he really is. And everyone who really believes this will try to stay pure because Christ is pure. ☐ For the free gift of eternal salvation is now being offered to everyone; and along with this gift comes the realization that God wants us to turn from godless living and sinful pleasures and to live good, God-fearing lives day after day, looking forward to that time when his glory shall be seen —the glory of our great God and Savior Jesus Christ. He died under God's judgment against our sins, so that he could rescue us from constant falling into sin and make us his very own people, with cleansed hearts and real enthusiasm for doing kind things to others.

Deut. 13:17. 2 Cor. 6:17. 1 Pet. 2:11. Jude 23. 1 Jn. 3:2, 3. Tit. 2:11–14.

*He spread out a cloud above them to shield
them from the burning sun, and gave them
a pillar of flame at night to give them light.*

He is like a father to us, tender and sympathetic to those who reverence him. For he knows
we are but dust.

He protects you day and night. □ Protecting
. . . from daytime heat and from rains and
storms.

Jehovah himself is caring for you! He is your
defender. He keeps his eye upon you as you
come and go, and always guards you. □ God
protected them in the howling wilderness as
though they were the apple of his eye. □ In your
great mercy you didn't abandon them to die in
the wilderness! The pillar of cloud led them forward day by day, and the pillar of fire showed
them the way through the night. You sent your
good Spirit to instruct them, and you did not
stop giving them bread from heaven or water for
their thirst. For forty years you sustained them
in the wilderness; they lacked nothing in all that
time. Their clothes didn't wear out and their feet
didn't swell! □ You have led the people you redeemed. In your lovingkindness you have guided
them wonderfully.

Jesus Christ is the same yesterday, today, and
forever.

*Ps. 105:39. Ps. 103:13, 14. Ps. 121:6. Is. 4:6. Ps. 121:5, 8. Deut.
32:10. Neh. 9:19–21. Ex. 15:13. Hebr. 13:8.*

When you hear of wars beginning, this does not signal my return; these must come, but the end is not yet.

God is our refuge and strength, a tested help in times of trouble. And so we need not fear even if the world blows up, and the mountains crumble into the sea. Let the oceans roar and foam; let the mountains tremble! □ Go home, my people, and lock the doors! Hide for a little while until the Lord's wrath against your enemies has passed. Look! The Lord is coming from the heavens to punish the people of the earth for their sins. □ I will hide beneath the shadow of your wings until this storm is past. □ Your real life is in heaven with Christ and God.

All who fear God and trust in him are blessed beyond expression. Such a man will not be overthrown by evil circumstances. God's constant care of him will make a deep impression on all who see it. He does not fear bad news, nor live in dread of what may happen. For he is settled in his mind that Jehovah will take care of him.

I have told you all this so that you will have peace of heart and mind. Here on earth you will have many trials and sorrows; but cheer up, for I have overcome the world.

Mt. 24:6. Ps. 46:1–3. Is. 26:20, 21. Ps. 57:1. Col. 3:3. Ps. 112:1, 6, 7. Jn. 16:33.

Get some sense and quit your sinning.

You are all children of the light and of the day, and do not belong to darkness and night. So be on your guard, not asleep like the others. Watch for his return and stay sober.

Another reason for right living is this: you know how late it is; time is running out. Wake up, for the coming of the Lord is nearer now than when we first believed. The night is far gone, the day of his return will soon be here. So quit the evil deeds of darkness and put on the armor of right living, as we who live in the daylight should! □ Use every piece of God's armor to resist the enemy whenever he attacks, and when it is all over, you will still be standing up. □ Turn from your sins . . . put them behind you and receive a new heart and a new spirit. □ Get rid of all that is wrong in your life, both inside and outside, and humbly be glad for the wonderful message we have received, for it is able to save our souls as it takes hold of our hearts.

My little children, stay in happy fellowship with the Lord so that when he comes you will be sure that all is well, and will not have to be ashamed and shrink back from meeting him.

1 Cor. 15:34. 1 Thess. 5:5, 6. Rom. 13:11, 12. Eph. 6:13. Ezk. 18:30, 31. Jas. 1:21. 1 Jn. 2:28.

Contempt has broken my heart.

He's just a carpenter's son. □ Nazareth! Can anything good come from there? □ The reason he can cast out demons is that he is demon-possessed himself—possessed by Satan, the demon king! □ We know Jesus is an evil person. □ He's duping the public. □ Blasphemy! This man is saying he is God! □ I, the Messiah, feast and drink, and you complain that I am a glutton and a drinking man, and hang around with the worst sort of sinners!

Praise the Lord if you are punished for doing right! Of course, you get no credit for being patient if you are beaten for doing wrong; but if you do right and suffer for it, and are patient beneath the blows, God is well pleased. This suffering is all part of the work God has given you. Christ, who suffered for you, is your example. Follow in his steps: he never sinned, never told a lie, never answered back when insulted; when he suffered he did not threaten to get even; he left his case in the hands of God who always judges fairly. □ Be happy if you are cursed and insulted for being a Christian.

The student shares his teacher's fate. The servant shares his master's!

Ps. 69:20. Mt. 13:55. Jn. 1:46. Mt. 9:34. Jn. 9:24. Jn. 7:12. Mt. 9:3. Mt. 11:19. 1 Pet. 2:19–23. 1 Pet. 4:14. Mt. 10:25.

I want men everywhere to pray with holy hands lifted up to God, free from sin and anger and resentment.

It's not *where* we worship that counts, but *how* we worship—is our worship spiritual and real? Do we have the Holy Spirit's help? For God is Spirit and we must have his help to worship as we should. The Father wants this kind of worship from us. □ When you call, the Lord will answer, "Yes, I am here." □ When you are praying, first forgive anyone you are holding a grudge against.

You can never please God without faith, without depending on him. Anyone who wants to come to God must believe that there is a God and that he rewards those who sincerely look for him. □ When you ask him, be sure that you really expect him to tell you, for a doubtful mind will be as unsettled as a wave of the sea that is driven and tossed by the wind. . . . If you don't ask with faith, don't expect the Lord to give you any solid answer.

He would not have listened if I had not confessed my sins. □ My little children, I am telling you this so that you will stay away from sin. But if you sin, there is someone to plead for you before the Father. His name is Jesus Christ, the one who is all that is good and who pleases God completely.

1 Tim. 2:8. Jn. 4:23, 24. Is. 58:9. Mk. 11:25. Hebr. 11:6. Jas. 1:6, 7. Ps. 66:18. 1 Jn. 2:1, 2.

My heart beats wildly, my strength fails.

O God, listen to me! Hear my prayer! For wherever I am, though far away at the ends of the earth, I will cry to you for help. When my heart is faint and overwhelmed, lead me to the mighty, towering Rock of safety.

I am with you; that is all you need. My power shows up best in weak people. Now I am glad to boast about how weak I am; I am glad to be a living demonstration of Christ's power, instead of showing off my own power and abilities. When I am weak, then I am strong—the less I have, the more I depend on him.

When he [Peter] looked around at the high waves, he was terrified and began to sink. "Save me, Lord!" he shouted. Instantly Jesus reached out his hand and rescued him. "O man of little faith," Jesus said, "Why did you doubt?" □ You are a poor specimen if you can't stand the pressure of adversity. □ He gives power to the tired and worn out, and strength to the weak. □ The eternal God is your Refuge, and underneath are the everlasting arms. □ Filled with his mighty, glorious strength so that you can keep going no matter what happens.

Ps. 38:10. Ps. 61:1, 2. 2 Cor. 12:9, 10. Mt. 14:30, 31. Prov. 24:10. Is. 40:29. Deut. 33:27. Col. 1:11.

I will bless the Lord who counsels me.

His royal titles: Wonderful, Counselor. □ I, Wisdom, give good advice and common sense. □ Your words are a flashlight to light the path ahead of me, and keep me from stumbling. □ Trust the Lord completely; don't ever trust yourself. In everything you do, put God first, and he will direct you and crown your efforts with success.

O Lord, I know it is not within the power of man to map his life and plan his course. □ If you leave God's paths and go astray, you will hear a Voice behind you say, "No, this is the way; walk here." □ Commit your work to the Lord, then it will succeed. □ Since the Lord is directing our steps, why try to understand everything that happens along the way?

You will keep on guiding me all my life with your wisdom and counsel; and afterwards receive me into the glories of heaven! □ Even when walking through the dark valley of death I will not be afraid, for you are close beside me, guarding, guiding all the way. □ For this great God is our God forever and ever. He will be our guide until we die.

Ps. 16:7. Is. 9:6. Prov. 8:14. Ps. 119:105. Prov. 3:5, 6. Jer. 10:23. Is. 30:21. Prov. 16:3. Prov. 20:24. Ps. 73:24. Ps. 23:4. Ps. 48:14.

*I am the Lord your God. Follow my laws;
keep my ordinances.*

Be holy now in everything you do, just as the
Lord is holy, who invited you to be his child. □
Anyone who says he is a Christian should live as
Christ did.

Not because we think we can do anything of
lasting value by ourselves. Our only power and
success comes from God. □ Take care to live in
me, and let me live in you. For a branch can't
produce fruit when severed from the vine. Nor
can you be fruitful apart from me.

Do the good things that result from being
saved, obeying God with deep reverence, shrinking back from all that might displease him. For
God is at work within you, helping you want to
obey him, and then helping you do what he wants.
□ The God of peace, who brought again from the
dead our Lord Jesus, the great shepherd of the
sheep, equip you with all you need for doing his
will, through the blood of the everlasting agreement between God and you. And may he produce
in you through the power of Christ all that is
pleasing to him.

*Ezk. 20:19. 1 Pet. 1:15. 1 Jn. 2:6. 2 Cor. 3:5. Jn. 15:4. Phil. 2:12,
13. Hebr. 13:20, 21.*

The Father has life in himself, and has granted his Son to have life in himself.

Our Savior Jesus Christ . . . broke the power of death and showed us the way of everlasting life through trusting him. □ I am the one who raises the dead and gives them life again. □ I will live again—and you will too. □ We will share in all that belongs to Christ. □ The first man, Adam, was given a natural, human body but Christ is more than that, for he was life-giving Spirit. I am telling you this strange and wonderful secret: we shall not all die, but we shall all be given new bodies! It will all happen in a moment, in the twinkling of an eye, when the last trumpet is blown. For there will be a trumpet blast from the sky and all the Christians who have died will suddenly become alive, with new bodies that will never, never die; and then we who are still alive shall suddenly have new bodies too.

Holy, holy, holy, Lord God Almighty—the one who was, and is, and is to come. Who lives forever and ever. □ The blessed and only Almighty God, the King of kings, and Lord of lords. □ Glory and honor to God for ever and ever. He is the King of the ages, the unseen one who never dies; he alone is God, and full of wisdom. Amen.

Jn. 5:26. 2 Tim. 1:10. Jn. 11:25. Jn. 14:19. Hebr. 3:14. 1 Cor. 15:45, 51, 52. Rev. 4:8, 9. 1 Tim. 6:15. 1 Tim. 1:17.

We won't need to look for honors.

Gideon replied . . . "I have one request. Give me all the earrings collected from your fallen foes,"—for the troops of Midian, being Ishmaelites, all wore golden earrings. "Gladly," they replied, and spread out a sheet for everyone to throw in the gold earrings he had gathered. Gideon made an ephod from the gold and put it in Ophrah, his home town. But all Israel soon began worshiping it, so it became an evil deed that Gideon and his family did.

Are you seeking great things for yourself? Don't. ☐ Because these experiences I had were so tremendous, God was afraid I might be puffed up by them; so I was given a physical condition which has been a thorn in my flesh, a messenger from Satan to hurt and bother me, and prick my pride. How weak I am; I am glad to be a living demonstration of Christ's power instead of showing off my own power and abilities.

Don't be selfish; don't live to make a good impression on others. Be humble, thinking of others as better than yourself. ☐ Love is very patient and kind, never jealous or envious, never boastful or proud, never haughty or selfish or rude. Love does not demand its own way.

Wear my yoke—for it fits perfectly—and let me teach you.

Gal. 5:26. Judg. 8:24, 25, 27. Jer. 45:5. 2 Cor. 12:7, 9. Phil. 2:3. 1 Cor. 13:4, 5. Mt. 11:29.

Keep a close watch on all you do and think.

To win the contest you must deny yourselves many things that would keep you from doing your best. An athlete goes to all this trouble just to win a blue ribbon or a silver cup, but we do it for a heavenly reward that never disappears. So I run straight to the goal with purpose in every step. I fight to win. I'm not just shadow-boxing or playing around. Like an athlete I punish my body, treating it roughly, training it to do what it should, not what it wants to. Otherwise I fear that after enlisting others for the race, I myself might be declared unfit and ordered to stand aside.

Put on all of God's armor so that you will be able to stand safe against all strategies and tricks of Satan. For we are not fighting against people made of flesh and blood, but against persons without bodies—the evil rulers of the unseen world, those mighty satanic beings and great evil princes of darkness who rule this world; and against huge numbers of wicked spirits in the spirit world.

Those who belong to Christ have nailed their natural evil desires to his cross and crucified them there. If we are living now by the Holy Spirit's power, let us follow the Holy Spirit's leading in every part of our lives.

1 Tim. 4:16. 1 Cor. 9:25–27. Eph. 6:11, 12. Gal. 5:24, 25.

The Holy Spirit helps us with our daily problems.

The Comforter . . . the Holy Spirit. □ Haven't you yet learned that your body is the home of the Holy Spirit God gave you, and that he lives within you? □ God is at work within you.

The Holy Spirit helps us with our daily problems and in our praying. For we don't even know what we should pray for, nor how to pray as we should; but the Holy Spirit prays for us with such feeling that it cannot be expressed in words. And the Father who knows all hearts knows, of course, what the Spirit is saying as he pleads for us in harmony with God's own will.

He knows we are but dust. □ He will not break the bruised reed, nor quench the dimly burning flame.

The spirit indeed is willing, but how weak the body is!

Because the Lord is my Shepherd, I have everything I need! He lets me rest in the meadow grass and leads me beside the quiet streams. He restores my failing health. He helps me do what honors him the most. Even when walking through the dark valley of death I will not be afraid, for you are close beside me, guarding, guiding all the way.

Rom. 8:26. Jn. 14:26. 1 Cor. 6:19. Phil. 2:13. Rom. 8:26, 27. Ps. 103:14. Is. 42:3. Mt. 26:41. Ps. 23:1–4.

When he calls on me I will answer; I will be with him in trouble, and rescue him and honor him.

Jabez . . . prayed to the God of Israel, "Oh, that you would wonderfully bless me and help me in my work; please be with me in all that I do, and keep me from all evil and disaster!" And God granted him his request. □ God appeared to Solomon and told him, "Ask me for anything, and I will give it to you." Solomon replied, "O God . . . give me wisdom and knowledge to rule . . . properly, for who is able to govern by himself such a great nation as this one of yours?" □ God gave Solomon great wisdom and understanding. His wisdom excelled that of any of the wise men of the East.

King Asa sent his troops to meet them there. "O Lord," he cried out to God, "no one else can help us! Here we are, powerless against this mighty army. Oh, help us, Lord our God! For we trust in you alone to rescue us and in your name we attack this vast horde. Don't let mere men defeat you!" Then the Lord defeated the Ethiopians, and Asa and the army of Judah triumphed as the Ethiopians fled.

Because you answer prayer, all mankind will come to you with their requests.

Ps. 91:15. 1 Chron. 4:9, 10. 2 Chron. 1:7, 8, 10. 1 Kgs. 4:29, 30. 2 Chron. 14:10–12. Ps. 65:2.

Put on the armor of right living.

Ask the Lord Jesus Christ to help you live as you should. □ I have put aside all else, counting it worth less than nothing, in order that I can have Christ, and become one with him, no longer counting on being saved by being good enough or by obeying God's laws, but by trusting Christ to save me; for God's way of making us right with himself depends on faith—counting on Christ alone. □ He will accept and acquit us—declare us not guilty—if we trust Jesus Christ to take away our sins. And we all can be saved in this same way, by coming to Christ, no matter who we are or what we have been like.

He has clothed me with garments of salvation and draped about me the robe of righteousness. □ I walk in the strength of the Lord God. I tell everyone that you alone are just and good.

For though once your heart was full of darkness, now it is full of light from the Lord, and your behavior should show it! Take no part in the worthless pleasures of evil and darkness, but instead, rebuke and expose them. But when you expose them, the light shines in upon their sin and shows it up, and when they see how wrong they really are, some of them may even become children of light!

Rom. 13:12, 14. Phil. 3:8, 9. Rom. 3:22. Is. 61:10. Ps. 71:16. Eph. 5:8, 11, 13–15.

*How great is your goodness . . . you have
stored up great blessings for those who trust
and reverence you.*

Since the world began no one has seen or heard
of such a God as ours, who works for those who
wait for him! □ No mere man has even seen,
heard or even imagined what wonderful things
God has ready for those who love the Lord. But
we know about these things because God has sent
his Spirit to tell us, and his Spirit searches out and
shows us all of God's deepest secrets. □ You have
let me experience the joys of life and the exquisite
pleasures of your own eternal presence.

How precious is your constant love, O God! All
humanity takes refuge in the shadow of your
wings. You feed them with blessings from your
own table and let them drink from your rivers of
delight.

Spend your time and energy in the exercise of
keeping spiritually fit. Bodily exercise is all right,
but spiritual exercise is much more important and
is a tonic for all you do. So exercise yourself
spiritually and practice being a better Christian,
because that will help you not only now in this
life, but in the next life too.

*Ps. 31:19. Is. 64:4. 1 Cor. 2:9, 10. Ps. 16:11. Ps. 36:7, 8. 1 Tim.
4:7, 8.*

The Son of God, whose eyes penetrate like flames of fire.

The heart is the most deceitful thing there is, and desperately wicked. No one can really know how bad it is! Only the Lord knows! He searches all hearts and examines deepest motives so he can give to each person his right reward, according to his deeds—how he has lived. □ You spread out our sins before you—our secret sins—and see them all. □ Jesus turned and looked at Peter. And Peter walked out of the courtyard, crying bitterly.

Jesus didn't trust them, for he knew mankind to the core. No one needed to tell him how changeable human nature is! □ He knows we are but dust. □ He will not break the bruised reed, nor quench the dimly burning flame.

The Lord knows those who are really his. □ I am the Good Shepherd and know my own sheep, and they know me. My sheep recognize my voice, and I know them, and they follow me. I give them eternal life and they shall never perish. No one shall snatch them away from me, for my Father has given them to me, and he is more powerful than anyone else, so no one can kidnap them from me.

Rev. 2:18. Jer. 17:9, 10. Ps. 90:8. Lk. 22:61, 62. Jn. 2:24, 25. Ps. 103:14. Is. 42:3. 2 Tim. 2:19. Jn. 10:14, 27–29.

Our Lord Jesus, the great Shepherd of the sheep.

The Head Shepherd. □ I am the Good Shepherd and know my own sheep, and they know me. My sheep recognize my voice, and I know them, and they follow me. I give them eternal life and they shall never perish. No one shall snatch them away from me. I have other sheep, too, in another fold. I must bring them also, and they will heed my voice.

Because the Lord is my Shepherd, I have everything I need! He lets me rest in the meadow grass and leads me beside the quiet stream. He restores my failing health. He helps me do what honors him the most.

We are the ones who strayed away like sheep! *We,* who left God's paths to follow our own. Yet God laid on *him* the guilt and sins of every one of us! □ I am the Good Shepherd. The Good Shepherd lays down his life for the sheep. □ I will seek my lost ones, those who strayed away, and bring them safely home again. I will put splints and bandages upon their broken limbs and heal the sick. □ Like sheep you wandered away from God, but now you have returned to your Shepherd, the Guardian of your souls who keeps you safe from all attacks.

Hebr. 13:20. 1 Pet. 5:4. Jn. 10:14, 27, 28, 16. Ps. 23:1–3. Is. 53:6. Jn. 10:11. Ezk. 34:16. 1 Pet. 2:25.

The city has no need of sun or moon to light it, for the glory of God and of the Lamb illuminate it.

A light from heaven brighter than the sun shone down on me and my companions. "Who are you, sir?" I asked. And the Lord replied, "I am Jesus, the one you are persecuting." □ Jesus took Peter, James, and his brother John to the top of a high and lonely hill, and as they watched, his appearance changed so that his face shone like the sun and his clothing became dazzling white. □ No longer will you need the sun or moon to give you light, for the Lord your God will be your everlasting light, and he will be your glory. Your sun shall never set; the moon shall not go down—for the Lord will be your everlasting light; your days of mourning all will end.

After you have suffered a little while, our God, who is full of kindness through Christ, will give you his eternal glory. He personally will come and pick you up, and set you firmly in place, and make you stronger than ever. To him be all power over all things, forever and ever. □ So be truly glad! There is wonderful joy ahead, even though the going is rough for a while down here.

Rev. 21:23. Acts 26:13, 15. Mt. 17:1, 2. Is. 60:19, 20. 1 Pet. 5:10. 1 Pet. 1:6.

The Lord is good. When trouble comes, he is the place to go! And he knows everyone who trusts in him!

Praise the Lord! For he is good and his mercy endures forever! □ God is our refuge and strength, a tested help in times of trouble. □ This I declare, that he alone is my refuge, my place of safety; he is my God, and I am trusting him. □ What blessings are yours, O Israel! Who else has been saved by the Lord? He is your shield and your helper! He is your excellent sword! □ As for God, his way is perfect; the word of the Lord is true. He shields all who hide behind him. Our Lord alone is God; we have no other Savior.

The person who truly loves God is the one who is open to God's knowledge. □ God's truth stands firm like a great rock, and nothing can shake it. It is a foundation stone with these words written on it: The Lord knows those who are really his, and a person who calls himself a Christian should not be doing things that are wrong. □ The Lord watches over all the plans and paths of godly men, but the paths of the godless lead to doom. □ You have certainly found favor with me, and you are my friend.

Nah. 1:7. Jer. 33:11. Ps. 46:1. Ps. 91:2. Deut. 33:29. 2 Sam. 22:31, 32. 1 Cor. 8:3. 2 Tim. 2:19. Ps. 1:6. Ex. 33:17.

I want you to be free from worry.

He is always thinking about you and watching everything that concerns you. □ The eyes of the Lord search back and forth across the whole earth, looking for people whose hearts are perfect toward him, so that he can show his great power in helping them.

Put God to the test and see how kind he is! See for yourself the way his mercies shower down on all who trust in him. Even strong young lions sometimes go hungry, but those of us who reverence the Lord will never lack any good thing. □ So my counsel is: Don't worry about *things*— food, drink, and clothes. For you already have life and a body—and they are far more important than what to eat and wear. Look at the birds! They don't worry about what to eat—they don't need to sow or reap or store up food—for your heavenly Father feeds them. And you are far more valuable to him than they are. □ Don't worry about anything; instead, pray about everything; tell God your needs and don't forget to thank him for his answers. If you do this you will experience God's peace, which is far more wonderful than the human mind can understand. His peace will keep your thoughts and your hearts quiet and at rest as you trust in Christ Jesus.

1 Cor. 7:32. 1 Pet. 5:7. 2 Chron. 16:9. Ps. 34:8, 10. Mt. 6:25, 26. Phil. 4:6, 7.

Stay in happy fellowship with the Lord.

A doubtful mind will be as unsettled as a wave of the sea that is driven and tossed by the wind; and every decision you then make will be uncertain, as you turn first this way, and then that.

I am amazed that you are turning away so soon from God who, in his love and mercy, invited you to share the eternal life he gives through Christ; you are already following a different "way to heaven," which really doesn't go to heaven at all.

Christ is useless to you if you are counting on clearing your debt to God by keeping those laws; you are lost from God's grace. You were getting along so well. Who has interfered with you to hold you back from following the truth?

Take care to live in me, and let me live in you. For a branch can't produce fruit when severed from the vine. Nor can you be fruitful apart from me. But if you stay in me and obey my commands, you may ask any request you like, and it will be granted! □ He carries out and fulfills all of God's promises, no matter how many of them there are; and we have told everyone how faithful he is, giving glory to his name.

1 Jn. 2:28. Jas. 1:6, 7. Gal. 1:6. Gal. 5:4, 7. Jn. 15:4, 7. 2 Cor. 1:20.

I am the Almighty; obey me and live as you should.

I [Paul] don't mean to say I am perfect. I haven't learned all I should even yet, but I keep working toward that day when I will finally be all that Christ saved me for and wants me to be. No, dear brothers, I am still not all I should be but I am bringing all my energies to bear on this one thing: Forgetting the past and looking forward to what lies ahead, I strain to reach the end of the race and receive the prize for which God is calling us up to heaven because of what Christ Jesus did for us.

Grow in spiritual strength and become better acquainted with our Lord and Savior Jesus Christ. □ Christians have no veil over our faces; we can be mirrors that brightly reflect the glory of the Lord. And as the Spirit of the Lord works within us, we become more and more like him. □ The good man walks along in the ever-brightening light of God's favor; the dawn gives way to morning splendor.

Jesus . . . looked up to heaven and said . . . "I'm not asking you to take them out of the world, but to keep them safe from Satan's power. I in them and you in me, all being perfected into one."

Gen. 17:1. Phil. 3:12–14. 2 Pet. 3:18. 2 Cor. 3:18. Prov. 4:18. Jn. 17:1, 15, 23.

Don't cause the Holy Spirit sorrow by the way you live.

Love . . . given to you by the Holy Spirit. □ The Comforter . . . the Holy Spirit. □ In all their affliction he was afflicted, and he personally saved them. In his love and pity he redeemed them and lifted them up and carried them through all the years.

He has put his own Holy Spirit into our hearts as a proof to us that we are living with him and he with us. □ Marked as belonging to Christ by the Holy Spirit, who long ago had been promised to all of us Christians. His presence within us is God's guarantee that he really will give us all that he promised; and the Spirit's seal upon us means that God has already purchased us and that he guarantees to bring us to himself. □ I advise you to obey only the Holy Spirit's instructions. He will tell you where to go and what to do, and then you won't always be doing the wrong things your evil nature wants you to. For we naturally love to do evil things that are just the opposite from the things that the Holy Spirit tells us to do; and the good things we want to do when the Spirit has his way with us are just the opposite of our natural desires.

The Holy Spirit helps us with our daily problems.

Eph. 4:30. Rom. 15:30. Jn. 14:26. Is. 63:9. 1 Jn. 4:13. Eph. 1:13, 14. Gal. 5:16, 17. Rom. 8:26.

*If you merely obey me, you should not con-
sider yourselves worthy of praise. For you
have simply done your duty!*

Then what can we boast about doing, to earn
our salvation? Nothing at all. Why? Because our
acquittal is not based on our good deeds; it is
based on what Christ has done and our faith in
him. □ What are you so puffed up about? What
do you have that God hasn't given you? And if all
you have is from God, why act as though you are
so great, and as though you have accomplished
something on your own? □ Because of his kindness you have been saved through trusting Christ.
And even trusting is not of yourselves; it too is a
gift from God. Salvation is not a reward for the
good we have done, so none of us can take any
credit for it. It is God himself who has made us
what we are and given us new lives from Christ
Jesus; and long ages ago he planned that we
should spend these lives in helping others.

But whatever I am now it is all because God
poured out such kindness and grace upon me. □
For everything comes from God alone. Everything
lives by his power, and everything is for his glory.
□ Everything we have has come from you, and
we only give you what is yours already!

*Lk. 17:10. Rom. 3:27. 1 Cor. 4:7. Eph. 2:8–10. 1 Cor. 15:10.
Rom. 11:36. 1 Chron. 29:14.*

Forgive my sins.

"Come, let's talk this over!" says the Lord; "no matter how deep the stain of your sins, I can take it out and make you as clean as freshly fallen snow. Even if you are stained as red as crimson, I can make you white as wool!"

Cheer up, son! For I have forgiven your sins! □ I, yes, I alone am he who blots away your sins for my own sake and will never think of them again.

So overflowing is his kindness towards us that he took away all our sins through the blood of his Son, by whom we are saved. □ He saved us—not because we were good enough to be saved, but because of his kindness and pity—by washing away our sins and giving us the new joy of the indwelling Holy Spirit whom he poured out upon us with wonderful fullness—and all because of what Jesus Christ our Savior did. □ He forgave all your sins, and blotted out the charges proved against you, the list of his commandments which you had not obeyed. He took this list of sins and destroyed it by nailing it to Christ's cross.

Yes, I will bless the Lord. . . . He forgives all my sins.

Ps. 25:18. Is. 1:18. Mt. 9:2. Is. 43:25. Eph. 1:7. Tit. 3:5, 6. Col. 2:13, 14. Ps. 103:2, 3.

This younger son packed all his belongings and took a trip to a distant land, and there wasted all his money.

There was a time when some of you were just like that but now your sins are washed away, and you are set apart for God, and he has accepted you because of what the Lord Jesus Christ and the Spirit of our God have done for you. □ All of us used to be just as they are, our lives expressing the evil within us. But God is so rich in mercy; he loved us so much that even though we were spiritually dead and doomed by our sins, he gave us back our lives again when he raised Christ from the dead—only by his undeserved favor have we ever been saved—and lifted us up from the grave into glory along with Christ, where we sit with him in the heavenly realms—all because of what Christ Jesus did.

In this act we see what real love is: it is not our love for God, but his love for us when he sent his Son to satisfy God's anger against our sins. □ God showed his great love for us by sending Christ to die for us while we were still sinners. And since, when we were his enemies, we were brought back to God by the death of his Son, what blessings he must have for us now that we are his friends, and he is living within us!

Lk. 15:13. 1 Cor. 6:11. Eph. 2:3–6. 1 Jn. 4:10. Rom. 5:8, 10.

*He returned home to his father. And while
he was still a long distance away, his father
saw him coming, and was filled with loving
pity and ran and embraced him and kissed
him.*

He is merciful and tender toward those who
don't deserve it; he is slow to get angry and full
of kindness and love. He never bears a grudge, nor
remains angry forever. He has not punished us as
we deserve for all our sins, for his mercy toward
those who fear and honor him is as great as the
height of the heavens above the earth. He has removed our sins as far away from us as the east is
from the west. He is like a father to us, tender and
sympathetic to those who reverence him.

And so we should not be like cringing, fearful
slaves, but we should behave like God's very own
children, adopted into the bosom of his family,
and calling to him, "Father, Father." For his Holy
Spirit speaks to us deep in our hearts, and tells
us that we really are God's children. □ Though
you once were far away from God, now you have
been brought very near to him because of what
Jesus Christ has done for you with his blood. Now
you are no longer strangers to God and foreigners
to heaven, but you are members of God's very
own family, citizens of God's country, and you
belong in God's household with every other
Christian.

Lk. 15:20. Ps. 103:8–13. Rom. 8:15, 16. Eph. 2:13, 19.

Remember, the Lord forgave you, so you must forgive others.

Then Jesus told him this story: A man loaned money to two people—$5,000 to one and $500 to the other. But neither of them could pay him back, so he kindly forgave them both, letting them keep the money. □ I forgave you all that tremendous debt, just because you asked me to—shouldn't you have mercy on others, just as I had mercy on you?

But when you are praying, first forgive anyone you are holding a grudge against, so that your Father in heaven will forgive you your sins too. □ Since you have been chosen by God who has given you this new kind of life, and because of his deep love and concern for you, you should practice tenderhearted mercy and kindness to others. Don't worry about making a good impression on them but be ready to suffer quietly and patiently. Be gentle and ready to forgive; never hold grudges.

"Sir, how often should I forgive a brother who sins against me? Seven times?" "No," Jesus replied, "seventy times seven."

Let love guide your life. □ Trust him and become full of the love of Christ Jesus.

Col. 3:13. Lk. 7:41, 42. Mt. 18:32, 33. Mk. 11:25. Col. 3:12, 13. Mt. 18:21, 22. Col. 3:14. 1 Tim. 1:14.

*When the Holy Spirit controls our lives he
will produce . . . peace.*

Following after the Holy Spirit leads to life
and peace.

God wants his children to live in peace. □ I am
leaving you with a gift—peace of mind and heart!
And the peace I give isn't fragile like the peace
the world gives. So don't be troubled or afraid.
□ I pray . . . that God who gives you hope will
keep you happy and full of peace as you believe
in him. I pray that God will help you overflow
with hope in him through the Holy Spirit's power
within you.

I know the one in whom I trust, and I am sure
that he is able to safely guard all that I have given
him until the day of his return. □ Christ himself
is our way of peace. □ He will keep in perfect
peace all those who trust in him, whose thoughts
turn often to the Lord!

Out of justice, peace. Quietness and confidence
will reign forevermore. My people will live in
safety, quietly at home. □ All who listen to me
shall live in peace and safety, unafraid.

Those who love your laws have great peace of
heart and mind. □ Peace flowing like a gentle
river, and great waves of righteousness.

*Gal. 5:22. Rom. 8:6. 1 Cor. 7:15. Jn. 14:27. Rom. 15:13. 2 Tim.
1:12. Eph. 2:14. Is. 26:3. Is. 32:17, 18. Prov. 1:33. Ps. 119:165.
Is. 48:18.*

I am making all things new.

Unless you are born again, you can never get into the Kingdom of God. □ When someone becomes a Christian he becomes a brand new person inside. He is not the same anymore. A new life has begun!

It will be as though I had sprinkled clean water on you, for you will be clean—your filthiness will be washed away. And I will give you a new heart —I will give you new and right desires—and put a new spirit within you. I will take out your stony hearts of sin and give you new hearts of love. And I will put my Spirit within you so that you will obey my laws and do whatever I command. □ Yes, you must be a new and different person, holy and good. Clothe yourself with this new nature.

God will confer on you a new name. He will hold you aloft in his hands for all to see—a splendid crown for the King of kings.

I am creating new heavens and a new earth— so wonderful that no one will even think about the old ones anymore. □ And so since everything around us is going to melt away, what holy, godly lives we should be living!

Rev. 21:5. Jn. 3:3. 2 Cor. 5:17. Ezk. 36:25–27. Eph. 4:24. Is. 62:2, 3. Is. 65:17. 2 Pet. 3:11.

*Anything that will stand heat . . . shall be
passed through fire in order to be made
ceremonially pure.*

The Lord is testing you to find out whether or
not you really love him with all your heart and
soul. □ Like a refiner of silver he will sit and
closely watch as the dross is burned away. He
will purify the Levites, the ministers of God, refining them like gold or silver, so that they will do
their work for God with pure hearts. □ There is
going to come a time of testing at Christ's Judgment Day to see what kind of material each
builder has used. Everyone's work will be put
through the fire so that all can see whether or not
it keeps its value, and what was really accomplished.

I myself will melt you in a smelting pot, and
skim off your slag. □ I will melt them in a crucible
of affliction. I will refine them and test them like
metal.

You have purified us with fire, O Lord, like
silver in a crucible. You sent troops to ride across
our broken bodies. We went through fire and
flood. But in the end, you brought us into wealth
and great abundance.

When you walk through the fire of oppression,
you will not be burned up—the flames will not
consume you.

Num. 31:22, 23. Deut. 13:3. Mal. 3:3. 1 Cor. 3:13. Is. 1:25. Jer.
9:7. Ps. 66:10, 12. Is. 43:2.

We can be finished with sin and live a good life.

Throw off your old evil nature—the old you that was a partner in your evil ways—rotten through and through, full of lust and sham. Now your attitudes and thoughts must all be constantly changing for the better. Yes, you must be a new and different person, holy and good. Clothe yourself with this new nature.

You should have as little desire for this world as a dead person does. Your real life is in heaven with Christ and God. □ Your old sin-loving nature was buried with him by baptism when he died, and when God the Father, with glorious power, brought him back to life again, you were given his wonderful new life to enjoy. Your old evil desires were nailed to the cross with him; that part of you that loves to sin was crushed and fatally wounded, so that your sin-loving body is no longer under sin's control, no longer needs to be a slave to sin; for when you are deadened to sin you are freed from all its allure and its power over you. So look upon your old sin nature as dead and unresponsive to sin, and instead be alive to God, alert to him, through Jesus Christ our Lord. Give yourselves completely to God—every part of you—for you are back from death and you want to be tools in the hands of God, to be used for his good purposes.

1 Pet. 2:24. Eph. 4:22–24. Col. 3:3. Rom. 6:4, 6, 7, 11, 13.

*Take care to live in me, and let me live in
you.*

I have been crucified with Christ: and I myself no longer live, but Christ lives in me. And
the real life I now have within this body is a result of my trusting in the Son of God, who loved
me and gave himself for me.

I know I am rotten through and through so
far as my old sinful nature is concerned. No matter which way I turn I can't make myself do right.
I want to but I can't. Oh, what a terrible predica-
ment I'm in! Who will free me from my slavery
to this deadly lower nature? Thank God! It has
been done by Jesus Christ our Lord. He has set
me free. □ Yet, even though Christ lives within
you, your body will die because of sin; but your
spirit will live, for Christ has pardoned it. □ The
only condition is that you fully believe the Truth,
standing in it steadfast and firm, strong in the
Lord, convinced of the Good News that Jesus
died for you, and never shifting from trusting him
to save you.

And now, my little children, stay in happy fellowship with the Lord so that when he comes you
will be sure that all is well, and will not have to be
ashamed and shrink back from meeting him. □
Anyone who says he is a Christian should live as
Christ did.

*Jn. 15:4. Gal. 2:20. Rom. 7:18, 24, 25. Rom. 8:10. Col. 1:23.
1 Jn. 2:28. 1 Jn. 2:6.*

Do you believe in the Messiah?

Who is he, sir?

God's Son shines out with God's glory, and all that God's Son is and does marks him as God. □ The blessed and only Almighty God, the King of kings and Lord of lords, who alone can never die, who lives in light so terrible that no human being can approach him. No mere man has ever seen him, nor ever will. Unto him be honor and everlasting power and dominion forever and ever. Amen. □ "I am the A and the Z, the Beginning and the Ending of all things," says God, who is the Lord, the All Powerful One who is, and was, and is coming again!

Yes, Lord, I believe! □ I know the one in whom I trust, and I am sure that he is able to safely guard all that I have given him until the day of his return. □ We believe because we have heard him ourselves, not just because of what you told us. He is indeed the Savior of the world.

I am sending Christ to be the carefully chosen, precious Cornerstone of my church, and I will never disappoint those who trust in him. Yes, he is very precious to you who believe.

Jesus Christ is the same yesterday, today, and forever.

Jn. 9:35. Jn. 9:36. Hebr. 1:3. 1 Tim. 6:15, 16. Rev. 1:8. Jn. 9:38. 2 Tim. 1:12. Jn. 4:42. 1 Pet. 2:6, 7. Hebr. 13:8.

*Martha, dear friend, you are so upset over
all these details!*

Look at the ravens—they don't plant or harvest
or have barns to store away their food, and yet
they get along all right—for God feeds them. And
you are far more valuable to him than any birds!
Look at the lilies! They don't toil and spin. And
don't worry about food—what to eat and drink;
don't worry at all that God will provide it for you.
All mankind scratches for its daily bread, but
your heavenly Father knows your needs.

We should be well satisfied without money if
we have enough food and clothing. People who
long to be rich soon begin to do all kinds of wrong
things to get money, things that hurt them and
make them evil-minded and finally send them to
hell itself. For the love of money is the first step
toward all kinds of sin. Some people have even
turned away from God because of their love for
it, and as a result have pierced themselves with
many sorrows.

The attractions of this world and the delights
of wealth, and the search for success and lure of
nice things come in and crowd out God's message from their hearts.

Let us strip off anything that slows us down or
holds us back . . . and let us run with patience
the particular race that God has set before us.

*Lk. 10:41. Lk. 12:24, 27, 29, 30. 1 Tim. 6:8–10. Mk. 4:19. Hebr.
12:1.*

Keep praying until the answer comes.

Then, teaching them more about prayer, he used this illustration: Suppose you went to a friend's house at midnight, wanting to borrow three loaves of bread. You would shout up to him, "A friend of mine has just arrived for a visit and I've nothing to give him to eat." He would call down from his bedroom, "Please don't ask me to get up. The door is locked for the night and we are all in bed. I just can't help you this time." But I'll tell you this—though he won't do it as a friend, if you keep knocking long enough he will get up and give you everything you want—just because of your persistence. ☐ Pray all the time. Ask God for anything in line with the Holy Spirit's wishes. Plead with him, reminding him of your needs, and keep praying earnestly for all Christians everywhere.

I will not let you go until you bless me. Because you have been strong with God, you shall prevail with men. ☐ Don't be weary in prayer; keep at it; watch for God's answers and remember to be thankful when they come.

[Jesus] went out into the mountains to pray, and prayed all night.

Lk. 18:1. Lk. 11:5–8. Eph. 6:18. Gen. 32:26, 28. Col. 4:2. Lk. 6:12.

Be careful how you act; these are difficult days. Don't be fools; be wise: make the most of every opportunity you have for doing good.

Be sure to continue to obey all of the commandments. . . . Love the Lord and follow his plan for your lives. Cling to him and serve him enthusiastically. □ Make the most of your chances to tell others the Good News. Be wise in all your contacts with them. Let your conversation be gracious as well as sensible, for then you will have the right answer for everyone. □ Keep away from every kind of evil.

When the bridegroom was delayed, they lay down to rest until midnight, when they were roused by the shout, "The bridegroom is coming! Come out to welcome him!" Stay awake and be prepared, for you do not know the date or moment of my return.

Work hard to prove that you really are among those God has called and chosen, and then you will never stumble or fall away. And God will open wide the gates of heaven for you to enter into the eternal kingdom of our Lord and Savior Jesus Christ. □ There will be great joy for those who are ready and waiting for his return. So be ready all the time. For I, the Messiah, will come when least expected.

Eph. 5:15, 16. Josh. 22:5. Col. 4:5, 6. 1 Thess. 5:22. Mt. 25:5, 6, 13. 2 Pet. 1:10, 11. Lk. 12:37, 40.

*All living things shall thank you, Lord, and
your people will bless you.*

I bless the holy name of God with all my heart.
Yes, I will bless the Lord and not forget the
glorious things he does for me. □ I will praise the
Lord no matter what happens. I will constantly
speak of his glories and grace. I will boast of all
his kindness to me. □ I will praise you, my God
and King, and bless your name each day and forever. Great is Jehovah! Greatly praise him! His
greatness is beyond discovery! Let each generation tell its children what glorious things he does.
I will meditate about your glory, splendor, majesty
and miracles. Your awe-inspiring deeds shall be
on every tongue; I will proclaim your greatness.

Your love and kindness are better to me than
life itself. How I praise you! I will bless you as
long as I live, lifting up my hands to you in prayer.
At last I shall be fully satisfied; I will praise you
with great joy.

Oh, how I praise the Lord. How I rejoice in
God my Savior!

O Lord, you are worthy to receive the glory
and the honor and the power, for you have created
all things. They were created and called into being
by your act of will.

*Ps. 145:10. Ps. 103:1, 2. Ps. 34:1, 2. Ps. 145:1–6. Ps. 63:3–5. Lk.
1:46, 47. Rev. 4:11.*

Seek to live a clean and holy life, for one who is not holy will not see the Lord.

Unless you are born again, you can never get into the Kingdom of God. □ Nothing evil will be permitted in it—no one immoral or dishonest.

You must be holy because I, the Lord your God, am holy. □ Obey God because you are his children; don't slip back into your old ways— doing evil because you knew no better. But be holy now in everything you do, just as the Lord is holy, who invited you to be his child. He himself has said, "You must be holy, for I am holy." And remember that your heavenly Father to whom you pray has no favorites when he judges. He will judge you with perfect justice for everything you do; so act in reverent fear of him from now on until you get to heaven. □ Throw off your old evil nature. Now your attitudes and thoughts must all be constantly changing for the better. Yes, you must be a new and different person, holy and good. Clothe yourself with this new nature. □ Long ago, even before he made the world, God chose us to be his very own, through what Christ would do for us; he decided then to make us holy in his eyes, without a single fault—we who stand before him covered with his love.

Hebr. 12:14. Jn. 3:3. Rev. 21:27. Lev. 19:2. 1 Pet. 1:14–17. Eph. 4:22–24. Eph. 1:4.

Gold purified by fire.

Let me assure you that no one has ever given up anything—home, brothers, sisters, mother, father, children, or property—for love of me and to tell others the Good News, who won't be given back, a hundred times over, homes, brothers, sisters, mothers, children, and land—with persecutions! All these will be his here on earth, and in the world to come he shall have eternal life.

Don't be bewildered or surprised when you go through the fiery trials ahead, for this is no strange, unusual thing that is going to happen to you. □ Be truly glad! There is wonderful joy ahead, even though the going is rough for a while down here. These trials are only to test your faith, to see whether or not it is strong and pure. If your faith remains strong after being tried in the test tube of fiery trials, it will bring you much praise and glory and honor on the day of his return.

After you have suffered a little while, our God, who is full of kindness through Christ, will give you his eternal glory. He personally will come and pick you up, and set you firmly in place, and make you stronger than ever. □ Here on earth you will have many trials and sorrows; but cheer up, for I have overcome the world.

Rev. 3:18. Mk. 10:29, 30. 1 Pet. 4:12. 1 Pet. 1:6, 7. 1 Pet. 5:10. Jn. 16:33.

Christ is your example. Follow in his steps.

For even I, the Messiah, am not here to be served, but to help others. □ And whoever wants to be greatest of all must be the slave of all. □ Jesus Christ . . . laid aside his mighty power and glory, taking the disguise of a slave.

Jesus of Nazareth . . . went around doing good. □ Share each other's troubles and problems, and so obey our Lord's command.

Gently, as Christ himself would do. □ Be humble, thinking of others as better than yourself.

Father, forgive these people, for they don't know what they are doing. □ Be kind to each other, tenderhearted, forgiving one another, just as God has forgiven you because you belong to Christ.

Anyone who says he is a Christian should live as Christ did. □ Keep your eyes on Jesus, our leader and instructor. He was willing to die a shameful death on the cross because of the joy he knew would be his afterwards; and now he sits in the place of honor by the throne of God.

1 Pet. 2:21. Mk. 10:45. Mk. 10:44. Phil. 2:5–7. Acts 10:38. Gal. 6:2. 2 Cor. 10:1. Phil. 2:3. Lk. 23:34. Eph. 4:32. 1 Jn. 2:6. Hebr. 12:2.

I searched for him but couldn't find him anywhere. I called to him, but there was no reply.

"O Lord, what am I to do now that Israel has fled from her enemies!" But the Lord said to Joshua, "Get up off your face! Israel has sinned and disobeyed my commandment and has taken loot when I said it was not to be taken; and they have not only taken it, they have lied about it and have hidden it among their belongings. That is why the people of Israel are being defeated. That is why your men are running from their enemies—for they are cursed. I will not stay with you any longer unless you completely rid yourselves of this sin."

Listen now! The Lord isn't too weak to save you. And he isn't getting deaf! He can hear you when you call! But the trouble is that your sins have cut you off from God. Because of sin he has turned his face away from you and will not listen anymore.

But, dearly loved friends, if our consciences are clear, we can come to the Lord with perfect assurance and trust, and get whatever we ask for because we are obeying him and doing the things that please him.

Song 5:6.   Josh. 7:8, 10–12.   Is. 59:1, 2.   1 Jn. 3:21, 22.

*I will ask the Father and he will give you
another Comforter, and he will never leave
you. He is the Holy Spirit, the Spirit who
leads into all truth.*

It is best for you that I go away, for if I don't,
the Comforter won't come. If I do, he will—for
I will send him to you.

His Holy Spirit speaks to us deep in our hearts,
and tells us that we really are God's children. □
And so we should not be like cringing, fearful
slaves, but we should behave like God's very own
children, adopted into the bosom of his family,
and calling to him, "Father, Father." □ The Holy
Spirit helps us with our daily problems and in our
praying. For we don't even know what we should
pray for, nor how to pray as we should; but the
Holy Spirit prays for us with such feeling that it
cannot be expressed in words.

I pray . . . that God who gives you hope will
keep you happy and full of peace as you believe
in him. I pray that God will help you overflow
with hope in him through the Holy Spirit's power
within you. □ We are able to hold our heads high
no matter what happens and know that all is well,
for we know how dearly God loves us, and we feel
this warm love everywhere within us because God
has given us the Holy Spirit to fill our hearts with
his love.

*Jn. 14:16, 17. Jn. 16:7. Rom. 8:16. Rom. 8:15. Rom. 8:26. Rom.
15:13. Rom. 5:5.*

Rest in the Lord; wait patiently for him.

There is a full complete rest *still waiting* for the people of God. □ My people will live in safety, quietly at home. □ They shall rest from all their toils and trials.

Christ has gone ahead to plead for us from his position as our High Priest, with the honor and rank of Melchizedek.

Come to me and I will give you rest—all of you who work so hard beneath a heavy yoke. Wear my yoke—for it fits perfectly—and let me teach you; for I am gentle and humble, and you shall find rest for your souls; for I give you only light burdens. □ Only in returning to me and waiting for me will you be saved; in quietness and confidence is your strength. □ Ask where the good road is, the godly paths you used to walk in, in the days of long ago. Travel there, and you will find rest for your souls.

Because the Lord is my Shepherd, I have everything I need! He lets me rest in the meadow grass and leads me beside the quiet streams. □ Now I can relax. For the Lord has done this wonderful miracle for me.

Ps. 37:7. Hebr. 4:9. Is. 32:18. Rev. 14:13. Hebr. 6:20. Mt. 11:28–30. Is. 30:15. Jer. 6:16. Ps. 23:1, 2. Ps. 116:7.

*Don't be anxious about tomorrow. Live one
day at a time.*

My times are in your hands. □ He subdues the
nations before us, and will personally select his
choicest blessings . . . the very best for those he
loves. □ Lord, lead me as you promised me you
would. Tell me clearly what to do, which way to
turn.

Commit everything you do to the Lord. Trust
him to help you do it and he will. □ In everything
you do, put God first, and he will direct you and
crown your efforts with success. □ If you leave
God's paths and go astray, you will hear a Voice
behind you say, "No, this is the way; walk here."

Because the Lord is my Shepherd, I have everything I need! He lets me rest in the meadow
grass and leads me beside the quiet streams. □
He is like a father to us, tender and sympathetic
to those who reverence him. For he knows we are
but dust. □ Don't worry at all about having
enough food and clothing. Your heavenly Father
already knows perfectly well that you need them.
□ Let him have all your worries and cares, for he
is always thinking about you and watching everything that concerns you.

*Mt. 6:34. Ps. 31:15. Ps. 47:3, 4. Ps. 5:8. Ps. 37:5. Prov. 3:6.
Is. 30:21. Ps. 23:1, 2. Ps. 103:13, 14. Mt. 6:31, 32. 1 Pet. 5:7.*

When he comes we will be like him, as a result of seeing him as he really is.

To all who received him, he gave the right to become children of God. All they needed to do was to trust him to save them. □ And by that same mighty power he has given us all the other rich and wonderful blessings he promised; for instance, the promise to . . . give us his own character.

For since the world began no one has seen or heard of such a God as ours, who works for those who wait for him!

We can see and understand only a little about God now, as if we were peering at his reflection in a poor mirror; but someday we are going to see him in his completeness, face to face. Now all that I know is hazy and blurred, but then I will see everything clearly, just as clearly as God sees into my heart right now. □ Christ . . . will take these dying bodies of ours and change them into glorious bodies like his own, using the same mighty power that he will use to conquer all else everywhere. □ But as for me, my contentment is not in wealth but in seeing you and knowing all is well between us. And when I awake in heaven, I will be fully satisfied, for I will see you face to face.

1 Jn. 3:2. Jn. 1:12. 2 Pet. 1:4. Is. 64:4. 1 Cor. 13:12. Phil. 3:20, 21. Ps. 17:15.

Who can survive?

Who can endure his coming? For he is like a blazing fire refining precious metal and he can bleach the dirtiest garments!

I saw a vast crowd, too great to count, from all nations and provinces and languages, standing in front of the throne and before the Lamb, clothed in white, with palm branches in their hands. "These are the ones coming out of the Great Tribulation," he said; "they washed their robes and whitened them by the blood of the Lamb. That is why they are here before the throne of God, serving him day and night in his temple. The one sitting on the throne will shelter them; they will never be hungry again, nor thirsty, and they will be fully protected from the scorching noontime heat. For the Lamb standing in front of the throne will feed them and be their Shepherd and lead them to the springs of the Water of Life. And God will wipe their tears away."

There is now no condemnation awaiting those who belong to Christ Jesus. □ So Christ has made us free. Now make sure that you stay free and don't get all tied up again in the chains of slavery.

Rev. 6:17. Mal. 3:2. Rev. 7:9, 14–17. Rom. 8:1. Gal. 5:1.

Don't bring me to trial! For as compared with you, no one is perfect.

"Come, let's talk this over," says the Lord; "no matter how deep the stain of your sins, I can take it out and make you as clean as freshly fallen snow. Even if you are stained as red as crimson, I can make you white as wool!"

He forgave all your sins, and blotted out the charges proved against you, the list of his commandments which you had not obeyed. He took this list of sins and destroyed it by nailing it to Christ's cross.

Since we have been made right in God's sight by faith in his promises, we can have real peace with him because of what Jesus Christ our Lord has done for us. □ So we, too, have trusted Jesus Christ, that we might be accepted by God. □ The more we know of God's laws, the clearer it becomes that we aren't obeying them; his laws serve only to make us see that we are sinners. No one can ever be made right in God's sight by doing what the law commands.

Everyone who trusts in him is freed from all guilt and declared righteous. □ How we thank God for all of this! It is he who makes us victorious through Jesus Christ our Lord!

Ps. 143:2. Is. 1:18. Col. 2:13, 14. Rom. 5:1. Gal. 2:16. Rom. 3:20. Acts 13:39. 1 Cor. 15:57.

The Holy Spirit tells us clearly that in the last times some in the church will turn away from Christ and become eager followers of teachers with devil-inspired ideas.

Be careful how you listen. □ Remember what Christ taught and let his words enrich your lives and make you wise. □ In every battle you will need faith as your shield to stop the fiery arrows aimed at you by Satan.

Those who love your laws have great peace of heart and mind and do not stumble. Your words are sweeter than honey. And since only your rules can give me wisdom and understanding, no wonder I hate every false teaching.

Your words are a flashlight to light the path ahead of me, and keep me from stumbling. They make me wiser than my enemies, because they are my constant guide.

Satan can change himself into an angel of light. □ Let God's curses fall on anyone, including myself, who preaches any other way to be saved than the one we told you about; yes, if an angel comes from heaven and preaches any other message, let him be forever cursed.

But as for me, I get as close to him [God] as I can! I have chosen him and I will tell everyone about the wonderful ways he rescues me.

1 Tim. 4:1. Lk. 8:18. Col. 3:16. Eph. 6:16. Ps. 119:165, 103, 104. Ps. 119:105, 98. 2 Cor. 11:14. Gal. 1:8. Ps. 73:28.

Loving God means doing what he tells us to do.

It is my Father's will that everyone who sees his Son and believes on him should have eternal life. □ We can come to the Lord with perfect assurance and trust, and get whatever we ask for because we are obeying him and doing the things that please him.

Wear my yoke—for it fits perfectly—and let me teach you; for I am gentle and humble, and you shall find rest for your souls; for I give you only light burdens. □ If you love me, obey me. The one who obeys me is the one who loves me; and because he loves me, my Father will love him; and I will too, and I will reveal myself to him.

The man who knows right from wrong and has good judgment and common sense is happier than the man who is immensely rich! Wisdom gives a long, good life, riches, honor, pleasure, peace. □ Those who love your laws have great peace of heart and mind and do not stumble. □ I love to do God's will.

And this is what God says we must do: Believe on the name of his Son Jesus Christ, and love one another. □ Love does no wrong to anyone. That's why it fully satisfies all of God's requirements. It is the only law you need.

1 Jn. 5:3. Jn. 6:40. 1 Jn. 3:21, 22. Mt. 11:29, 30. Jn. 14:15, 21. Prov. 3:13, 17. Ps. 119:165. Rom. 7:22. 1 Jn. 3:23. Rom. 13:10.

Overlook my youthful sins, O Lord.

I've blotted out your sins; they are gone like morning mist at noon! □ I, yes, I alone am he who blots away your sins for my own sake and will never think of them again. □ "Come, let's talk this over!" says the Lord; "no matter how deep the stain of your sins, I can take it out and make you as clean as freshly fallen snow. Even if you are stained as red as crimson, I can make you white as wool!" □ I will forgive and forget their sins. □ You will tread our sins beneath your feet; you will throw them into the depths of the ocean!

It was good for me to undergo this bitterness, for you have lovingly delivered me from death; you have forgiven all my sins. □ Where is another God like you, who pardons the sins of the survivors among his people? You cannot stay angry with your people for you love to be merciful. □ All praise to him who always loves us and who set us free from our sins by pouring out his lifeblood for us. He has gathered us into his kingdom and made us priests of God his Father. Give to him everlasting glory! He rules forever! Amen!

Ps. 25:6, 7. Is. 44:22. Is. 43:25. Is. 1:18. Jer. 31:34. Mic. 7:19. Is. 38:17. Mic. 7:18. Rev. 1:5, 6.

*I continually discipline and punish everyone
I love.*

My son, don't be angry when the Lord punishes
you. Don't be discouraged when he has to show
you where you are wrong. For when he punishes
you, it proves that he loves you. When he whips
you it proves you are really his child. □ His punishment is proof of his love. Just as a father
punishes a son he delights in to make him better,
so the Lord corrects you. □ For though he
wounds, he binds and heals again. □ If you will
humble yourselves under the mighty hand of God,
in his good time he will lift you up. □ I refined
you in the furnace of affliction. □ I am the Lord
your God, who punishes you for your own good
and leads you along the paths that you should
follow.

He does not enjoy afflicting men and causing
sorrow. □ He has not punished us as we deserve
for all our sins, for his mercy toward those who
fear and honor him is as great as the height of
the heavens above the earth. He has removed
our sins as far away from us as the east is from the
west. He is like a father to us, tender and sympathetic to those who reverence him. For he knows
we are but dust.

*Rev. 3:19. Hebr. 12:5, 6. Prov. 3:12. Job 5:18. 1 Pet. 5:6. Is.
48:10. Is. 48:17. Lam. 3:33. Ps. 103:10–14.*

He is in heaven and you are only here on earth, so let your words be few.

Don't recite the same prayer over and over as the heathen do, who think prayers are answered only by repeating them again and again. Remember, your Father knows exactly what you need even before you ask him!

They called to Baal all morning, shouting, "O Baal, hear us!"

Two men went to the Temple to pray. One was a proud, self-righteous Pharisee, and the other a cheating tax collector. The proud Pharisee prayed this prayer: "Thank God, I am not a sinner like everyone else, especially like that tax collector over there! For I never cheat, I don't commit adultery." But the corrupt tax collector stood at a distance and dared not even lift his eyes to heaven as he prayed, but beat upon his chest in sorrow, exclaiming, "God, be merciful to me, a sinner." I tell you, this sinner, not the Pharisee, returned home forgiven! For the proud shall be humbled, but the humble shall be honored.

We don't even know what we should pray for, nor how to pray as we should. □ Lord, teach us.

Eccl. 5:2. Mt. 6:7, 8. 1 Kgs. 18:26. Lk. 18:10, 11, 13, 14. Rom. 8:26. Lk. 11:1.

*When you draw close to God, God will draw
close to you.*

Enoch . . . lived . . . in fellowship with
God. □ How can we walk together with your sins
between us? □ But as for me, I get as close to
him as I can! I have chosen him and I will tell
everyone about the wonderful ways he rescues
me.

The Lord will stay with you as long as you
stay with him! Whenever you look for him, you
will find him. But if you forsake him, he will
forsake you. Whenever they have turned again
to the Lord God of Israel in their distress, and
searched for him, he has helped them.

I know the plans I have for you, says the Lord.
They are plans for good and not for evil, to give
you a future and a hope. In those days when you
pray, I will listen. You will find me when you
seek me, if you look for me in earnest.

Now we may walk right into the very Holy of
Holies where God is, because of the blood of
Jesus. This is the fresh, new, life-giving way which
Christ has opened up for us by tearing the curtain—his human body—to let us into the holy
presence of God. And since this great High Priest
of ours rules over God's household, let us go right
in, to God himself, with true hearts fully trusting
him to receive us.

*Jas. 4:8. Gen. 5:24. Amos 3:3. Ps. 73:28. 2 Chron. 15:2, 4. Jer.
29:11–13. Hebr. 10:19–22.*

[Jesus] went back to prayer the third time.

While Christ was here on earth he pleaded with God, praying with tears and agony of soul to the only one who would save him from [premature] death.

Oh, that we might know the Lord! Let us press on to know him, and he will respond to us as surely as the coming of dawn or the rain of early spring. □ Be patient in trouble, and prayerful always. □ Pray all the time. Ask God for anything in line with the Holy Spirit's wishes. Plead with him, reminding him of your needs. □ Don't worry about anything; instead, pray about everything; tell God your needs and don't forget to thank him for his answers. If you do this you will experience God's peace, which is far more wonderful than the human mind can understand. His peace will keep your thoughts and your hearts quiet and at rest as you trust in Christ Jesus.

I want your will, not mine. □ We are sure of this, that he will listen to us whenever we ask him for anything in line with his will. □ Be delighted with the Lord. Then he will give you all your heart's desires. Commit everything you do to the Lord. Trust him to help you do it and he will.

Mt. 26:44. Hebr. 5:7. Hos. 6:3. Rom. 12:12. Eph. 6:18. Phil. 4:6, 7. Mt. 26:39. 1 Jn. 5:14. Ps. 37:4, 5.

Since we are his children, we will share his treasures—for all God gives to his Son Jesus is now ours too.

Now that we are Christ's we are the true descendants of Abraham, and all of God's promises to him belong to us.

See how very much our heavenly Father loves us, for he allows us to be called his children. □ Now we are no longer slaves, but God's own sons. And since we are his sons, everything he has belongs to us, for that is the way God planned. □ His unchanging plan has always been to adopt us into his own family by sending Jesus Christ to die for us. And he did this because he wanted to!

Father, I want them with me—these you've given me—so that they can see my glory. You gave me the glory because you loved me before the world began!

To every one who overcomes—who to the very end keeps on doing things that please me—I will give power over the nations. You will rule them with a rod of iron just as my Father gave me the authority to rule them; they will be shattered like a pot of clay that is broken into tiny pieces. □ I will let every one who conquers sit beside me on my throne, just as I took my place with my Father on his throne when I had conquered.

Rom. 8:17. Gal. 3:29. 1 Jn. 3:1. Gal. 4:7. Eph. 1:5. Jn. 17:24. Rev. 2:26, 27. Rev. 3:21.

He has chosen a plan despised by the world.

How can this be? . . . These men are all from Galilee, and yet we hear them speaking all the native languages of the lands where we were born!

[Jesus] saw two brothers . . . fishing with a net, for they were commercial fishermen. Jesus called out, "Come along with me and I will show you how to fish for the souls of men!" □ When the Council saw the boldness of Peter and John, and could see that they were obviously uneducated non-professionals, they were amazed and realized what being with Jesus had done for them!

My preaching was very plain, not with a lot of oratory and human wisdom, but the Holy Spirit's power was in my words, proving to those who heard them that the message was from God.

You didn't choose me! I chose you! I appointed you to go and produce lovely fruit always. Whoever lives in me and I in him shall produce a large crop of fruit. For apart from me you can't do a thing. □ This precious treasure—this light and power that now shine within us—is held in a perishable container, that is, in our weak bodies. Everyone can see that the glorious power within must be from God and is not our own.

1 Cor. 1:28. Acts 2:7. Mt. 4:18, 19. Acts 4:13. 1 Cor. 2:4. Jn. 15:16, 5. 2 Cor. 4:7.

Don't try to get into the good graces of important people, but enjoy the company of ordinary folks.

How can you claim that you belong to the Lord Jesus Christ, the Lord of glory, if you show favoritism to rich people and look down on poor people? Listen to me, dear brothers: God has chosen poor people to be rich in faith, and the Kingdom of Heaven is theirs, for that is the gift God has promised to all those who love him.

Don't think only of yourself. Try to think of the other fellow, too, and what is best for him. □ We should be well satisfied without money if we have enough food and clothing. People who long to be rich soon begin to do all kinds of wrong things to get money, things that hurt them and make them evil-minded and finally send them to hell itself.

God has deliberately chosen to use ideas the world considers foolish and of little worth in order to shame those people considered by the world as wise and great. He has chosen a plan despised by the world, counted as nothing at all, and used it to bring down to nothing those the world considers great, so that no one anywhere can ever brag in the presence of God.

For it is from God alone that you have your life through Christ Jesus.

Rom. 12:16. Jas. 2:1, 5. 1 Cor. 10:24. 1 Tim. 6:8, 9. 1 Cor. 1:27–29. 1 Cor. 1:30.

When the Holy Spirit controls our lives he will produce . . . patience, kindness.

I am Jehovah, the merciful and gracious God, slow to anger and rich in steadfast love and truth.

Live and act in a way worthy of those who have been chosen for such wonderful blessings. Be humble and gentle. Be patient with each other, making allowance for each other's faults because of your love. □ Be kind to each other, tender-hearted, forgiving one another, just as God has forgiven you because you belong to Christ. □ The wisdom that comes from heaven is first of all pure and full of quiet gentleness. Then it is peace-loving and courteous. It allows discussion and is willing to yield to others; it is full of mercy and good deeds. It is wholehearted and straight-forward and sincere. □ Love is very patient and kind.

Let us not get tired of doing what is right, for after a while we will reap a harvest of blessing if we don't get discouraged and give up. □ Now as for you, dear brothers who are waiting for the Lord's return, be patient, like a farmer who waits until the autumn for his precious harvest to ripen. Yes, be patient. And take courage, for the coming of the Lord is near.

Gal. 5:22. Ex. 34:6. Eph. 4:1, 2. Eph. 4:32. Jas. 3:17. 1 Cor. 13:4. Gal. 6:9. Jas. 5:7, 8.

*You love me so much. You are constantly
so kind! You have rescued me from deepest
hell.*

Don't be afraid, for I have ransomed you; I
have called you by name; you are mine. I am the
Lord, and there is no other Savior. I, yes, I alone
am he who blots away your sins for my own sake
and will never think of them again. □ They trust
in their wealth and boast about how rich they are,
yet not one of them, though rich as kings, can
ransom his own brother from the penalty of sin!
For God's forgiveness does not come that way.
For a soul is far too precious to be ransomed by
mere earthly wealth. □ I have found a substitute.
□ God is so rich in mercy; he loved us so much
that even though we were spiritually dead and
doomed by our sins, he gave us back our lives
again when he raised Christ from the dead.

There is salvation in no one else! Under all
heaven there is no other name for men to call
upon to save them. □ God our Savior . . . longs
for all to be saved and to understand this truth:
That God is on one side, and all the people on the
other side, and Christ Jesus, himself man, is between them to bring them together, by giving his
life for all mankind.

Your love and kindness are forever; your truth
is as enduring as the heavens.

*Ps. 86:13. Is. 43:1, 11, 25. Ps. 49:6–8. Job 33:24. Eph. 2:4, 5.
Acts 4:12. 1 Tim. 2:3–6. Ps. 89:2.*

I have taken your lovingkindness and your truth as my ideals.

Jehovah is kind and merciful, slow to get angry, full of love. □ Your Father in heaven . . . gives his sunlight to both the evil and the good, and sends rain on the just and on the unjust too. □ Follow God's example in everything you do just as a much loved child imitates his father. Be full of love for others, following the example of Christ who loved you and gave himself to God as a sacrifice to take away your sins. And God was pleased, for Christ's love for you was like sweet perfume to him. □ Be tenderhearted, forgiving one another, just as God has forgiven you because you belong to Christ. □ Now you can have real love for everyone because your souls have been cleansed from selfishness and hatred when you trusted Christ to save you; so see to it that you really do love each other warmly, with all your hearts. □ Whatever we do, it is certainly not for our own profit, but because Christ's love controls us now.

Love your *enemies!* Do good to *them!* Lend to *them!* And don't be concerned about the fact that they won't repay. Then your reward from heaven will be very great, and you will truly be acting as sons of God: for he is kind to the *unthankful* and to those who are *very wicked.*

Ps. 26:3. Ps. 145:8. Mt. 5:45. Eph. 5:1, 2. Eph. 4:32. 1 Pet. 1:22. 2 Cor. 5:14. Lk. 6:35.

*Jesus was led out into the wilderness by the
Holy Spirit, to be tempted there by Satan.*

While Christ was here on earth he pleaded with
God, praying with tears and agony of soul to the
only one who would save him from [premature]
death. And God heard his prayers because of his
strong desire to obey God at all times. And even
though Jesus was God's Son, he had to learn from
experience what it was like to obey, when obeying
meant suffering. It was after he had proved himself perfect in this experience that Jesus became
the Giver of eternal salvation to all those who
obey him. □ This High Priest of ours understands
our weaknesses, since he had the same temptations we do, though he never once gave way to
them and sinned.

The wrong desires that come into your life
aren't anything new and different. Many others
have faced exactly the same problems before you.
And no temptation is irresistible. You can trust
God to keep the temptation from becoming so
strong that you can't stand up against it, for he
has promised this and will do what he says. He
will show you how to escape temptation's power
so that you can bear up patiently against it. □ I
am with you; that is all you need. My power
shows up best in weak people.

Mt. 4:1. Hebr. 5:7–9. Hebr. 4:15. 1 Cor. 10:13. 2 Cor. 12:9.

*I, the Messiah, did not come to be served,
but to serve, and to give my life as a ransom
for many.*

If under the old system the blood of bulls and
goats and the ashes of young cows could cleanse
men's bodies from sin, just think how much more
surely the blood of Christ will transform our lives
and hearts. His sacrifice frees us from the worry
of having to obey the old rules, and makes us
want to serve the living God.

He was brought as a lamb to the slaughter. □ I
lay down my life for the sheep. No one can kill
me without my consent—I lay down my life
voluntarily. For I have the right and power to lay
it down when I want to and also the right and
power to take it again.

The life of the flesh is in the blood, and I have
given you the blood to sprinkle upon the altar as
an atonement for your souls; it is the blood that
makes atonement, because it is the life. □ Without
the shedding of blood there is no forgiveness of
sins.

God showed his great love for us by sending
Christ to die for us while we were still sinners.
And since by his blood he did all this for us as
sinners, how much more will he do for us now
that he has declared us not guilty? Now he will
save us from all of God's wrath to come.

*Mt. 20:28. Hebr. 9:13, 14. Is. 53:7. Jn. 10:15, 18. Lev. 17:11.
Hebr. 9:22. Rom. 5:8, 9.*

*If we confess our sins to him, he can be
depended on to forgive us and to cleanse us
from every wrong.*

Have pity upon me and take away the awful
stain of my transgressions. Oh, wash me, cleanse
me from this guilt. Let me be pure again. For I
admit my shameful deed—it haunts me day and
night. It is against you and you alone I sinned.

He returned home to his father. And while he
was still a long distance away, his father saw him
coming, and was filled with loving pity and ran
and embraced him and kissed him. □ I've blotted
out your sins; they are gone like morning mist at
noon! Oh, return to me, for I have paid the price
to set you free. □ Your sins have been forgiven
in the name of Jesus our Savior. □ God has forgiven you because you belong to Christ.

It will be as though I had sprinkled clean water
on you, for you will be clean. And I will give you
a new heart—I will give you new and right desires
—and put a new spirit within you. I will take
out your stony hearts of sin and give you new
hearts of love. And I will put my Spirit within
you so that you will obey my laws and do whatever I command. □ They shall walk with me in
white, for they are worthy.

1 Jn. 1:9. Ps. 51:1–4. Lk. 15:20. Is. 44:22. 1 Jn. 2:12. Eph. 4:32.
Ezk. 36:25–27. Rev. 3:4.

A servant is not above his master.

You call me Master and Lord, and you do well to say it, for it is true.

The student shares his teacher's fate. The servant shares his master's! □ So since they persecuted me, naturally they will persecute you. And if they had listened to me, they would listen to you! □ I have given them your commands. And the world hates them because they don't fit in with it, just as I don't.

If you want to keep from becoming fainthearted and weary, think about his patience as sinful men did such terrible things to him. After all, you have never yet struggled against sin and temptation until you sweat great drops of blood.

Let us run with patience the particular race that God has set before us. Keep your eyes on Jesus, our leader and instructor. He was willing to die a shameful death on the cross because of the joy he knew would be his afterwards; and now he sits in the place of honor by the throne of God. □ Since Christ suffered and underwent pain, you must have the same attitude he did; you must be ready to suffer, too.

Mt. 10:24. Jn. 13:13. Mt. 10:25. Jn. 15:20. Jn. 17:14. Hebr. 12:3, 4. Hebr. 12:1, 2. 1 Pet. 4:1.

My son, trust my advice.

Oh, that they would always have such a heart for me, wanting to obey my commandments. Then all would go well with them in the future, and with their children throughout all generations!

Your heart is not right before God. □ The old sinful nature within us is against God. It never did obey God's laws and it never will. That's why those who are still under the control of their old sinful selves, bent on following their old evil desires, can never please God.

Their first action was to dedicate themselves to the Lord. □ *Above all else, guard your affections.* For they influence everything else in your life.

Work hard and cheerfully at all you do, just as though you were working for the Lord and not merely for your masters. □ Don't work hard only when your master is watching and then shirk when he isn't looking; work hard and with gladness all the time, as though working for Christ, doing the will of God with all your hearts.

If you will only help me to want your will, then I will follow your laws more closely.

Prov. 23:26. Deut. 5:29. Acts 8:21. Rom. 8:7, 8. 2 Cor. 8:5. Prov. 4:23. Col. 3:23. Eph. 6:6, 7. Ps. 119:32.

I am with you to protect and deliver you.

Who can snatch the prey from the hands of a mighty man? Who can demand that a tyrant let his captives go? But the Lord says, "Even the captives of the most mighty and most terrible shall all be freed; for I will fight those who fight you, and I will save your children. I will feed your enemies with their own flesh and they shall be drunk with rivers of their own blood. All the world shall know that I, the Lord, am your Savior and Redeemer, the Mighty One of Israel." □ Fear not, for I am with you. Do not be dismayed. I am your God. I will strengthen you; I will help you; I will uphold you with my victorious right hand.

This High Priest of ours understands our weaknesses, since he had the same temptations we do, though he never once gave way to them and sinned. □ For since he himself has now been through suffering and temptation, he knows what it is like when we suffer and are tempted, and he is wonderfully able to help us. □ The steps of good men are directed by the Lord. He delights in each step they take. If they fall it isn't fatal, for the Lord holds them with his hand.

Jer. 15:20. Is. 49:24–26. Is. 41:10. Hebr. 4:15. Hebr. 2:18. Ps. 37:23, 24.

*He satisfies the thirsty soul and fills the hun-
gry soul with good.*

Realize how kind the Lord has been to you.

O God, my God! How I search for you! How
I thirst for you in this parched and weary land
where there is no water. How I long to find you!
How I wish I could go into your sanctuary to
see your strength and glory, for your love and
kindness are better to me than life itself. How I
praise you! I will bless you as long as I live,
lifting up my hands to you in prayer. □ I long,
yes, faint with longing to be able to enter your
courtyard and come near to the Living God. □ I
long to go and be with Christ.

When I awake in heaven, I will be fully satisfied. □ They will never be hungry again, nor
thirsty, and they will be fully protected from the
scorching noontime heat. For the Lamb standing
in front of the throne will feed them and be
their Shepherd and lead to the springs of the
Water of life. And God will wipe their tears
away. □ You feed them with blessings from your
own table and let them drink from your rivers of
delight. □ "I will satisfy my people with my
bounty," says the Lord.

*Ps. 107:9. 1 Pet. 2:2, 3. Ps. 63:1–4. Ps. 84:2. Phil. 1:23. Ps. 17:15.
Rev. 7:16, 17. Ps. 36:8. Jer. 31:14.*

I myself will go with you and give you success.

Be strong! Be courageous! Do not be afraid of them! For the Lord your God will be with you. He will neither fail you nor forsake you. Don't be afraid, for the Lord will go before you and will be with you; he will not fail nor forsake you. □ Yes, be bold and strong! Banish fear and doubt! For remember, the Lord your God is with you wherever you go. □ If you want favor with both God and man, and a reputation for good judgment and common sense, then trust the Lord completely; don't ever trust yourself. In everything you do, put God first, and he will direct you and crown your efforts with success. □ The man who knows right from wrong and has good judgment and common sense is happier than the man who is immensely rich! For such wisdom is far more valuable than precious jewels. Nothing else compares with it.

God has said, "I will never, *never* fail you nor forsake you." That is why we can say without any doubt or fear, "The Lord is my Helper and I am not afraid of anything that mere man can do to me." □ Our only power and success comes from God.

O Lord, I know it is not within the power of man to map his life and plan his course.

Ex. 33:14. Deut. 31:6, 8. Josh. 1:9. Prov. 3:4–6. Prov. 3:13–15. Hebr. 13:5, 6. 2 Cor. 3:5. Jer. 10:23.

Let us outdo each other in being helpful and kind to each other and in doing good.

Timely advice is as lovely as golden apples in a silver basket.

Those who feared and loved the Lord spoke often of him to each other. And he had a Book of Remembrance drawn up in which he recorded the names of those who feared him and loved to think about him. □ If two of you agree down here on earth concerning anything you ask for, my Father in heaven will do it for you.

The Lord God said, "It isn't good for man to be alone." □ Two can accomplish more than twice as much as one, for the results can be much better. If one falls, the other pulls him up; but if a man falls when he is alone, he's in trouble.

Live in such a way that you will never make your brother stumble by letting him see you doing something he thinks is wrong. If your brother is bothered by what you eat, you are not acting in love if you go ahead and eat it. Don't undo the work of God for a chunk of meat. Remember, there is nothing wrong with the meat, but it is wrong to eat it if it makes another stumble. □ Share each other's troubles and problems, and so obey our Lord's command.

Hebr. 10:24. Prov. 25:11. Mal. 3:16. Mt. 18:19. Gen. 2:18. Eccl. 4:9, 10. Rom. 14:13, 15, 20. Gal. 6:2.

Search the Book of the Lord.

Keep these commandments carefully in mind. Tie them to your hand to remind you to obey them, and tie them to your forehead between your eyes! □ Constantly remind the people about these laws, and you yourself must think about them every day and every night so that you will be sure to obey all of them. For only then will you succeed.

The godly man is a good counselor. □ I have followed your commands and have not gone along with cruel and evil men. □ I have thought much about your words, and stored them in my heart so that they would hold me back from sin.

We have seen and proved that what the prophets said came true. You will do well to pay close attention to everything they have written, for, like lights shining into dark corners, their words help us to understand many things that otherwise would be dark and difficult. But when you consider the wonderful truth of the prophets' words, then the light will dawn in your souls and Christ the Morning Star will shine in your hearts. □ These things that were written in the Scriptures so long ago are to teach us patience and to encourage us.

Is. 34:16. Deut. 11:18. Josh. 1:8. Ps. 37:30. Ps. 17:4. Ps. 119:11. 2 Pet. 1:19. Rom. 15:4.

A man's heart determines his speech.

Remember what Christ taught and let his words enrich your lives and make you wise. ☐ A good man's speech reveals the rich treasures within him.

Those who love to talk will suffer the consequences. Men have died for saying the wrong thing! ☐ A good man produces good deeds from a good heart. Whatever is in the heart overflows into speech. ☐ The godly man is a good counselor because he is just and fair and knows right from wrong. ☐ Don't use bad language. Say only what is good and helpful to those you are talking to, and what will give them a blessing.

You must give account on Judgment Day for every idle word you speak. Your words now reflect your fate then: either you will be justified by them or you will be condemned.

If anyone publicly acknowledges me as his friend, I will openly acknowledge him as my friend before my Father in heaven. ☐ Make the most of your chances to tell others the Good News. Be wise in all your contacts with them. Let your conversation be gracious as well as sensible, for then you will have the right answer for everyone.

Mt. 12:34. Col. 3:16. Mt. 12:35. Prov. 18:21. Lk. 6:45. Ps. 37:30, 31. Eph. 4:29. Mt. 12:36–37. Mt. 10:32. Col. 4:5, 6.

*We prayed to our God and guarded the city
day and night to protect ourselves.*

Keep alert and pray. Otherwise temptation will
overpower you. □ Don't be weary in prayer; keep
at it; watch for God's answers and remember to
be thankful when they come. □ Let him have all
your worries and cares, for he is always thinking
about you and watching everything that concerns
you. Be careful—watch out for attacks from Satan, your great enemy. He prowls around like a
hungry, roaring lion, looking for some victim to
tear apart. Stand firm when he attacks.

Why do you call me Lord when you won't obey
me? □ It is a message to obey, not just to listen
to.

Then the Lord said to Moses, "Quit praying
and get the people moving! Forward, march!"

Don't worry about anything; instead, pray
about everything; tell God your needs and don't
forget to thank him for his answers. If you do
this you will experience God's peace, which is far
more wonderful than the human mind can understand. His peace will keep your thoughts and your
hearts quiet and at rest as you trust in Christ
Jesus.

*Neh. 4:9. Mt. 26:41. Col. 4:2. 1 Pet. 5:7–9. Lk. 6:46. Jas. 1:22.
Ex. 14:15. Phil. 4:6, 7.*

*A gracious God, merciful, slow to get angry,
and full of kindness.*

Oh, please, show the great power [of your
patience] by forgiving our sins and showing us
your steadfast love. Forgive us, even though you
have said that you don't let sin go unpunished,
and that you punish the father's fault in the children to the third and fourth generation.

Oh, do not hold us guilty for our former sins!
Let your tenderhearted mercies meet our needs,
for we are brought low to the dust. Help us, God
of our salvation! Help us for the honor of your
name. Oh, save us and forgive our sins. □ O Lord,
we have sinned against you grievously, yet help us
for the sake of your own reputation! O Lord, we
confess our wickedness, and that of our fathers
too. □ Oh, be not so angry with us, Lord, nor
forever remember our sins. Oh, look and see that
we are all your people.

Lord, if you keep in mind our sins then who
can ever get an answer to his prayers? But you
forgive! What an awesome thing this is!

*Jon. 4:2. Num. 14:17, 18. Ps. 79:8, 9. Jer. 14:7, 20. Is. 64:9.
Ps. 130:3, 4.*

She has done what she could.

This poor widow has given more than all the rest of them combined. □ If anyone so much as gives you a cup of water because you are Christ's —I say this solemnly—he won't lose his reward. □ If you are really eager to give, then it isn't important how much you have to give. God wants you to give what you have, not what you haven't.

Let us stop just *saying* we love people; let us *really* love them, and *show* it by our *actions*. □ If you have a friend who is in need of food and clothing, and you say to him, "Well, good-bye and God bless you; stay warm and eat hearty," and then don't give him clothes or food, what good does that do? □ If you give little, you will get little. A farmer who plants just a few seeds will get only a small crop, but if he plants much, he will reap much. Every one must make up his own mind as to how much he should give. Don't force anyone to give more than he really wants to, for cheerful givers are the ones God prizes.

Just so, if you merely obey me, you should not consider yourselves worthy of praise. For you have simply done your duty!

Mk. 14:8. Lk. 21:3. Mk. 9:41. 2 Cor. 8:12. 1 Jn. 3:18. Jas. 2:15, 16. 2 Cor. 9:6, 7. Lk. 17:10.

*He, the mighty Holy One, has done great
things to me.*

Who else is like the Lord among the gods? Who
is glorious in holiness like him? Who is so awesome in splendor, a wonder-working God? □
Where among the heathen gods is there a god like
you? Where are their miracles? □ Who shall not
fear, O Lord, and glorify your Name? For you
alone are holy. □ We honor your holy name.

Praise the Lord, the God of Israel, for he has
come to visit his people and has redeemed them.

Who is this who comes from Edom, from the
city of Bozrah, with his magnificent garments of
crimson? Who is this in kingly robes, marching in
the greatness of his strength? It is I, the Lord,
announcing your salvation; I, the Lord, the one
who is mighty to save! □ For the Lord your God
has arrived to live among you. He is a mighty
Savior. He will give you victory.

Now glory be to God who by his mighty power
at work within us is able to do far more than we
would ever dare to ask or even dream of—in-
finitely beyond our highest prayers, desires,
thoughts, or hopes. May he be given glory forever
and ever.

*Lk. 1:49. Ex. 15:11. Ps. 86:8. Rev. 15:4. Mt. 6:9. Lk. 1:68. Is.
63:1. Zeph. 3:17. Eph 3:20, 21.*

Whatever you do or say, let it be as a representative of the Lord Jesus.

We despised him and rejected him—a man of sorrows, acquainted with bitterest grief. □ Here on earth you will have many trials and sorrows; but cheer up, for I have overcome the world.

He is, therefore, exactly the kind of High Priest we need; for he is holy and blameless, unstained by sin, undefiled by sinners, and to him has been given the place of honor in heaven. □ That no one can speak a word of blame against you. You are to live clean, innocent lives as children of God in a dark world full of people who are crooked and stubborn.

Jesus of Nazareth . . . went around doing good and healing all who were possessed by demons, for God was with him. □ Whenever we can we should always be kind to everyone, and especially to our Christian brothers.

The true Light arrived to shine on everyone coming into the world. □ You are the world's light—a city on a hill, glowing in the night for all to see. Let your good deeds glow for all to see, so that they will praise your heavenly Father.

Col. 3:17. Is. 53:3. Jn. 16:33. Hebr. 7:26. Phil. 2:15. Acts 10:38. Gal. 6:10. Jn. 1:9. Mt. 5:14, 16.

Stay always within the boundaries where God's love can reach and bless you.

Take care to live in me, and let me live in you. For a branch can't produce fruit when severed from the vine. Nor can you be fruitful apart from me. Yes, I am the Vine; you are the branches. Whoever lives in me and I in him shall produce a large crop of fruit. For apart from me you can't do a thing.

When the Holy Spirit controls our lives he will produce . . . love.

My true disciples produce bountiful harvests. This brings great glory to my Father. I have loved you even as the Father has loved me. Live within my love. When you obey me you are living in my love, just as I obey the Father and live in his love. ☐ Those who do what Christ tells them to will learn to love God more and more.

I demand that you love each other as much as I love you. ☐ God showed his great love for us by sending Christ to die for us while we were still sinners. ☐ We know how much God loves us because we have felt his love and because we believe him when he tells us that he loves us dearly. God is love, and anyone who lives in love is living with God and God is living in him.

Jude 21. Jn. 15:4, 5. Gal. 5:22. Jn. 15:8–10. 1 Jn. 2:5. Jn. 15:12. Rom. 5:8. 1 Jn. 4:16.

*We have been delivered from hell and given
eternal life.*

Anyone who listens to my message and believes
in God who sent me has eternal life, and will
never be damned for his sins, but has already
passed out of death into life. □ Whoever has
God's Son has life; whoever does not have his
Son, does not have life.

It is this God who has made you and me into
faithful Christians and commissioned us apostles
to preach the Good News. He has put his brand
upon us—his mark of ownership—and given us
his Holy Spirit in our hearts as guarantee that we
belong to him. □ Then we will know for sure, by
our actions, that we are on God's side, and our
consciences will be clear. If our consciences are
clear, we can come to the Lord with perfect assurance and trust. □ We know that we are children of God.

Once you were under God's curse, doomed forever for your sins. Even though we were spiritually
dead and doomed by our sins, he gave us back
our lives again when he raised Christ from the
dead—only by his undeserved favor have we
ever been saved. □ He has rescued us out of the
darkness and gloom of Satan's kingdom and
brought us into the kingdom of his dear Son.

*1 Jn. 3:14. Jn. 5:24. 1 Jn. 5:12. 2 Cor. 1:21, 22. 1 Jn. 3:19, 21.
1 Jn. 5:19. Eph. 2:1, 5. Col. 1:13.*

You have let me experience the joys of life.

The Lord says: "Take your choice of life or death!" □ I will continue to teach you those things which are good and right. □ I am the Way —yes, and the Truth and the Life. No one can get to the Father except by means of me. □ Come . . . with me.

Before every man there lies a wide and pleasant road that seems right but ends in death. □ Heaven can be entered only through the narrow gate! The highway to hell is broad, and its gate is wide enough for all the multitudes who choose its easy way. But the Gateway to Life is small, and the road is narrow, and only a few ever find it.

A main road will go through that once-deserted land; it will be named "The Holy Highway." No evil-hearted men may walk upon it. God will walk there with you; even the most stupid cannot miss the way. □ Oh, that we might know the Lord! Let us press on to know him.

There are many homes up there where my Father lives, and I am going to prepare them for your coming.

Ps. 16:11. Jer. 21:8. 1 Sam. 12:23. Jn. 14:6. Mt. 4:19. Prov. 14:12. Mt. 7:13, 14. Is. 35:8. Hos. 6:3. Jn. 14:2.

Abraham trusted God, and when God told him to leave home and go far away to another land which he promised to give him, Abraham obeyed.

He . . . will personally select his choicest blessings . . . the very best for those he loves. □ God protected them in the howling wilderness as though they were the apple of his eye. He spreads his wings over them, even as an eagle overspreads her young. She carries them upon her wings— as does the Lord his people! When the Lord alone was leading them, and they lived without foreign gods, God gave them fertile hilltops.

I am the Lord your God, who punishes you for your own good and leads you along the paths that you should follow. □ Who is a teacher like him?

We know these things are true by believing, not by seeing. □ For this world is not our home; we are looking forward to our everlasting home in heaven. □ Dear brothers, you are only visitors here. Since your real home is in heaven I beg you to keep away from the evil pleasures of this world; they are not for you, for they fight against your very souls.

Hebr. 11:8. Ps. 47:4. Deut. 32:10–13. Is. 48:17. Job 36:22. 2 Cor. 5:7. Hebr. 13:14. 1 Pet. 2:11.

*Be happy in the Lord and crown him, our
holy God.*

Even the heavens can't be absolutely pure compared with him! How much less someone like you,
who is corrupt and sinful, drinking in sin as a
sponge soaks up water! □ Even the moon and stars
are less than nothing as compared to him. How
much less is man, who is but a worm in his sight?

Who else is like the Lord among the gods? Who
is glorious in holiness like him? □ Holy, holy, holy
is the Lord of Hosts.

Be holy now in everything you do, just as the
Lord is holy, who invited you to be his child. He
himself has said, "You must be holy, for I am
holy." □ Share his holiness.

God's home is holy and clean, and you are that
home. □ What holy, godly lives we should be
living! Try hard to live without sinning; and be
at peace with everyone so that he will be pleased
with you when he returns.

Say only what is good and helpful to those you
are talking to, and what will give them a blessing.
Don't cause the Holy Spirit sorrow by the way you
live. Remember, he is the one who marks you to
be present on that day when salvation from sin will
be complete.

*Ps. 97:12. Job 15:15, 16. Job 25:5, 6. Ex. 15:11. Is. 6:3. 1 Pet.
1:15, 16. Hebr. 12:10. 1 Cor. 3:17. 2 Pet. 3:11, 14. Eph. 4:29, 30.*

*You have armed me with strong armor for
the battle.*

When I am weak, then I am strong.

"O Lord," he cried out to God, "no one else
can help us! Here we are, powerless against this
mighty army. Oh, help us, Lord our God! For we
trust in you alone to rescue us, and in your name
we attack this vast horde. Don't let mere men defeat you!" □ Jehoshaphat cried out to the Lord to
save him, and the Lord made the charioteers see
their mistake and leave him.

It is better to trust the Lord than to put confidence in men. It is better to take refuge in him
than in the mightiest king! □ The best-equipped
army cannot save a king—for great strength is
not enough to save anyone. A war horse is a poor
risk for winning victories—it is strong but it
cannot save.

For we are not fighting against people made of
flesh and blood, but against persons without
bodies—the evil rulers of the unseen world, those
mighty satanic beings and great evil princes of
darkness who rule this world; and against huge
numbers of wicked spirits in the spirit world.

*Ps. 18:39. 2 Cor. 12:10. 2 Chron. 14:11. 2 Chron. 18:31. Ps
118:8, 9. Ps. 33:16, 17. Eph. 6:12.*

Be full of love.

I am giving a new commandment to you now —love each other just as much as I love you. □ Show deep love for each other, for love makes up for many of your faults. □ Love overlooks insults.

When you are praying, first forgive anyone you are holding a grudge against, so that your Father in heaven will forgive you your sins too. □ Love your *enemies!* Do good to *them!* Lend to *them!* And don't be concerned about the fact that they won't repay. □ Do not rejoice when your enemy meets trouble. Let there be no gladness when he falls. □ Don't repay evil for evil. Don't snap back at those who say unkind things about you. Instead, pray for God's help for them, for we are to be kind to others, and God will bless us for it. □ Be at peace with everyone, just as much as possible. □ Be kind to each other, tenderhearted, forgiving one another, just as God has forgiven you because you belong to Christ.

Little children, let us stop just *saying* we love people; let us *really* love them, and *show* it by our *actions.* Then we will know for sure, by our actions, that we are on God's side, and our consciences will be clear, even when we stand before the Lord.

Eph. 5:2. Jn. 13:34. 1 Pet. 4:8. Prov. 10:12. Mk. 11:25. Lk. 6:35. Prov. 24:17. 1 Pet. 3:9. Rom. 12:18. Eph. 4:32. 1 Jn. 3:18, 19.

*May God's love and the Holy Spirit's friend-
ship be yours.*

I will ask the Father and he will give you another Comforter, and he will never leave you. He
is the Holy Spirit, the Spirit who leads into all
truth. The world at large cannot receive him, for
it isn't looking for him and doesn't recognize him.
But you do, for he lives with you now and some
day shall be in you. □ He will not be presenting
his own ideas, but will be passing on to you what
he has heard. He shall praise me and bring me
great honor by showing you my glory.

We know how dearly God loves us, and we feel
this warm love everywhere within us because God
has given us the Holy Spirit to fill our hearts with
his love.

If you give yourself to the Lord, you and Christ
are joined together as one person. Haven't you
yet learned that your body is the home of the Holy
Spirit God gave you, and that he lives within you?
Your own body does not belong to you.

Don't cause the Holy Spirit sorrow by the way
you live. Remember, he is the one who marks you
to be present on that day when salvation from
sin will be complete. □ And in the same way—
by our faith—the Holy Spirit helps us with our
daily problems and in our praying.

*2 Cor. 13:14. Jn. 14:16, 17. Jn. 16:13, 14. Rom. 5:5. 1 Cor. 6:17,
19. Eph. 4:30. Rom. 8:26.*

The God of peace . . . produce in you through the power of Christ all that is pleasing to him.

Be happy. Grow in Christ. Pay attention to what I have said. Live in harmony and peace.

Because of his kindness you have been saved through trusting Christ. And even trusting is not of yourselves; it too is a gift from God. Salvation is not a reward for the good we have done, so none of us can take any credit for it. □ But whatever is good and perfect comes to us from God, the Creator of all light, and he shines forever without change or shadow.

Do the good things that result from being saved, obeying God with deep reverence, shrinking back from all that might displease him. For God is at work within you, helping you want to obey him, and then helping you do what he wants. □ Be a new and different person with a fresh newness in all you do and think. Then you will learn from your own experience how his ways will really satisfy you. □ May you always be doing those good, kind things which show that you are a child of God, for this will bring much praise and glory to the Lord.

Not because we think we can do anything of lasting value by ourselves. Our only power and success comes from God.

Hebr. 13:20, 21. 2 Cor. 13:11. Eph. 2:8, 9. Jas. 1:17. Phil. 2:12. 13. Rom. 12:2. Phil. 1:11. 2 Cor. 3:5.

The Temple of the Lord must be a marvelous structure, famous and glorious.

You have become living building-stones for God's use in building his house. □ Don't you realize that all of you together are the house of God, and that the Spirit of God lives among you in his house? If anyone defiles and spoils God's home, God will destroy him. For God's home is holy and clean, and you are that home. □ Haven't you yet learned that your body is the home of the Holy Spirit God gave you, and that he lives within you? Your own body does not belong to you. For God has bought you with a great price. So use every part of your body to give glory back to God, because he owns it. □ What union can there be between God's temple and idols? For you are God's temple, the home of the living God. □ You are members of God's very own family, citizens of God's country, and you belong in God's household with every other Christian. What a foundation you stand on now: the apostles and the prophets; and the cornerstone of the building is Jesus Christ himself. We who believe are carefully joined together with Christ as parts of a beautiful, constantly growing temple for God. And you also are joined with him and with each other by the Spirit, and are part of this dwelling place of God.

1 Chron. 22:5. 1 Pet. 2:5. 1 Cor. 3:16, 17. 1 Cor. 6:19, 20. 2 Cor. 6:16. Eph. 2:19–22.

You did not abandon us.

Dear friends, don't be bewildered or surprised when you go through the fiery trials ahead, for this is no strange, unusual thing that is going to happen to you. □ Let God train you, for he is doing what any loving father does for his children. Whoever heard of a son who was never corrected? If God doesn't punish you when you need it, as other fathers punish their sons, then it means that you aren't really God's son at all—that you don't really belong in his family.

The Lord is testing you to find out whether or not you really love him with all your heart and soul.

The Lord will not abandon his chosen people, for that would dishonor his great name. He made you a special nation for himself—just because he wanted to! □ Can a mother forget her little child and not have love for her own son? Yet even if that should be, I will not forget you. □ Happy is the man who has the God of Jacob as his helper, whose hope is in the Lord his God.

Don't you think that God will surely give justice to his people who plead with him day and night? Yes! He will answer them quickly!

Ezra 9:9. 1 Pet. 4:12. Hebr. 12:7, 8. Deut. 13:3. 1 Sam. 12:22. Is. 49:15. Ps. 146:5. Lk. 18:7, 8.

*My Father! If it is possible, let this cup be
taken away from me. But I want your will,
not mine.*

Now my soul is deeply troubled. Shall I pray,
Father, save me from what lies ahead? But that is
the very reason why I came!

I have come here from heaven to do the will of
God who sent me, not to have my own way. □
He humbled himself even further, going so far as
actually to die a criminal's death on a cross. □
Yet while Christ was here on earth he pleaded
with God, praying with tears and agony of soul
to the only one who would save him from [prema-
ture] death. And God heard his prayers because
of his strong desire to obey God at all times. And
even though Jesus was God's Son, he had to learn
from experience what it was like to obey, when
obeying meant suffering.

Don't you realize that I could ask my Father
for thousands of angels to protect us, and he
would send them instantly? Yes, it was written
long ago that the Messiah must suffer and die
and rise again from the dead on the third day;
and that this message of salvation should be taken
from Jerusalem to all the nations: *There is forgiveness of sins for all who turn to me.*

*Mt. 26:39. Jn. 12:27. Jn. 6:38. Phil. 2:8. Hebr. 5:7, 8. Mt. 26:53.
Lk. 24:46, 47.*

When the Holy Spirit controls our lives he will produce . . . goodness.

Follow God's example in everything you do just as a much loved child imitates his father. □ Love your *enemies!* Pray for those who *persecute* you! In that way you will be acting as true sons of your Father in heaven. For he gives his sunlight to both the evil and the good, and sends rain on the just and on the unjust too. □ Try to show as much compassion as your Father does.

Because of this light within you, you should do only what is good and right and true.

When the time came for the kindness and love of God our Savior to appear, then he saved us—not because we were good enough to be saved, but because of his kindness and pity—by washing away our sins and giving us the new joy of the indwelling Holy Spirit whom he poured out upon us with wonderful fullness—and all because of what Jesus Christ our Savior did. □ He is good to everyone, and his compassion is intertwined with everything he does. □ Since he did not spare even his own Son for us but gave him up for us all, won't he also surely give us everything else?

Gal. 5:22, 23. Eph. 5:1. Mt. 5:44, 45. Lk. 6:36. Eph. 5:9. Tit. 3:4–6. Ps. 145:9. Rom. 8:32.

You have given me the blessings you reserve for those who reverence your name.

No weapon turned against you shall succeed, and you will have justice against every courtroom lie. This is the heritage of the servants of the Lord. "This is the blessing I have given you," says the Lord. □ For the Angel of the Lord guards and rescues all who reverence him. Oh, put God to the test and see how kind he is! See for yourself the way his mercies shower down on all who trust in him. If you belong to the Lord, reverence him; for everyone who does this has everything he needs. Even strong young lions sometimes go hungry, but those of us who reverence the Lord will never lack any good thing. □ He sees that I am given pleasant brooks and meadows as my share! What a wonderful inheritance!

For you who fear my name, the Sun of Righteousness will rise with healing in his wings. And you will go free, leaping with joy like calves let out to pasture. □ Since he did not spare even his own Son for us but gave him up for us all, won't he also surely give us everything else?

Ps. 61:5. Is. 54:17. Ps. 34:7–10. Ps. 16:6. Mal. 4:2. Rom. 8:32.

I will praise you with great joy.

How precious it is, Lord, to realize that you are thinking about me constantly! I can't even count how many times a day your thoughts turn towards me. And when I waken in the morning, you are still thinking of me. □ Your words are sweeter than honey. □ Your love is sweeter than wine.

Your steadfast love, O Lord, is as great as all the heavens. Your faithfulness reaches beyond the clouds. Your justice is as solid as God's mountains. Your decisions are as full of wisdom as the oceans are with water. You are concerned for men and animals alike. How precious is your constant love, O God! All humanity takes refuge in the shadow of your wings. You feed them with blessings from your own table and let them drink from your rivers of delight. □ Whom have I in heaven but you? And I desire no one on earth as much as you! □ You have let me experience the joys of life and the exquisite pleasures of your own eternal presence.

Oh, what a wonderful God we have! How great are his wisdom and knowledge and riches! For everything comes from God alone. Everything lives by his power, and everything is for his glory. To him be glory evermore.

Ps. 63:5, 6. Ps. 139:17, 18. Ps. 119:103. Song 1:2. Ps. 36:5–8. Ps. 73:25. Ps. 16:11. Rom. 11:33, 36.

Nicodemus . . . came secretly to interview Jesus.

Peter was following far to the rear. □ Even many of the Jewish leaders believed him to be the Messiah but wouldn't admit it to anyone because of their fear that the Pharisees would excommunicate them from the synagogue; for they loved the praise of men more than the praise of God. □ Fear of man is a dangerous trap, but to trust in God means safety.

Some will come to me––those the Father has given me––and I will never, never reject them. □ He will not break the bruised reed, nor quench the dimly burning flame. □ Faith even as small as a tiny mustard seed.

The Holy Spirit, God's gift, does not want you to be afraid of people, but to be wise and strong, and to love them and enjoy being with them. If you will stir up this inner power, you will never be afraid to tell others about our Lord. □ And now, my little children, stay in happy fellowship with the Lord so that when he comes you will be sure that all is well, and will not have to be ashamed and shrink back from meeting him. □ If anyone publicly acknowledges me as his friend, I will openly acknowledge him as my friend before my Father in heaven.

Jn. 7:50. Mt. 26:58. Jn. 12:42, 43. Prov. 29:25. Jn. 6:37. Is. 42:3. Mt. 17:20. 2 Tim. 1:7, 8. 1 Jn. 2:28. Mt. 10:32.

Take your share of suffering as a good soldier of Jesus Christ.

Jesus, our leader and instructor. He was willing to die a shameful death on the cross. □ It was right and proper that God, who made everything for his own glory, should allow Jesus to suffer, for in doing this he was bringing vast multitudes of God's people to heaven; for his suffering made Jesus a perfect Leader, one fit to bring them into their salvation. □ They must enter into the Kingdom of God through many tribulations.

For we are not fighting against people made of flesh and blood, but against persons without bodies—the evil rulers of the unseen world, those mighty satanic beings and great evil princes of darkness who rule this world; and against huge numbers of wicked spirits in the spirit world. So use every piece of God's armor. □ I don't use human plans and methods to win my battles. I use God's mighty weapons, not those made by men, to knock down the devil's strongholds.

After you have suffered a little while, our God, who is full of kindness through Christ, will give you his eternal glory. He personally will come and pick you up, and set you firmly in place, and make you stronger than ever.

2 *Tim. 2:3. Hebr. 12:2. Hebr. 2:10. Acts 14:22. Eph. 6:12, 13.*
2 *Cor. 10:3, 4. 1 Pet. 5:10.*

The Lord . . . is full of tenderness and mercy.

He is like a father to us, tender and sympathetic to those who reverence him. □ Who can forget the wonders he performs—deeds of mercy and of grace? He gives food to those who trust him; he never forgets his promises.

He will never let me stumble, slip or fall. For he is always watching, never sleeping. □ He spreads his wings over them, even as an eagle overspreads her young. She carries them upon her wings—as does the Lord his people!

His compassion never ends. It is only the Lord's mercies that have kept us from complete destruction. Great is his faithfulness; his lovingkindness begins afresh each day.

So when Jesus came out of the wilderness, a vast crowd was waiting for him and he pitied them and healed their sick. □ Jesus Christ is the same yesterday, today, and forever.

And the very hairs of your head are all numbered. Not one sparrow (What do they cost? Two for a penny?) can fall to the ground without your Father knowing it. So don't worry! You are more valuable to him than many sparrows.

Jas. 5:11. Ps. 103:13. Ps. 111:4, 5. Ps. 121:3, 4. Deut. 32:11. Lam. 3:22, 23. Mt. 14:14. Hebr. 13:8. Mt. 10:30, 29, 31.

I have trodden the winepress alone.

Who else is like the Lord among the gods? Who is glorious in holiness like him? Who is so awesome in splendor, a wonder-working God? □ He saw no one was helping you, and wondered that no one intervened. Therefore he himself stepped in to save you through his mighty power and justice. □ He personally carried the load of our sins in his own body when he died on the cross, so that we can be finished with sin and live a good life from now on. For his wounds have healed ours!

Sing a new song to the Lord telling about his mighty deeds! For he has won a mighty victory by his power and holiness. □ God took away Satan's power to accuse you of sin, and God openly displayed to the whole world Christ's triumph at the cross where your sins were all taken away. □ And when he sees all that is accomplished by the anguish of his soul, he shall be satisfied; and because of what he has experienced, my righteous Servant shall make many to be counted righteous before God, for he shall bear all their sins.

March on, my soul, with strength! □ Overwhelming victory is ours through Christ who loved us enough to die for us.

Is. 63:3. Ex. 15:11. Is. 59:16. 1 Pet. 2:24. Ps. 98:1. Col. 2:15. Is. 53:11. Judg. 5:21. Rom. 8:37.

Just as a father punishes a son he delights in to make him better, so the Lord corrects you.

Don't you see that I alone am God? I kill and make live. I wound and heal—no one delivers from my power. □ "For I know the plans I have for you," says the Lord. "They are plans for good and not for evil, to give you a future and a hope." □ This plan of mine is not what you would work out, neither are my thoughts the same as yours!

But I will court her again, and bring her into the wilderness, and speak to her tenderly there. □ So you should realize that, as a man punishes his son, the Lord punishes you to help you. □ For when he punishes you, it proves that he loves you. When he whips you it proves you are really his child. □ Being punished isn't enjoyable while it is happening—it hurts! But afterwards we can see the result, a quiet growth in grace and character. □ If you will humble yourselves under the mighty hand of God, in his good time he will lift you up.

I know, O Lord, that your decisions are right and that your punishment was right and did me good.

Prov. 3:12. Deut. 32:39. Jer. 29:11. Is. 55:8. Hos. 2:14. Deut. 8:5. Hebr. 12:6. Hebr. 12:11. 1 Pet. 5:6. Ps. 119:75.

*The earth belongs to God! Everything in all
the world is his!*

She doesn't realize that all she has, has come
from me. It was I who gave her all the gold and
silver that she used in worshiping Baal, her god!
But now I will take back the wine and ripened
corn I constantly supplied, and the clothes I gave
her to cover her nakedness—I will no longer give
her rich harvests of grain in its season, or wine at
the time of the grape harvest.

Everything we have has come from you, and
we only give you what is yours already! For we
are here for but a moment, strangers in the land
as our fathers were before us; our days on earth
are like a shadow, gone so soon, without a trace.
O Lord our God, all of this material . . . comes
from you! It all belongs to you! □ For everything
lives by his power, and everything is for his glory.
To him be glory evermore.

The living God . . . always richly gives us
all we need for our enjoyment.

And it is he who will supply all your needs
from his riches in glory, because of what Christ
Jesus has done for us.

*Ps. 24:1. Hos. 2:8, 9. 1 Chron. 29:14–16. Rom. 11:36. 1 Tim. 6:17.
Phil. 4:19.*

Broken cisterns that can't hold water!

The people who lived there began to talk about building a great city, with a temple-tower reaching to the skies—a proud, eternal monument to themselves. God scattered them all over the earth; and that ended the building of the city. □ I worked hard to be wise instead of foolish—but now I realize that even this was like chasing the wind. For the more my wisdom, the more my grief; to increase knowledge only increases distress. □ Then I tried to find fulfillment by inaugurating a great public works program: homes, vineyards, gardens, parks and orchards for myself, and reservoirs to hold the water to irrigate my plantations. I collected silver and gold as taxes from many kings and provinces. But as I looked at everything I had tried, it was all so useless, a chasing of the wind, and there was nothing really worthwhile anywhere.

If anyone is thirsty, let him come to me and drink. □ For he satisfies the thirsty soul and fills the hungry soul with good.

Let heaven fill your thoughts; don't spend your time worrying about things down here.

Jer. 2:13. Gen. 11:3, 4, 8. Eccl. 1:17, 18. Eccl. 2:4–6, 8, 11. Jn. 7:37. Ps. 107:9. Col. 3:2.

I'm not asking you to take them out of the world, but to keep them safe from Satan's power.

Live clean, innocent lives as children of God in a dark world full of people who are crooked and stubborn. Shine out among them like beacon lights. □ You are the world's seasoning . . . you are the world's light. Let your good deeds glow for all to see, so that they will praise your heavenly Father.

I held you back from sinning against me. □ No temptation is irresistible. You can trust God to keep the temptation from becoming so strong that you can't stand up against it, for he has promised this and will do what he says. He will show you how to escape temptation's power.

The Lord is faithful; he will make you strong and guard you from satanic attacks of every kind. □ He died for our sins just as God our Father planned, and rescued us from this evil world in which we live. □ And now—all glory to him who alone is God, who saves us through Jesus Christ our Lord; yes, splendor and majesty, all power and authority are his from the beginning; his they are and his they evermore shall be. And he is able to keep you from slipping and falling away, and to bring you, sinless and perfect, into his glorious presence with mighty shouts of everlasting joy. Amen.

Jn. 17:15. Phil. 2:15. Mt. 5:13, 14, 16. Gen. 20:6. 1 Cor. 10:13. 2 Thess. 3:3. Gal. 1:4. Jude 24, 25.

To trust in God means safety.

The Lord is very great, and lives in heaven. □ He is high above the nations; his glory is far greater than the heavens. Far below him are the heavens and the earth; he stoops to look, and lifts the poor from the dirt, and the hungry from the garbage dump, and sets them among princes!

But God is so rich in mercy; he loved us so much that even though we were spiritually dead and doomed by our sins, he gave us back our lives again when he raised Christ from the dead —only by his undeserved favor have we ever been saved—and lifted us up from the grave into glory along with Christ, where we sit with him in the heavenly realms—all because of what Christ Jesus did.

Since he did not spare even his own Son for us but gave him up for us all, won't he also surely give us everything else? For I am convinced that nothing can ever separate us from his love. Death can't, and life can't. The angels won't, and all the powers of hell itself cannot keep God's love away. Our fears for today, our worries about tomorrow, or where we are—high above the sky, or in the deepest ocean—nothing will ever be able to separate us from the love of God demonstrated by our Lord Jesus Christ when he died for us.

Prov. 29:25. Is. 33:5. Ps. 113:4, 6, 7, 8. Eph. 2:4–6. Rom. 8:32, 38, 39.

God has deliberately chosen to use ideas the world considers foolish and of little worth in order to shame those people considered by the world as wise and great.

When they cried to the Lord, he sent them a savior, Ehud (son of Gera, a Benjaminite), who was left-handed. The next judge after Ehud was Shamgar (son of Anath). He once killed six hundred Philistines with an ox goad, thereby saving Israel from disaster.

Then the Lord turned to him [Gideon] and said, "I will make you strong! Go and save Israel from the Midianites! I am sending you!" But Gideon replied, "Sir, how can I save Israel? My family is the poorest in the whole tribe of Manasseh, and I am the least thought of in the entire family!"

The Lord then said to Gideon, "There are too many of you! I can't let all of you fight the Midianites, for then the people of Israel will boast to me that they saved themselves by their own strength!"

"Not by might, nor by power, but by my Spirit," says the Lord of Hosts—"you will succeed because of my Spirit, though you are few and weak." □ Your strength must come from the Lord's mighty power within you.

1 Cor. 1:27. Judg. 3:15, 31. Judg. 6:14, 15. Judg. 7:2. Zech. 4:6. Eph. 6:10.

The joy of the Lord is your strength.

Sing for joy, O heavens; shout, O earth. Break forth with song, O mountains, for the Lord has comforted his people, and will have compassion upon them in their sorrow. □ God has come to save me! I will trust and not be afraid, for the Lord is my strength and song; he is my salvation. □ He is my strength, my shield from every danger. I trusted in him, and he helped me. Joy rises in my heart until I burst out in songs of praise to him.

We rejoice in our wonderful new relationship with God—all because of what our Lord Jesus Christ has done in dying for our sins—making us friends of God. □ Even though the fig trees are all destroyed, and there is neither blossom left nor fruit, and though the olive crops all fail, and the fields lie barren; even if the flocks die in the fields and the cattle barns are empty, yet I will rejoice in the Lord; I will be happy in the God of my salvation. The Lord God is my Strength, and he will give me the speed of a deer and bring me safely over the mountain.

Neh. 8:10. Is. 49:13. Is. 12:2. Ps. 28:7. Rom. 5:11. Hab. 3:17–19.

He was before all else began.

The faithful and true witness [of all that is or was or evermore shall be], the primeval source of God's creation. □ He is the Head of . . . his church—which he began; and he is the Leader of all those who arise from the dead, so that he is first in everything.

The Lord formed me in the beginning, before he created anything else. From ages past, I am. I existed before the earth began. I was there when he established the heavens and formed the great springs in the depths of the oceans. I was there when he set the limits of the seas and gave them his instructions not to spread beyond their boundaries. I was there when he made the blueprint for the earth and oceans. I was always at his side like a little child. I was his constant delight, laughing and playing in his presence. □ From eternity to eternity I am God.

Jesus, our leader. He was willing to die a shameful death on the cross because of the joy he knew would be his afterwards; and now he sits in the place of honor by the throne of God.

Col. 1:17. Rev. 3:14. Col. 1:18. Prov. 8:22, 23, 27–30. Is. 43:13. Hebr. 12:2.

*What God in all of heaven or earth can do
what you have done for us?*

Who in all of heaven can be compared with
God? What mightiest angel is anything like him?
O Jehovah, Commander of the heavenly armies,
where is there any other Mighty One like you?
Faithfulness is your very character. □ Where
among the heathen gods is there a god like you?
Where are their miracles? □ All heaven shall
praise your miracles, O Lord; myriads of angels
will praise you for your faithfulness. □ You are
doing all these things just because you promised
to and because you want to! How great you are,
Lord God! We have never heard of any other god
like you.

No mere man has ever seen, heard or even
imagined what wonderful things God has ready
for those who love the Lord. But we know about
these things because God has sent his Spirit to
tell us, and his Spirit searches out and shows us
all of God's deepest secrets.

Don't you yet understand? Don't you know
by now that the everlasting God, Creator of the
farthest parts of the earth, never grows faint or
weary?

*Deut. 3:25. Ps. 89:6, 8. Ps. 86:8. Ps. 89:5. 2 Sam. 7:21, 22. 1 Cor.
2:9, 10. Is. 40:28.*

*If anyone is going to boast, let him boast
only of what the Lord has done.*

Let not the wise man bask in his wisdom, nor
the mightly man in his might, nor the rich man in
his riches. Let them boast in this alone: That they
truly know me, and understand that I am the
Lord.

Everything else is worthless when compared
with the priceless gain of knowing Christ Jesus
my Lord. I have put aside all else, counting it
worth less than nothing, in order that I can have
Christ. □ His unchanging plan has always been
to adopt us into his own family by sending Jesus
Christ to die for us. □ I am not ashamed of this
Good News about Christ. It is God's powerful
method of bringing all who believe it to heaven.
This message was preached first to the Jews alone,
but now everyone is invited to come to God in this
same way.

Whom have I in heaven but you? And I desire
no one on earth as much as you! □ How I rejoice in the Lord!

Glorify your name, not ours, O Lord! Cause
everyone to praise your lovingkindness and your
truth. □ He must become greater and greater, and
I must become less and less.

*1 Cor. 1:31.   Jer. 9:23, 24.   Phil. 3:8.   Eph. 1:5.   Rom. 1:16.   Ps.
73:25.   1 Sam. 2:1.   Ps. 115:1.   Jn. 3:30.*

Jehovah is mine!

God has already given you everything you need . . . and you belong to Christ, and Christ is God's. ☐ Jesus Christ . . . died under God's judgment against our sins, so that he could rescue us from constant falling into sin. ☐ God has put all things under his feet and made him the supreme Head of the church. ☐ Christ . . . died [for the church] so that he could give her to himself as a glorious church without a single spot or wrinkle or any other blemish, being holy and without a single fault.

I will boast of all his kindness to me. ☐ How happy God has made me! For he has clothed me with garments of salvation and draped about me the robe of righteousness.

Whom have I in heaven but you? And I desire no one on earth as much as you! My health fails; my spirits droop, yet God remains! He is the strength of my heart; he is mine forever! ☐ I said to him, "You are my Lord; I have no other help but yours." The Lord himself is my inheritance, my prize. He is my food and drink, my highest joy! He guards all that is mine. He sees that I am given pleasant brooks and meadows as my share! What a wonderful inheritance.

Ps. 119:57. 1 Cor. 3:21, 23. Tit. 2:13, 14. Eph. 1:22. Eph. 5:25, 27. Ps. 34:2. Is. 61:10. Ps. 73:25, 26. Ps. 16:2, 5, 6.

Before every man there lies a wide and pleasant road that seems right but ends in death.

A man is a fool to trust himself!

Your words are a flashlight to light the path ahead of me, and keep me from stumbling. □ I have followed your commands and have not gone along with cruel and evil men.

If there is a prophet among you, or one who claims to foretell the future by dreams, and if his predictions come true but he says, "Come, let us worship the gods of the other nations," don't listen to him. For the Lord is testing you to find out whether or not you really love him with all your heart and soul. You must *never* worship any God but Jehovah; obey only his commands and cling to him.

I will instruct you (says the Lord) and guide you along the best pathway for your life; I will advise you and watch your progress. Don't be like a senseless horse or mule that has to have a bit in its mouth to keep it in line! Many sorrows come to the wicked, but abiding love surrounds those who trust in the Lord. So rejoice in him, all those who are his, and shout for joy, all those who try to obey him.

Prov. 14:12. Prov. 28:26. Ps. 119:105. Ps. 17:4. Deut. 13:1–4. Ps. 32:8–11.

God gave Solomon great wisdom and under standing.

Now a greater than Solomon is here. □ The Prince of Peace.

Even if we were good, we really wouldn't expect anyone to die for us, though, of course, that might be barely possible. But God showed his great love for us by sending Christ to die for us while we were still sinners. □ Jesus Christ, who, though he was God, did not demand and cling to his rights as God, but laid aside his mighty power and glory, taking the disguise of a slave and becoming like men. And he humbled himself even further, going so far as actually to die a criminal's death on a cross. □ How long, how wide, how deep, and how high his love really is.

Christ is the mighty power of God to save them; Christ himself is the center of God's wise plan for their salvation. □ In him lie hidden all the mighty, untapped treasures of wisdom and knowledge. □ The endless treasures available . . . in Christ. □ It is from God alone that you have your life through Christ Jesus. He showed us God's plan of salvation; he was the one who made us acceptable to God; he made us pure and holy and gave himself to purchase our salvation.

1 Kgs. 4:29. Mt. 12:42. Is. 9:6. Rom. 5:7, 8. Phil. 2:5–8. Eph. 3:19. 1 Cor. 1:24. Col. 2:3. Eph. 3:8. 1 Cor. 1:30.

I made you and I will care for you.

The Lord who created you, O Israel, says, "Don't be afraid, for I have ransomed you; I have called you by name; you are mine. When you go through deep waters and great trouble, I will be with you. When you go through rivers of difficulty, you will not drown! When you walk through the fire of oppression, you will not be burned up —the flames will not consume you." □ I will be your God through all your lifetime, yes, even when your hair is white with age.

He spreads his wings over them, even as an eagle overspreads her young. She carries them upon her wings—as does the Lord his people! □ In his love and pity he redeemed them and lifted them up and carried them through all the years.

Jesus Christ is the same yesterday, today, and forever. □ I am convinced that . . . nothing will ever be able to separate us from the love of God demonstrated by our Lord Jesus Christ when he died for us.

Can a mother forget her little child and not have love for her own son? Yet even if that should be, I will not forget you.

Is. 46:4. Is. 43:1, 2. Is. 46:4. Deut. 32:11, 12. Is. 63:9. Hebr. 13:8. Rom. 8:38, 39. Is. 49:15.

Consider the quarry from which you were mined, the rock from which you were cut!

I was born a sinner, yes, from the moment my mother conceived me. □ No one pitied you or cared for you. On that day when you were born, you were dumped out into a field and left to die, unwanted. But I came by and saw you there, covered with your own blood, and I said, "Live! Thrive like a plant in the field!"

He lifted me out of the pit of despair, out from the bog and the mire, and set my feet on a hard, firm path and steadied me as I walked along. He has given me a new song to sing, of praises to our God.

When we were utterly helpless with no way of escape, Christ came at just the right time and died for us sinners who had no use for him. Even if we were good, we really wouldn't expect anyone to die for us, though, of course, that might be barely possible. But God showed his great love for us by sending Christ to die for us while we were still sinners. □ God is so rich in mercy; he loved us so much that even though we were spiritually dead and doomed by our sins, he gave us back our lives again when he raised Christ from the dead.

Is. 51:1. Ps. 51:5. Ezk. 16:5, 6. Ps. 40:2, 3. Rom. 5:6–8. Eph. 2:4, 5.

How happy God has made me!

I will praise the Lord no matter what happens. I will constantly speak of his glories and grace. I will boast of all his kindness to me. Let all who are discouraged take heart. Let us praise the Lord together, and exalt his name. □ For Jehovah God is our Light and our Protector. He gives us grace and glory. No good thing will he withhold from those who walk along his paths. O Lord of the armies of heaven, blessed are those who trust in you. □ I bless the holy name of God with all my heart.

Those who have reason to be thankful should continually be singing praises to the Lord. □ Be filled . . . with the Holy Spirit, and controlled by him. Talk with each other much about the Lord, quoting psalms and hymns and singing sacred songs, making music in your hearts to the Lord. Always give thanks for everything to our God and Father in the name of our Lord Jesus Christ. □ Singing to the Lord with thankful hearts.

Around midnight . . . Paul and Silas were praying and singing hymns to the Lord. □ Always be full of joy in the Lord; I say it again, rejoice!

Is. 61:10. Ps. 34:1–3. Ps. 84:11, 12. Ps. 103:1. Jas. 5:13. Eph. 5:18–20. Col. 3:16. Acts 16:25. Phil. 4:4.

Blessings overflow!

Oh, put God to the test and see how kind he is! See for yourself the way his mercies shower down on all who trust in him. If you belong to the Lord, reverence him; for everyone who does this has everything he needs. Even strong, young lions sometimes go hungry, but those of us who reverence the Lord will never lack any good thing. ☐ *His compassion never ends.* Great is his faithfulness; his lovingkindness begins afresh each day.

The Lord himself is my inheritance, my prize. He is my food and drink, my highest joy! He guards all that is mine. He sees that I am given pleasant brooks and meadows as my share! What a wonderful inheritance! ☐ He has given you the whole world to use, and life and even death are your servants. He has given you all of the present and all of the future. All are yours. ☐ How we praise God, the Father of our Lord Jesus Christ, who has blessed us with every blessing in heaven because we belong to Christ.

I have learned how to get along happily whether I have much or little. ☐ Do you want to be truly rich? You already are if you are happy and good. ☐ God . . . will supply all your needs from his riches in glory, because of what Christ Jesus has done for us.

Ps. 23:5. Ps. 34:8-10. Lam. 3:22, 23. Ps. 16:5, 6. 1 Cor. 3:22. Eph. 1:3. Phil. 4:11. 1 Tim. 6:6. Phil. 4:18, 19.

Your words are a flashlight to light the path ahead of me, and keep me from stumbling.

Every day and all night long their counsel will lead you and save you from harm; when you wake up in the morning, let their instructions guide you into the new day. For their advice is a beam of light directed into the dark corners of your mind to warn you of danger and to give you a good life. □ And if you leave God's paths and go astray, you will hear a Voice behind you say, "No, this is the way; walk here."

I am the Light of the world. So if you follow me, you won't be stumbling through the darkness, for living light will flood your path. □ We have seen and proved that what the prophets said came true. You will do well to pay close attention to everything they have written, for, like lights shining into dark corners, their words help us to understand many things that otherwise would be dark and difficult. □ We can see and understand only a little about God now, as if we were peering at his reflection in a poor mirror; but someday we are going to see him in his completeness, face to face. Now all that I know is hazy and blurred, but then I will see everything clearly, just as clearly as God sees into my heart right now.

Ps. 119:105. Prov. 6:22, 23. Is. 30:21. Jn. 8:12. 2 Pet. 1:19. 1 Cor. 13:12.

Happy the man who puts his trust in the Lord.

Abraham never doubted. He believed God, for his faith and trust grew ever stronger, and he praised God for this blessing even before it happened. He was completely sure that God was well able to do anything he promised. □ Judah, depending upon the Lord God of their fathers, defeated Israel.

God is our refuge and strength, a tested help in times of trouble. And so we need not fear even if the world blows up, and the mountains crumble into the sea. □ It is better to trust the Lord than to put confidence in men. It is better to take refuge in him than in the mightiest king! □ The steps of good men are directed by the Lord. He delights in each step they take. If they fall it isn't fatal, for the Lord holds them with his hand.

Oh, put God to the test and see how kind he is! See for yourself the way his mercies shower down on all who trust in him. If you belong to the Lord, reverence him; for everyone who does this has everything he needs.

Prov. 16:20. Rom. 4:20, 21. 2 Chron. 13:18. Ps. 46:1, 2. Ps. 118:8, 9. Ps. 37:23, 24. Ps. 34:8, 9.

*I will lie down in peace and sleep, for though
I am alone, O Lord, you will keep me safe.*

You don't need to be afraid of the dark any
more, nor fear the dangers of the day; nor dread
the plagues of darkness, nor disasters in the morning. He will shield you with his wings. They will
shelter you. His faithful promises are your armor.
☐ He will never let me stumble, slip or fall. For he
is always watching, never sleeping. Jehovah himself is caring for you! He is your defender. He
protects you day and night. He keeps his eye
upon you as you come and go, and always guards
you.

I shall live forever in your tabernacle; oh, to
be safe beneath the shelter of your wings! ☐ Darkness cannot hide from God; to you the night shines
as bright as day. Darkness and light are both
alike to you.

Since he did not spare even his own Son for us
but gave him up for us all, won't he also surely
give us everything else? ☐ You belong to Christ,
and Christ is God's. ☐ I will trust and not be
afraid.

*Ps. 4:8. Ps. 91:5, 6, 4. Ps. 121:3–8. Ps. 61:4. Ps. 139:12. Rom.
8:32. 1 Cor. 3:23. Is. 12:2.*

Anyone who wants to follow me must put aside his own desires and conveniences and carry his cross with him every day and keep close to me!

Whether others honor us or despise us, whether they criticize us or commend us. □ Those who decide to please Christ Jesus by living godly lives will suffer at the hands of those who hate him. □ The fact that I am still being persecuted proves that I am still preaching salvation through faith in the cross of Christ alone.

Be happy if you are cursed and insulted for being a Christian, for when that happens the Spirit of God will come upon you with great glory. Don't let me hear of your suffering for murdering or stealing or making trouble or being a busybody and prying into other people's affairs. But it is no shame to suffer for being a Christian. Praise God for the privilege of being in Christ's family and being called by his wonderful name! If you are suffering according to God's will, keep on doing what is right and trust yourself to the God who made you.

For to you has been given the privilege not only of trusting him but also of suffering for him. □ And if we think that our present service for him is hard, just remember that some day we are going to sit with him and rule with him.

Lk. 9:23. 2 Cor. 6:8. 2 Tim. 3:12. Gal. 5:11. 1 Pet. 4:14–16, 19. Phil. 1:29. 2 Tim. 2:12.

*Don't be impatient. Wait for the Lord, and
he will come and save you! Be brave, stouthearted and courageous.*

Don't you yet understand? Don't you know by
now that the everlasting God, the Creator of the
farthest parts of the earth, never grows faint or
weary? He gives power to the tired and worn out,
and strength to the weak. □ Fear not, for I am
with you. Do not be dismayed. I am your God.
I will strengthen you; I will help you; I will uphold you with my victorious right hand. □ To
the poor, O Lord, you are a refuge from the
storm, a shadow from the heat, a shelter from
merciless men who are like a driving rain that
melts down an earthen wall.

When the way is rough, your patience has a
chance to grow. So let it grow, and don't try to
squirm out of your problems. For when your
patience is finally in full bloom, then you will be
ready for anything, strong in character, full and
complete. □ Do not let this happy trust in the
Lord die away, no matter what happens. Remember your reward! You need to keep on patiently doing God's will if you want him to do for
you all that he has promised. His coming will not
be delayed much longer.

*Ps. 27:14. Is. 40:28, 29. Is. 41:10. Is. 25:4. Jas. 1:3, 4. Hebr.
10:35–37.*

You don't understand now why I am doing it; someday you will.

Do you remember how the Lord led you through the wilderness for all those forty years, humbling you and testing you to find out how you would respond, and whether or not you would really obey him?

I signed a covenant with you, and you became mine. □ When he punishes you, it proves that he loves you.

Dear friends, don't be bewildered or surprised when you go through the fiery trials ahead, for this is no strange, unusual thing that is going to happen to you. Instead, be really glad—because these trials will make you partners with Christ in his suffering, and afterwards you will have the wonderful joy of sharing his glory in that coming day when it will be displayed. □ These troubles and sufferings of ours are, after all, quite small and won't last very long. Yet this short time of distress will result in God's richest blessing upon us forever and ever! So we do not look at what we can see right now, the troubles all around us, but we look forward to the joys in heaven which we have not yet seen. The troubles will soon be over, but the joys to come will last forever.

Jn. 13:7. Deut. 8:2. Ezk. 16:8. Hebr. 12:6. 1 Pet. 4:12, 13. 2 Cor. 4:17, 18.

Let us lift our hearts and hands to him in heaven.

Who can be compared with God enthroned on high? Far below him are the heavens and the earth; he stoops to look, and lifts the poor from the dirt, and the hungry from the garbage dump, and sets them among princes! □ To you, O Lord, I pray. □ I reach out for you. I thirst for you as parched land thirsts for rain. Come quickly, Lord, and answer me, for my depression deepens; don't turn away from me or I shall die. Let me see your kindness to me in the morning, for I am trusting you. Show me where to walk, for my prayer is sincere.

For your love and kindness are better to me than life itself. How I praise you! I will bless you as long as I live, lifting up my hands to you in prayer. □ Give me happiness, O Lord, for I worship only you. O Lord, you are so good and kind, so ready to forgive; so full of mercy for all who ask your aid. Listen closely to my prayer, O God. Hear my urgent cry. I will call to you whenever trouble strikes, and you will help me.

If our consciences are clear, we can come to the Lord with perfect assurance and trust, and get whatever we ask for because we are obeying him and doing the things that please him.

Lam. 3:41. Ps. 113:5–8. Ps. 25:1. Ps. 143:6–8. Ps. 63:3, 4. Ps. 86:4–7. 1 Jn. 3:21, 22.

*When the Holy Spirit controls our lives he
will produce . . . faithfulness.*

Because of his kindness you have been saved
through trusting Christ. And even trusting is not
of yourselves; it too is a gift from God. □ You
can never please God without faith, without depending on him. Anyone who wants to come to
God must believe that there is a God and that he
rewards those who sincerely look for him. □
There is no eternal doom awaiting those who trust
him to save them. But those who don't trust him
have already been tried and condemned for not
believing in the only Son of God. □ I *do* have
faith; oh, help me to have *more!*

Those who do what Christ tells them to will
learn to love God more and more. That is the
way to know whether or not you are a Christian.

We know these things are true by believing,
not by seeing. □ I have been crucified with Christ:
and I myself no longer live, but Christ lives in me.
And the real life I now have within this body is a
result of my trusting in the Son of God, who loved
me and gave himself for me. □ You love him
even though you have never seen him; though not
seeing him, you trust him; and even now you are
happy with the inexpressible joy that comes from
heaven itself.

*Gal. 5:22. Eph. 2:8. Hebr. 11:6. Jn. 3:18. Mk. 9:24. 1 Jn. 2:5.
2 Cor. 5:7. Gal. 2:20. 1 Pet. 1:8.*

Watchman, what of the night?

Time is running out. Wake up, for the coming of the Lord is nearer now than when we first believed. The night is far gone, the day of his return will soon be here. So quit the evil deeds of darkness and put on the armor of right living, as we who live in the daylight should!

Now learn a lesson from the fig tree. When her branch is tender and the leaves begin to sprout, you know that summer is almost here. Just so, when you see all these things beginning to happen, you can know that my return is near, even at the doors. Heaven and earth will disappear, but my words remain forever.

I wait expectantly, trusting God to help, for he has promised. I long for him more than sentinels long for the dawn.

He who has said all these things declares: "Yes, I am coming soon!" Amen! Come, Lord Jesus!

So stay awake and be prepared, for you do not know the date or moment of my return.

Is. 21:11. Rom. 13:11, 12. Mt. 24:32, 33, 35. Ps. 130:5, 6. Rev. 22:20. Mt. 25:13.

Be glad for all God is planning for you.

Looking forward to the joys of heaven. □ If being a Christian is of value to us only now in this life, we are the most miserable of creatures. □ They must enter into the Kingdom of God through many tribulations. □ No one can be my disciple who does not carry his own cross and follow me. □ You know that such troubles are a part of God's plan for us Christians.

Always be full of joy in the Lord; I say it again, rejoice! □ I pray . . . that God who gives you hope will keep you happy and full of peace as you believe in him. □ All honor to God, the God and Father of our Lord Jesus Christ; for it is his boundless mercy that has given us the privilege of being born again, so that we are now members of God's own family. Now we live in the hope of eternal life because Christ rose again from the dead. □ You love him even though you have never seen him; though not seeing him, you trust him; and even now you are happy with the inexpressible joy that comes from heaven itself. □ For because of our faith, he has brought us into this place of highest privilege where we now stand, and we confidently and joyfully look forward to actually becoming all that God has in mind for us to be.

Rom. 12:12. Col. 1:5. 1 Cor. 15:19. Acts 14:22. Lk. 14:27. 1 Thess. 3:3. Phil. 4:4. Rom. 15:13. 1 Pet. 1:3. 1 Pet. 1:8. Rom. 5:2.

The Lord is thinking about me right now!

"I know the plans I have for you," says the Lord. "They are plans for good and not for evil." □ This plan of mine is not what you would work out, neither are my thoughts the same as yours! For just as the heavens are higher than the earth, so are my ways higher than yours, and my thoughts than yours.

How precious it is, Lord, to realize that you are thinking about me constantly! I can't even count how many times a day your thoughts turn towards me. And when I waken in the morning, you are still thinking of me! □ O Lord, what miracles you do! And how deep are your thoughts! □ O Lord my God, many and many a time you have done great miracles for us, and we are ever in your thoughts.

Few of you who follow Christ have big names or power or wealth. □ God has chosen poor people to be rich in faith, and the Kingdom of Heaven is theirs, for that is the gift God has promised to all those who love him. □ We own nothing, and yet we enjoy everything. □ The endless treasures available . . . in Christ.

Ps. 40:17. Jer. 29:11. Is. 55:8, 9. Ps. 139:17, 18. Ps. 92:5. Ps. 40:5. 1 Cor. 1:26. Jas. 2:5. 2 Cor. 6:10. Eph. 3:8.

My feet were slipping and I was almost gone.

I screamed, "I'm slipping, Lord!" and he was kind and saved me. □ Simon, Simon, Satan has asked to have you, to sift you like wheat, but I have pleaded in prayer for you that your faith should not completely fail.

Don't you know that this good man, though you trip him up seven times, will each time rise again? □ If they fall it isn't fatal, for the Lord holds them with his hand.

Do not rejoice against me, O my enemy, for though I fall, I will rise again! When I sit in darkness, the Lord himself will be my Light.

He will deliver you again and again, so that no evil can touch you.

If you sin, there is someone to plead for you before the Father. His name is Jesus Christ, the one who is all that is good and who pleases God completely. □ He is able to save completely all who come to God through him. Since he will live forever. he will always be there to remind God that he has paid for their sins with his blood.

Ps. 73:2. Ps. 94:18. Lk. 22:31, 32. Prov. 24:16. Ps. 37:24. Mic. 7:8. Job 5:19. 1 Jn. 2:1. Hebr. 7:25.

I will give them one heart and mind to worship me forever.

I will give you a new heart—I will give you new and right desires—and put a new spirit within you. I will take out your stony hearts of sin and give you new hearts of love. □ The Lord is good and glad to teach the proper path to all who go astray; he will teach the ways that are right and best to those who humbly turn to him. And when we obey him, every path he guides us on is fragrant with his lovingkindness and his truth.

That they will be of one heart and mind, just as you and I are, Father—that just as you are in me and I am in you, so they will be in us, and the world will believe you sent me.

Live and act in a way worthy of those who have been chosen for such wonderful blessings as these. Be humble and gentle. Be patient with each other, making allowance for each other's faults because of your love. Try always to be led along together by the Holy Spirit, and so be at peace with one another. We are all parts of one body, we have the same Spirit, and we have all been called to the same glorious future. For us there is only one Lord, one faith, one baptism, and we all have the same God and Father who is over us all and in us all, and living through every part of us.

Jer. 32:39. Ezk. 36:26. Ps. 25:8–10. Jn. 17:21. Eph. 4:1–6.

*They that wait upon the Lord shall renew
their strength.*

When I am weak, then I am strong. □ The Lord
. . . has given me the strength to perform this task.

I am with you; that is all you need. My power
shows up best in weak people. Now I am glad to
boast about how weak I am; I am glad to be a
living demonstration of Christ's power, instead of
showing off my own power and abilities. □ Trust
in the Lord God always, for in the Lord Jehovah
is your everlasting strength.

Give your burdens to the Lord. He will carry
them. He will not permit the godly to slip or fall.
□ Their weapons were shattered by the Mighty
One of Jacob, the Shepherd, the Rock of Israel.

You come to me with a sword and a spear, but
I come to you in the name of the Lord of the
armies of heaven and of Israel—the very God
whom you have defied. □ I will rejoice in the Lord.
He shall rescue me! From the bottom of my heart
praise rises to him. Where is his equal in all of
heaven and earth? Who else protects the weak and
helpless from the strong?

*Is. 40:31.   2 Cor. 12:10.   Is. 49:5.   2 Cor. 12:9.   Is. 26:4.   Ps. 55:22.
Gen. 49:24.   1 Sam. 17:45.   Ps. 35:9, 10.*

Don't copy the behavior and customs of this world, but be a new and different person with a fresh newness in all you do and think.

Don't you realize that making friends with God's enemies—the evil pleasures of this world —makes you an enemy of God? I say it again, that if your aim is to enjoy the evil pleasure of the unsaved world, you cannot also be a friend of God.

Don't be teamed with those who do not love the Lord, for what do the people of God have in common with the people of sin? How can light live with darkness? And what harmony can there be between Christ and the devil? How can a Christian be a partner with one who doesn't believe? ☐ Stop loving this evil world and all that it offers you, for when you love these things you show that you do not really love God. This world is fading away, and these evil, forbidden things will go with it, but whoever keeps doing the will of God will live forever.

You went along with the crowd and were just like all the others, full of sin, obeying Satan, the mighty prince of the power of the air. ☐ That isn't the way Christ taught you! If you have really heard his voice and learned from him the truths concerning himself, then throw off your old evil nature.

Rom. 12:2. Jas. 4:4. 2 Cor. 6:14, 15. 1 Jn. 2:15, 17. Eph. 2:2. Eph. 4:20–22.

The Lord is on my side.

In your day of trouble, may the Lord be with you! May the God of Jacob keep you from all harm. May he send you aid from his sanctuary in Zion. May there be shouts of joy when we hear the news of your victory, flags flying with praise to God for all that he has done for you. May he answer all your prayers! Some nations boast of armies and of weaponry, but our boast is in the Lord our God. Those nations will collapse and perish; we will arise to stand firm and sure!

He will come like a flood-tide driven by Jehovah's breath. □ Remember this—the wrong desires that come into your life aren't anything new and different. Many others have faced exactly the same problems before you. And no temptation is irresistible. You can trust God to keep the temptation from becoming so strong that you can't stand up against it, for he has promised this and will do what he says. He will show you how to escape temptation's power so that you can bear up patiently against it.

If God is on our side, who can ever be against us? □ He is for me! How can I be afraid? What can mere man do to me?

Our God is able to deliver us; and he will deliver us out of your hand.

Ps. 118:7. Ps. 20:1, 2, 5, 7, 8. Is. 59:19. 1 Cor. 10:13. Rom. 8:31. Ps. 118:6. Dan. 3:17.

You are the world's seasoning.

Be beautiful inside, in your hearts, with the lasting charm of a gentle and quiet spirit which is so precious to God. □ For you have a new life. It was not passed on to you from your parents, for the life they gave you will fade away. This new one will last forever, for it comes from Christ, God's ever-living Message to men. □ Anyone who believes in me, even though he dies like anyone else, shall live again. □ Sons of God, for they are raised up in new life from the dead. □ The glorious, ever-living God.

If anyone doesn't have the Spirit of Christ living in him, he is not a Christian at all. Yet, even though Christ lives within you, your body will die because of sin; but your spirit will live for Christ has pardoned it. And if the Spirit of God, who raised up Jesus from the dead, lives in you, he will make your dying bodies live again after you die, by means of this same Holy Spirit living within you. □ Our earthly bodies which die and decay are different from the bodies we shall have when we come back to life again, for they will never die.

Good salt is worthless if it loses its saltiness; it can't season anything. So don't lose your flavor! Live in peace with each other.

Mt. 5:13. 1 Pet. 3:4. 1 Pet. 1:23. Jn. 11:25. Lk. 20:36. Rom. 1:23. Rom. 8:9–11. 1 Cor. 15:42. Mk. 9:50.

I, even I, am he who comforts you.

What a wonderful God we have—he is the Father of our Lord Jesus Christ, the source of every mercy, and the one who so wonderfully comforts and strengthens us in our hardships and trials. And why does he do this? So that when others are troubled, needing our sympathy and encouragement, we can pass on to them this same help and comfort God has given us. □ He is like a father to us, tender and sympathetic to those who reverence him. For he knows we are but dust. □ I will comfort you there as a little one is comforted by its mother. □ Let him have all your worries and cares, for he is always thinking about you and watching everything that concerns you.

But you are merciful and gentle, Lord, slow in getting angry, full of constant lovingkindness and of truth.

Another Comforter . . . the Holy Spirit, the Spirit who leads into all truth. □ The Holy Spirit helps us with our daily problems.

He will wipe away all tears from their eyes, and there shall be no more death, nor sorrow, nor crying, nor pain. All of that has gone forever.

Is. 51:12. 2 Cor. 1:3, 4. Ps. 103:13, 14. Is. 66:13. 1 Pet. 5:7. Ps. 86:15. Jn. 14:16, 17. Rom. 8:26. Rev. 21:4.

*A doubtful mind will be as unsettled as a
wave of the sea that is driven and tossed by
the wind.*

Anyone who lets himself be distracted from the
work I plan for him is not fit for the Kingdom of
God.

You can never please God without faith, without depending on him. Anyone who wants to
come to God must believe that there is a God and
that he rewards those who sincerely look for him.
□ When you ask him, be sure that you really
expect him to tell you. If you don't ask with faith,
don't expect the Lord to give you any solid
answer. □ You can pray for anything, and *if you
believe, you have it;* it's yours!

We will no longer be like children, forever
changing our minds about what we believe because someone has told us something different,
or has cleverly lied to us and made the lie sound
like the truth. Instead, we will lovingly follow the
truth at all times—speaking . . . in every way
like Christ who is the Head of his body, the
church.

Live in me. □ Be strong and steady, always
abounding in the Lord's work, for you know that
nothing you do for the Lord is ever wasted.

*Jas. 1:6. Lk. 9:62. Hebr. 11:6. Jas. 1:6, 7. Mk. 11:24. Eph. 4:14,
15. Jn. 15:4. 1 Cor. 15:58.*

Weeping may go on all night, but in the morning there is joy.

Troubles are a part of God's plan for us Christians. Even while we were still with you we warned you ahead of time that suffering would soon come—and it did. ☐ I have told you all this so that you will have peace of heart and mind. Here on earth you will have many trials and sorrows; but cheer up, for I have overcome the world.

When I awake in heaven, I will be fully satisfied, for I will see you face to face. ☐ The night is far gone, the day of his return will soon be here. ☐ He shall be as the light of the morning; a cloudless sunrise when the tender grass springs forth upon the earth; as sunshine after rain.

He will swallow up death forever. The Lord God will wipe away all tears. ☐ He will wipe away all tears from their eyes, and there shall be no more death, nor sorrow, nor crying, nor pain. All of that has gone forever. ☐ We who are still alive and remain on the earth will be caught up with them in the clouds to meet the Lord in the air and remain with him forever. So comfort and encourage each other with this news.

Ps. 30:5. 1 Thess. 3:3, 4. Jn. 16:33. Ps. 17:15. Rom. 13:12. 2 Sam. 23:4. Is. 25:8. Rev. 21:4. 1 Thess. 4:17, 18.

He does not crush the weak.

It is a broken spirit you want—remorse and penitence. A broken and a contrite heart, O God, you will not ignore. □ He heals the broken-hearted, binding up their wounds. □ The high and lofty one who inhabits eternity, the Holy One, says this: "I live in that high and holy place where those with contrite, humble spirits dwell; and I refresh the humble and give new courage to those with repentant hearts. For I will not fight against you forever, nor always show my wrath; if I did, all mankind would perish—the very souls that I have made."

I will seek my lost ones, those who strayed away, and bring them safely home again. I will put splints and bandages upon their broken limbs and heal the sick. □ When they walk through the Valley of Weeping it will become a place of springs where pools of blessing and refreshment collect after rains! □ So take a new grip with your tired hands, stand firm on your shaky legs, and mark out a straight, smooth path for your feet so that those who follow you, though weak and lame, will not fall and hurt themselves, but become strong. □ Your God . . . is coming to save you.

Mt. 12:20. Ps. 51:17. Ps. 147:3. Is. 57:15, 16. Ezk. 34:16. Ps. 84:6. Hebr. 12:12, 13. Is. 35:4.

*Open my eyes to see wonderful things in
your Word.*

He opened their minds to understand at last
these many scriptures. □ Then he explained to
them that only they were permitted to understand
about the Kingdom of Heaven, and others were
not. □ And Jesus prayed this prayer: "O Father,
Lord of heaven and earth, thank you for hiding
the truth from those who think themselves so wise,
and for revealing it to little children. Yes, Father,
for it pleased you to do it this way." □ And God
has actually given us his Spirit (not the world's
spirit) to tell us about the wonderful free gifts of
grace and blessing that God has given us. □ How
precious it is, Lord, to realize that you are thinking about me constantly. I can't even count how
many times a day your thoughts turn towards me.
And when I waken in the morning, you are still
thinking of me! □ Oh, what a wonderful God we
have! How great are his wisdom and knowledge
and riches! How impossible it is for us to understand his decisions and his methods! For who
among us can know the mind of the Lord? Who
knows enough to be his counselor and guide? For
everything comes from God alone. Everything
lives by his power, and everything is for his glory.
To him be glory evermore.

*Ps. 119:18. Lk. 24:45. Mt. 13:11. Mt. 11:25, 26. 1 Cor. 2:12.
Ps. 139:17, 18. Rom. 11:33, 34, 36.*

"The Spring of the Man Who Prayed."

If you only knew what a wonderful gift God has for you, and who I am, you would ask me for some *living* water! □ "If anyone is thirsty, let him come to me and drink." He was speaking of the Holy Spirit, who would be given to everyone believing in him.

Bring all the tithes into the storehouse so that there will be food enough in my Temple; if you do, I will open up the windows of heaven for you and pour out a blessing so great you won't have room enough to take it in! Try it! Let me prove it to you! □ If even sinful persons like yourselves give children what they need, don't you realize that your heavenly Father will do at least as much, and give the Holy Spirit to those who ask for him? □ Keep on asking and you will keep on getting; keep on looking and you will keep on finding.

And because we are his sons God has sent the Spirit of his Son into our hearts, so now we can rightly speak of God as our dear Father. □ And so we should not be like cringing, fearful slaves, but we should behave like God's very own children, adopted into the bosom of his family, and calling to him, "Father, Father."

Judg. 15:19. Jn. 4:10. Jn. 7:37, 39. Mal. 3:10. Lk. 11:13. Lk. 11:9. Gal. 4:6. Rom. 8:15.

God . . . full of kindness through Christ.

I will make my goodness pass before you, and I will announce to you the meaning of my name Jehovah, the Lord. I show kindness and mercy to anyone I want to. □ God pities him and says, "Set him free. Do not make him die, for I have found a substitute." □ Yet now God declares us "not guilty" of offending him if we trust in Jesus Christ, who in his kindness freely takes away our sins. For God sent Christ Jesus to take the punishment for our sins and to end all God's anger against us. He used Christ's blood and our faith as the means of saving us from his wrath. In this way he was being entirely fair, even though he did not punish those who sinned in former times. For he was looking forward to the time when Christ would come and take away those sins. □ Jesus Christ brought us loving forgiveness.

Because of his kindness you have been saved through trusting Christ. And even trusting is not of yourselves; it too is a gift from God. □ May God our Father and Jesus Christ our Lord show you his kindness and mercy and give you great peace of heart and mind. □ God has given each of you some special abilities; be sure to use them to help each other, passing on to others God's many kinds of blessings. □ He gives us more and more strength.

1 Pet. 5:10. Ex. 33:19. Job 33:24. Rom. 3:24, 25. Jn. 1:17. Eph. 2:8. 1 Tim. 1:2. 1 Pet. 4:10. Jas. 4:6.

*Shall I look to the mountain gods for help?
No! My help is from Jehovah who made the
mountains! And the heavens too!*

Just as the mountains surround and protect
Jerusalem, so the Lord surrounds and protects his
people. □ He protects you day and night. He
keeps you from all evil, and preserves your life.
He keeps his eye upon you as you come and go,
and always guards you.

O God enthroned in heaven, I lift my eyes to
you. We look to Jehovah our God for his mercy
and kindness just as a servant keeps his eyes upon
his master or a slave girl watches her mistress for
the slightest signal. □ How much you have helped
me—and how I rejoice through the night beneath the protecting shadow of your wings.

O our God, won't you stop them? We have no
way to protect ourselves against this mighty army.
We don't know what to do, but we are looking
to you. □ Oh, help us, Lord our God! For we
trust in you alone to rescue us, and in your name
we attack this vast horde. □ My eyes are ever
looking to the Lord for help, for he alone can
rescue me. □ Our help is from the Lord who
made heaven and earth.

*Ps. 121:1, 2. Ps. 125:2. Ps. 121:6–8. Ps. 123:1, 2. Ps. 63:7.
2 Chron. 20:12. 2 Chron. 14:11. Ps. 25:15. Ps. 124:8.*

But as for me, I get as close to him as I can!

Lord, I love your home, this shrine where the brilliant, dazzling splendor of your presence lives. □ A single day spent in your Temple is better than a thousand anywhere else! I would rather be a doorman of the Temple of my God than live in palaces of wickedness. □ How greatly to be envied are those you have chosen to come and live with you within the holy tabernacle courts! What joys await us among all the good things there.

The Lord is wonderfully good to those who wait for him, to those who seek for him. □ Yet the Lord still waits for you to come to him, so he can show you his love; he will conquer you to bless you, just as he said. For the Lord is faithful to his promises.

And so, dear brothers, now we may walk right into the very Holy of Holies where God is, because of the blood of Jesus. This is the fresh, new, life-giving way which Christ has opened up for us by tearing the curtain—his human body—to let us into the holy presence of God . . . let us go right in, to God himself, with true hearts fully trusting him to receive us, because we have been sprinkled with Christ's blood to make us clean, and because our bodies have been washed with pure water.

Ps. 73:28. Ps. 26:8. Ps. 84:10. Ps. 65:4. Lam. 3:25. Is. 30:18. Hebr. 10:19, 20, 22.

When your patience is finally in full bloom,
then you will be ready for anything, strong
in character, full and complete.

There is wonderful joy ahead, even though the going is rough for a while down here. These trials are only to test your faith, to see whether or not it is strong and pure. It is being tested as fire tests gold and purifies it—and your faith is far more precious to God than mere gold; so if your faith remains strong after being tried in the test tube of fiery trials, it will bring you much praise and glory and honor on the day of his return. □ We can rejoice, too, when we run into problems and trials for we know that they are good for us—they help us learn to be patient. And patience develops strength of character in us and helps us trust God more each time we use it until finally our hope and faith are strong and steady.

It is good both to hope and wait quietly for the salvation of the Lord. □ You were actually joyful when all you owned was taken from you, knowing that better things were awaiting you in heaven, things that would be yours forever. Do not let this happy trust in the Lord die away, no matter what happens. Remember your reward! You need to keep on patiently doing God's will if you want him to do for you all that he has promised.

Jas. 1:4. 1 Pet. 1:6, 7. Rom. 5:3, 4. Lam. 3:26. Hebr. 10:34–36.

If you will humble yourselves under the mighty hand of God, in his good time he will lift you up.

Pride disgusts the Lord. Take my word for it—*proud men shall be punished.*

And yet, O Lord, you are our Father. We are the clay and you are the Potter. We are all formed by your hand. Oh, be not so angry with us, Lord, nor forever remember our sins. Oh, look and see that we are all your people. ☐ You have punished me greatly; but I needed it all, as a calf must be trained for the yoke. Turn me again to you and restore me, for you alone are the Lord, my God. I turned away from God but I was sorry afterwards. I kicked myself for my stupidity. I was thoroughly ashamed of all I did in younger days. ☐ It is good for a young man to be under discipline, for it causes him to sit apart in silence beneath the Lord's demands, to lie face downward in the dust; then at last there is hope for him.

Misery comes upon them to punish them for sowing seeds of sin. Mankind heads for sin and misery as predictably as flames shoot upwards from a fire. ☐ Although God gives him grief, yet he will show compassion too, according to the greatness of his lovingkindness. For he does not enjoy afflicting men and causing sorrow.

1 Pet. 5:6. Prov. 16:5. Is. 64:8, 9. Jer. 13:18, 19. Lam. 3:27–29. Job 5:6, 7.. Lam. 3:32, 33.

*The heavens are telling the glory of God;
they are a marvelous display of his craftsmanship.*

Since earliest times men have seen the earth
and sky and all God made, and have known of his
existence and great eternal power. □ He never
left himself without a witness. □ Day and night
they keep on telling about God. Without a sound
or word, silent in the skies, their message reaches
out to all the world.

When I look up into the night skies and see the
work of your fingers—the moon and the stars you
have made—I cannot understand how you can
bother with mere puny man, to pay any attention
to him!

The sun has one kind of glory while the moon
and stars have another kind. And the stars differ
from each other in their beauty and brightness. In
the same way, our earthly bodies which die and
decay are different from the bodies we shall have
when we come back to life again, for they will
never die. □ And those who are wise—the people
of God—shall shine as brightly as the sun's brilliance, and those who turn many to righteousness
will glitter like stars forever.

*Ps. 19:1. Rom. 1:20. Acts 14:17. Ps. 19:2, 3. Ps. 8:3, 4. 1 Cor.
15:41, 42. Dan. 12:3.*

The Son can do nothing by himself. He does
only what he sees the Father doing, and in
the same way.

The Lord grants wisdom! His every word is a
treasure of knowledge and understanding. He
grants good sense to the godly—his saints. He is
their shield, protecting them and guarding their
pathway. □ I will give you the right words and
such logic that none of your opponents will be
able to reply!

Wait for the Lord, and he will come and save
you! Be brave, stouthearted and courageous. Yes,
wait and he will help you. □ I am with you; that
is all you need. My power shows up best in weak
people.

Beloved of God and chosen by him. □ We who
have been made holy by Jesus, now have the same
Father he has. That is why Jesus is not ashamed
to call us his brothers.

Am I not everywhere in all of heaven and
earth? □ His body, filled with himself, the Author
and Giver of everything everywhere.

I am the Lord, and there is no other Savior. □
He is indeed the Savior of the world.

May God the Father and Christ Jesus our Savior give you his blessings and his peace.

Jn. 5:19. Prov. 2:6–8. Lk. 21:15. Ps. 27:14. 2 Cor. 12:9. Jude 1.
Hebr. 2:11. Jer. 23:24. Eph. 1:23. Is. 43:11. Jn. 4:42. Tit. 1:4.

*Show me the path where I should go, O
Lord; point out the right road for me to
walk.*

Moses talked there with the Lord and said to
him . . . "You say you are my friend, and that
I have found favor before you; please, if this is
really so, guide me clearly along the way you
want me to travel so that I will understand you
and walk acceptably before you." And the Lord
replied, "I myself will go with you and give you
success." □ He revealed his will and nature to
Moses and the people of Israel.

He will teach the ways that are right and best
to those who humbly turn to him. Where is the
man who fears the Lord? God will teach him how
to choose the best. □ Trust the Lord completely;
don't ever trust yourself. In everything you do,
put God first, and he will direct you and crown
your efforts with success.

You have let me experience the joys of life and
the exquisite pleasures of your own eternal presence. □ I will instruct you (says the Lord) and
guide you along the best pathway for your life; I
will advise you and watch your progress. □ The
good man walks along in the ever-brightening light
of God's favor; the dawn gives way to morning
splendor.

*Ps. 25:4. Ex. 33:12–14. Ps. 103:7. Ps. 25:9, 12. Prov. 3:5, 6. Ps.
16:11. Ps. 32:8. Prov. 4:18.*

*What are you so puffed up about? What do
you have that God hasn't given you?*

Whatever I am now it is all because God
poured out such kindness and grace upon me. □
It was a happy day for him when he gave us our
new lives, through the truth of his Word. □ God's
blessings are not given just because someone de-
cides to have them or works hard to get them. □
Then what can we boast about doing, to earn our
salvation? Nothing at all. □ For it is from God
alone that you have your life through Christ Jesus.
If anyone is going to boast, let him boast only of
what the Lord has done.

Once you were under God's curse, doomed
forever for your sins. You went along with the
crowd and were just like all the others, full of
sin, obeying Satan, the mighty prince of the power
of the air, who is at work right now in the hearts
of those who are against the Lord. All of us used
to be just as they are, our lives expressing the evil
within us, doing every wicked thing that our pas-
sions or our evil thoughts might lead us into. We
started out bad, being born with evil natures, and
were under God's anger just like everyone else. □
Now your sins are washed away, and you are set
apart for God, and he has accepted you because
of what the Lord Jesus Christ and the Spirit of
our God have done for you.

*1 Cor. 4:7. 1 Cor. 15:10. Jas. 1:18. Rom. 9:16. Rom. 3:27. 1 Cor.
1:30, 31. Eph. 2:1-3. 1 Cor. 6:11.*

All praise to him who always loves us and who set us free from our sins by pouring out his lifeblood for us.

Many waters cannot quench the flame of love, neither can the floods drown it. Love is strong as death. □ The greatest love is shown when a person lays down his life for his friends.

He personally carried the load of our sins in his own body when he died on the cross, so that we can be finished with sin and live a good life from now on. For his wounds have healed ours! □ So overflowing is his kindness towards us that he took away all our sins through the blood of his Son, by whom we are saved.

Your sins are washed away, and you are set apart for God, and he has accepted you because of what the Lord Jesus Christ and the Spirit of our God have done for you. □ You have been chosen by God himself—you are priests of the King, you are holy and pure, you are God's very own—all this so that you may show to others how God called you out of the darkness into his wonderful light. □ I plead with you to give your bodies to God. Let them be a living sacrifice, holy —the kind he can accept. When you think of what he has done for you, is this too much to ask?

Rev. 1:5. Song 8:7, 6. Jn. 15:13. 1 Pet. 2:24. Eph. 1:7. 1 Cor. 6:11. 1 Pet. 2:9. Rom. 12:1.

*There are different kinds of service to God,
but it is the same Lord we are serving.*

Azmaveth (son of Adi-el) was the chief finan-
cial officer in charge of the palace treasuries, and
Jonathan (son of Uzziah) was chief of the re-
gional treasuries throughout the cities, villages,
and fortresses of Israel. Ezri (son of Chelub) was
manager of the laborers on the king's estates. And
Shime-i from Ramath had the oversight of the
king's vineyards; and Zabdi from Shiphma was
responsible for his wine production and storage.
These men were King David's overseers.

Here is a list of some of the parts he has
placed in his church, which is his body: apostles,
prophets—those who preach God's Word, teachers, those who do miracles, those who have the
gift of healing, those who can help others, those
who can get others to work together, those who
speak in languages they have never learned.

God has given each of you some special abilities; be sure to use them to help each other, passing on to others God's many kinds of blessings.
Are you called to preach? Then preach as though
God himself were speaking through you. Are you
called to help others? Do it with all the strength
and energy that God supplies, so that God will
be glorified through Jesus Christ—to him be glory
and power forever and ever. Amen.

1 Cor. 12:5. 1 Chron. 27:25–27, 31. 1 Cor. 12:28. 1 Pet. 4:10, 11.

*Moses didn't realize as he came back down
the mountain with the tablets that his face
glowed from being in the presence of God.*

Glorify your name, not ours, O Lord! Cause
everyone to praise your lovingkindness and your
truth. □ Sir, when did we ever see you hungry
and feed you? Or thirsty and give you anything to
drink? □ When you did it to these my brothers
you were doing it to me! □ Be humble, thinking
of others as better than yourself. □ Serve each
other with humble spirits.

His [Jesus'] appearance changed so that his face
shone like the sun and his clothing became dazzling white. □ Everyone in the Council chamber
saw Stephen's face become as radiant as an angel's! □ I have given them the glory you gave me.
□ We Christians have no veil over our faces; we
can be mirrors that brightly reflect the glory of
the Lord. And as the Spirit of the Lord works
within us, we become more and more like him.

You are the world's light—a city on a hill,
glowing in the night for all to see. Don't hide your
light! □ Shine out among them like beacon lights,
holding out to them the Word of Life.

*Ex. 34:29. Ps. 115:1. Mt. 25:37. Mt. 25:40. Phil. 2:3. 1 Pet. 5:5.
Mt. 17:2. Acts 6:15. Jn. 17:22. 2 Cor. 3:18. Mt. 5:14, 15. Phil.
2:15, 16.*

There are many ways in which God works in our lives, but it is the same God who does the work in and through all of us who are his.

Some men from Manasseh deserted the Israeli army and joined David. They were brave and able warriors, and they assisted David when he fought against the Amalek raiders at Ziklag. □ The Holy Spirit displays God's power through each of us as a means of helping the entire church.

From the tribe of Issachar there were 200 leaders of the tribe with their relatives—all men who understood the temper of the times and knew the best course for Israel to take. □ To one person the Spirit gives the ability to give wise advice; someone else may be especially good at studying and teaching, and this is his gift from the same Spirit.

From the tribe of Zebulun there were 50,000 trained warriors; they were fully armed and totally loyal to David. □ I delight to do your will, my God, for your law is written upon my heart!

God . . . has made many parts for our bodies and has put each part just where he wants it. If one part suffers, all parts suffer with it, and if one part is honored, all the parts are glad.

One Lord, one faith, one baptism.

1 Cor. 12:6. 1 Chron. 12:19, 21. 1 Cor. 12:7. 1 Chron. 12:32. 1 Cor. 12:8. 1 Chron. 12:33 Ps. 40:8. 1 Cor. 12:18, 26. Eph. 4:5.

His coming will not be delayed much longer.

Write my answer on a billboard, large and clear, so that anyone can read it at a glance and rush to tell the others. But these things I plan won't happen right away. Slowly, steadily, surely, the time approaches when the vision will be fulfilled. If it seems slow, do not despair, for these things will surely come to pass. Just be patient! They will not be overdue a single day!

But don't forget this, dear friends, that a day or a thousand years from now is like tomorrow to the Lord. He isn't really being slow about his promised return, even though it sometimes seems that way. But he is waiting, for the good reason that he is not willing that any should perish, and he is giving more time for sinners to repent. □ But you are merciful and gentle, Lord, slow in getting angry, full of constant lovingkindness and of truth. □ Oh, that you should burst forth from the skies and come down! How the mountains would quake in your presence! For since the world began no one has seen or heard of such a God as ours, who works for those who wait for him!

Hebr. 10:37. Hab. 2:2, 3. 2 Pet. 3:8, 9. Ps. 86:15. Is. 64:1, 4.

When the Holy Spirit controls our lives he will produce . . . gentleness.

The meek will be filled with fresh joy from the Lord, and the poor shall exult in the Holy One of Israel.

Unless you turn to God from your sins and become as little children, you will never get into the Kingdom of Heaven. Therefore anyone who humbles himself as this little child, is the greatest in the Kingdom of Heaven. □ Be beautiful inside, in your hearts, with the lasting charm of a gentle and quiet spirit which is so precious to God. □ Love is very patient and kind, never jealous or envious, never boastful or proud.

Be patient and gentle. □ Wear my yoke—for it fits perfectly—and let me teach you; for I am gentle and humble. □ He was oppressed and he was afflicted, yet he never said a word. He was brought as a lamb to the slaughter; and as a sheep before her shearers is dumb, so he stood silent before the ones condemning him.

This suffering is all part of the work God has given you. Christ, who suffered for you, is your example. Follow in his steps: He never sinned, never told a lie, never answered back when insulted; when he suffered he did not threaten to get even; he left his case in the hands of God who always judges fairly.

Gal. 5:22, 23. Is. 29:19. Mt. 18:3, 4. 1 Pet. 3:4. 1 Cor. 13:4. 1 Tim. 6:11. Mt. 11:29. Is. 53:7. 1 Pet. 2:21–23.

He will teach the ways that are right and best to those who humbly turn to him.

The meek and lowly are fortunate!

Again I looked throughout the earth and saw that the swiftest person does not always win the race, nor the strongest man the battle, and that wise men are often poor, and skillful men are not necessarily famous. □ We should make plans—counting on God to direct us.

O God enthroned in heaven, I lift my eyes to you. We look to Jehovah our God for his mercy and kindness just as a servant keeps his eyes upon his master or a slave girl watches her mistress for the slightest signal. □ Show me where to walk, for my prayer is sincere.

O our God, won't you stop them? We have no way to protect ourselves against this mighty army. We don't know what to do, but we are looking to you.

If you want to know what God wants you to do, ask him, and he will gladly tell you, for he is always ready to give a bountiful supply of wisdom to all who ask him; he will not resent it.

When the Holy Spirit, who is truth, comes, he shall guide you into all truth.

Ps. 25:9. Mt. 5:5. Eccl. 9:11. Prov. 16:9. Ps. 123:1, 2. Ps. 143:8. 2 Chron. 20:12. Jas. 1:5. Jn. 16:13.

He . . . set my feet on a hard, firm path.

Christ . . . a mighty Rock of spiritual refreshment. □ Simon Peter answered, "The Christ, the Messiah, the Son of the living God." Upon this rock I will build my church; and all the powers of hell shall not prevail against it. □ There is salvation in no one else! Under all heaven there is no other name for men to call upon to save them.

Fully trusting him. No longer any room for doubt. □ A doubtful mind will be as unsettled as a wave of the sea that is driven and tossed by the wind.

Who then can ever keep Christ's love from us? When we have trouble or calamity, when we are hunted down or destroyed, is it because he doesn't love us anymore? And if we are hungry, or penniless, or in danger, or threatened with death, has God deserted us? Despite all this, overwhelming victory is ours through Christ who loved us enough to die for us. I am convinced that . . . nothing will ever be able to separate us from the love of God demonstrated by our Lord Jesus Christ when he died for us.

Ps. 40:2. 1 Cor. 10:4. Mt. 16:16, 18. Acts 4:12. Hebr. 10:22, 23. Jas. 1:6. Rom. 8:35, 37–39.

The Lord's promise is sure. He speaks no careless word; all he says is purest truth.

I have thoroughly tested your promises and that is why I love them so much. ☐ God's laws are perfect. They protect us, make us wise, and give us joy and light. ☐ Every word of God proves true. He defends all who come to him for protection. Do not add to his words, lest he rebuke you, and you be found a liar.

I have thought much about your words, and stored them in my heart so that they would hold me back from sin. I will meditate upon them and give them my full respect. ☐ God's laws are pure, eternal, just. They are more desirable than gold. They are sweeter than honey dripping from a honeycomb. ☐ Fix your thoughts on what is true and good and right. Think about things that are pure and lovely, and dwell on the fine, good things in others. Think about all you can praise God for and be glad about. ☐ Long to grow up into the fullness of your salvation; cry for this as a baby cries for his milk.

What a God he is! How perfect in every way! All his promises prove true. He is a shield for everyone who hides behind him. For who is God except our Lord? Who but he is as a rock?

Ps. 12:6. Ps. 119:140. Ps. 19:7, 8. Prov. 30:5, 6. Ps. 119:11, 15. Ps. 19:9, 10. Phil. 4:8. 1 Pet. 2:3. Ps. 18:30, 31.

You are my place of safety.

Jehovah is my rock, my fortress and my Savior. I will hide in God, who is my rock and my refuge. He is my shield and my salvation, my refuge and high tower. ☐ He is my strength, my shield from every danger. I trusted in him, and he helped me. Joy rises in my heart until I burst out in songs of praise to him.

They will reverence and glorify the name of God from west to east. For he will come like a flood-tide driven by Jehovah's breath. ☐ That is why we can say without any doubt or fear, "The Lord is my Helper and I am not afraid of anything that mere man can do to me."

The Lord is my light and my salvation; whom shall I fear? ☐ When I sit in darkness, the Lord himself will be my Light.

Just as the mountains surround and protect Jerusalem, so the Lord surrounds and protects his people. ☐ How I rejoice through the night beneath the protecting shadow of your wings.

Honor your name by leading me. ☐ Be our strength each day and our salvation in the time of trouble.

Ps. 59:9. 2 Sam. 22:2, 3. Ps. 28:7. Is. 59:19. Hebr. 13:6. Ps. 27:1. Mic. 7:8. Ps. 125:2. Ps. 63:7. Ps. 31:3. Is. 33:2.

Never be lazy in your work but serve the Lord enthusiastically.

Whatever you do, do well, for in death, where you are going, there is no working or planning, or knowing, or understanding. ☐ Work hard and cheerfully at all you do, just as though you were working for the Lord and not merely for your masters, remembering that it is the Lord Christ who is going to pay you, giving you your full portion of all he owns. He is the one you are really working for. ☐ Remember, the Lord will pay you for each good thing you do.

All of us must quickly carry out the tasks assigned us by the one who sent me, for there is little time left before the night falls and all work comes to an end.

So, dear brothers, work hard to prove that you really are among those God has called and chosen, and then you will never stumble or fall away. ☐ And we are anxious that you keep right on loving others as long as life lasts, so that you will get your full reward. Then, knowing what lies ahead for you, you won't become bored with being a Christian, nor become spiritually dull and indifferent, but you will be anxious to follow the example of those who receive all that God has promised them because of their strong faith and patience. ☐ So run your race to win.

Rom. 12:11. Eccl. 9:10. Col. 3:23, 24. Eph. 6:8. Jn. 9:4. 2 Pet. 1:10. Hebr. 6:11, 12. 1 Cor. 9:24.

Don't leave me now, for trouble is near.

How long will you forget me, Lord? Forever? How long will you look the other way when I am in need? How long must I be hiding daily anguish in my heart? □ Oh, do not hide yourself when I am trying to find you. Do not angrily reject your servant. You have been my help in all my trials before; don't leave me now. Don't forsake me, O God of my salvation.

When he calls on me I will answer; I will be with him in trouble, and rescue him and honor him. □ He is close to all who call on him sincerely. He fulfills the desires of those who reverence and trust him; he hears their cries for help and rescues them.

I will not abandon you or leave you as orphans in the storm—I will come to you. □ I am with you always, even to the end of the world.

God is our refuge and strength, a tested help in times of trouble. □ I stand silently before the Lord, waiting for him to rescue me. For salvation comes from him alone. Yes, he alone is my Rock, my rescuer, defense and fortress—why then should I be tense with fear when troubles come?

Ps. 22:11. Ps. 13:1, 2. Ps. 27:9. Ps. 91:15. Ps. 145:18, 19. Jn. 14:18. Mt. 28:20. Ps. 46:1. Ps. 62:5, 6.

I am the First and Last, the Living One who died, who is now alive forevermore.

Jehovah is King! He is robed in majesty and strength. The world is his throne. O Lord, you have reigned from prehistoric times, from the everlasting past.

His power is incredible. □ If God is on our side, who can ever be against us? □ Our God is able to deliver us; and he will deliver us out of your hand. □ My Father has given them to me, and he is more powerful than anyone else, so no one can kidnap them from me. □ You belong to God and have already won your fight with those who are against Christ, because there is someone in your hearts who is stronger than any evil teacher in this wicked world.

Glorify your name, not ours, O Lord! □ Yours is the mighty power and glory and victory and majesty. Everything in the heavens and earth is yours, O Lord, and this is your kingdom. We adore you as being in control of everything. O our God, we thank you and praise your glorious name, but who am I and who are my people that we should be permitted to give anything to you? Everything we have has come from you, and we only give you what is yours already!

Rev. 1:18. Ps. 93:1, 2. Nah. 1:3. Rom. 8:31. Dan. 3:17. Jn. 10:29. 1 Jn. 4:4. Ps. 115:1. 1 Chron. 29:11, 13, 14.

The Lord is with you; he protects you.

Man's futile wrath will bring you glory. You will use it as an ornament! □ Just as water is turned into irrigation ditches, so the Lord directs the king's thoughts. He turns them wherever he wants to. □ When a man is trying to please God, God makes even his worst enemies to be at peace with him.

I wait expectantly, trusting God to help, for he has promised. I long for him more than sentinels long for the dawn. □ I cried to him and he answered me! He freed me from all my fears.

The eternal God is your Refuge, and underneath are the everlasting arms. He thrusts out your enemies before you; it is he who cries, "Destroy them!" □ Blessed is the man who trusts in the Lord and has made the Lord his hope and confidence. He is like a tree planted along a riverbank, with its roots reaching deep into the water —a tree not bothered by the heat nor worried by long months of drought. Its leaves stay green and it goes right on producing all its luscious fruit.

What can we ever say to such wonderful things as these? If God is on our side, who can ever be against us?

Prov. 3:26. Ps. 76:10. Prov. 21:1. Prov. 16:7. Ps. 130:5, 6. Ps. 34:4. Deut. 33:27. Jer. 17:7, 8. Rom. 8:31.

A servant is not greater than his master. Nor is the messenger more important than the one who sends him. You know these things—now do them! That is the path of blessing.

They began to argue among themselves as to who would have the highest rank [in the coming Kingdom]. Jesus told them, "In this world the kings and great men order their slaves around, and the slaves have no choice but to like it! But among you, the one who serves you best will be your leader. Out in the world the master sits at the table and is served by his servants. But not here! For I am your servant." □ Your care for others is the measure of your greatness. □ Anyone wanting to be a leader among you must be your servant. And if you want to be right at the top, you must serve like a slave. Your attitude must be like my own, for I, the Messiah, did not come to be served, but to serve, and to give my life as a ransom for many.

He [Jesus] got up from the supper table, took off his robe, wrapped a towel around his loins, poured water into a basin, and began to wash the disciples' feet and to wipe them with the towel he had around him.

Lead them by your good example.

Jn. 13:16, 17. Lk. 22:24–27. Lk. 9:48. Mt. 20:26–28. Jn. 13:4–5. 1 Pet. 5:3.

O God, my heart is ready to praise you!

The Lord is my light and my salvation; whom shall I fear?

He will keep in perfect peace all those who trust in him, whose thoughts turn often to the Lord! For good men the path is not uphill and rough! God does not give them a rough and treacherous path, but smooths the road before them. □ He does not fear bad news, nor live in dread of what may happen. For he is settled in his mind that Jehovah will take care of him. That is why he is not afraid, but can calmly face his foes.

But when I am afraid, I will put my confidence in you. Yes, I will trust the promises of God. □ There I'll be when troubles come. He will hide me. He will set me on a high rock out of reach of all my enemies. Then I will bring him sacrifices and sing his praises with much joy.

After you have suffered a little while, our God, who is full of kindness through Christ, will give you his eternal glory. He personally will come and pick you up, and set you firmly in place, and make you stronger than ever. To him be all power over all things, forever and ever. Amen.

Ps. 108:1. Ps. 27:1. Is. 26:3, 7. Ps. 112:7, 8. Ps. 56:3. Ps. 27:5, 6. 1 Pet. 5:10, 11.

Real life and real living are not related to how rich we are.

It is better to have little and be godly than to own an evil man's wealth. □ Better a little with reverence for God, than great treasure and trouble with it. □ Do you want to be truly rich? You already are if you are happy and good. We should be well satisfied without money if we have enough food and clothing.

Give me neither poverty nor riches! Give me just enough to satisfy my needs! For if I grow rich, I may become content without God. And if I am too poor, I may steal, and thus insult God's holy name. □ Give us our food again today, as usual.

Don't worry about *things*—food, drink, and clothes. For you already have life and a body— and they are far more important than what to eat and wear. □ "When I sent you out to preach the Good News and you were without money, duffle bag, or extra clothing, how did you get along?" "Fine," they replied. □ Stay away from the love of money; be satisfied with what you have. For God has said, "I will never, *never* fail you nor forsake you."

Lk. 12:15. Ps. 37:16. Prov. 15:16. 1 Tim. 6:6, 8. Prov. 30:8, 9.
Mt. 6:11. Mt. 6:25. Lk. 22:35. Hebr. 13:5.

Only the Holy Spirit gives eternal life.

The Scriptures tell us that the first man, Adam, was given a natural, human body but Christ is more than that, for he was life-giving Spirit. □ Men can only reproduce human life, but the Holy Spirit gives new life from heaven. □ He saved us —not because we were good enough to be saved, but because of his kindness and pity—by washing away our sins and giving us the new joy of the indwelling Holy Spirit.

You are controlled by your new nature if you have the Spirit of God living in you. Yet, even though Christ lives within you, your body will die because of sin; but your spirit will live, for Christ has pardoned it. And if the Spirit of God, who raised up Jesus from the dead, lives in you, he will make your dying bodies live again after you die, by means of this same Holy Spirit living within you.

I have been crucified with Christ: and I myself no longer live, but Christ lives in me. And the real life I now have within this body is a result of my trusting in the Son of God, who loved me and gave himself for me. □ So look upon your old sin nature as dead and unresponsive to sin, and instead be alive to God, alert to him, through Jesus Christ our Lord.

Jn. 6:63. 1 Cor. 15:45. Jn. 3:6. Tit. 3:5. Rom. 8:9–11. Gal. 2:20. Rom. 6:11.

The end of the world is coming soon.

I saw a great white throne and the one who sat upon it, from whose face the earth and sky fled away, but they found no place to hide. □ God has commanded that the earth and the heavens be stored away for a great bonfire at the judgment day, when all ungodly men will perish.

God is our refuge and strength, a tested help in times of trouble. And so we need not fear even if the world blows up, and the mountains crumble into the sea. Let the oceans roar and foam; let the mountains tremble! □ When you hear of wars beginning, this does not signal my return; these must come, but the end is not yet.

We will have wonderful new bodies in heaven, homes that will be ours forevermore, made for us by God himself, and not by human hands. □ We are looking forward to God's promise of new heavens and a new earth afterwards, where there will be only goodness. Dear friends, while you are waiting for these things to happen and for him to come, try hard to live without sinning; and be at peace with everyone so that he will be pleased with you when he returns.

1 Pet. 4:7. Rev. 20:11. 2 Pet. 3:7. Ps. 46:1–3. Mt. 24:6. 2 Cor. 5:1. 2 Pet. 3:13, 14.

Jehovah is King!

Have you no respect at all for me? the Lord God asks. How can it be that you don't even tremble in my presence? I set the shorelines of the world by perpetual decrees, so that the oceans, though they toss and roar, can never pass those bounds. Isn't such a God to be feared and worshiped? □ For promotion and power come from nowhere on earth, but only from God. He promotes one and deposes another.

World events are under his control. He removes kings and sets others on their thrones. He gives wise men their wisdom, and scholars their intelligence. □ When you hear of wars beginning, this does not signal my return; these must come, but the end is not yet.

If God is on our side, who can ever be against us? □ Not one sparrow (What do they cost? Two for a penny?) can fall to the ground without your Father knowing it. And the very hairs of your head are all numbered. So don't worry! You are more valuable to him than many sparrows.

Ps. 99:1. Jer. 5:22. Ps. 75:6, 7. Dan. 2:21. Mt. 24:6. Rom. 8:31.
Mt. 10:29–31.

The Enemy.

Be careful—watch out for attacks from Satan, your great enemy. He prowls around like a hungry, roaring lion, looking for some victim to tear apart. □ Resist the devil and he will flee from you.

Put on all of God's armor so that you will be able to stand safe against all strategies and tricks of Satan. For we are not fighting against people made of flesh and blood, but against persons without bodies—the evil rulers of the unseen world, those mighty satanic beings and great evil princes of darkness who rule this world; and against huge numbers of wicked spirits in the spirit world. So use every piece of God's armor to resist the enemy whenever he attacks, and when it is all over, you will still be standing up. But to do this, you will need the strong belt of truth and the breastplate of God's approval. Wear shoes that are able to speed you on as you preach the Good News of peace with God. In every battle you will need faith as your shield to stop the fiery arrows aimed at you by Satan.

Do not rejoice against me, O my enemy, for though I fall, I will rise again!

Lk. 10:19. 1 Pet. 5:8. Jas. 4:7. Eph. 6:11–16. Mic. 7:8.

David took strength from the Lord.

Master, to whom shall we go? You alone have the words that give eternal life. □ I know the one in whom I trust, and I am sure that he is able to safely guard all that I have given him until the day of his return.

In my distress I screamed to the Lord for his help. And he heard me from heaven; my cry reached his ears. On the day when I was weakened, they attacked. But the Lord held me steady. He led me to a place of safety, for he delights in me. He reached down from heaven and took me and drew me out of my great trials. He rescued me from deep waters. He delivered me from my strong enemy, from those who hated me—I who was helpless in their hands.

I will praise the Lord no matter what happens. I will constantly speak of his glories and grace. I will boast of all his kindness to me. Let all who are discouraged take heart. Let us praise the Lord together, and exalt his name. For I cried to him and he answered me! He freed me from all my fears. Oh, put God to the test and see how kind he is! See for yourself the way his mercies shower down on all who trust in him.

1 Sam. 30:6. Jn. 6:68. 2 Tim. 1:12. Ps. 18:6, 18, 19, 16, 17. Ps. 34:1–4, 8.

It is good both to hope and wait quietly for the salvation of the Lord.

Has he forgotten to be kind to one so un-deserving? Has he slammed the door in anger on his love? □ I spoke too hastily when I said, "The Lord has deserted me," for you listened to my plea and answered me. Oh, love the Lord, all of you who are his people; for the Lord protects those who are loyal to him, but harshly punishes all who haughtily reject him. So cheer up! Take courage if you are depending on the Lord.

Don't you think that God will surely give justice to his people who plead with him day and night? Yes! He will answer them quickly! □ Wait for the Lord to handle the matter. □ Rest in the Lord; wait patiently for him to act. Don't be envious of evil men who prosper.

You will not need to fight! Take your places; stand quietly and see the incredible rescue opera-tion God will perform for you.

Let us not get tired of doing what is right, for after a while we will reap a harvest of blessing if we don't get discouraged and give up. □ Be patient, like a farmer who waits until the autumn for his precious harvest to ripen.

Lam. 3:26. Ps. 77:9. Ps. 31:22–24. Lk. 18:7, 8. Prov. 20:22. Ps. 37:7. 2 Chron. 20:17. Gal. 6:9. Jas. 5:7.

May my spoken words and unspoken thoughts be pleasing even to you, O Lord, my Rock and my Redeemer.

How can I ever know what sins are lurking in my heart? Cleanse me from these hidden faults. □ Look after each other so that not one of you will fail to find God's best blessings. Watch out that no bitterness takes root among you, for as it springs up it causes deep trouble, hurting many in their spiritual lives.

God who began the good work within you will keep right on helping you grow in his grace until his task within you is finally finished on that day when Jesus Christ returns. Remember always to live as Christians should. □ So also the tongue is a small thing, but what enormous damage it can do. A great forest can be set on fire by one tiny spark. And the tongue is a flame of fire. It is full of wickedness, and poisons every part of the body. And the tongue is set on fire by hell itself, and can turn our whole lives into a blazing flame of destruction and disaster. No human being can tame the tongue. It is always ready to pour out its deadly poison. □ Let your conversation be gracious as well as sensible.

Ps. 19:14. Ps. 19:12. Hebr. 12:15. Phil. 1:6, 27. Jas. 3:5, 6, 8. Col. 4:6.

Not by might, nor by power, but by my Spirit, says the Lord of Hosts.

Who can advise the Spirit of the Lord or be his teacher or give him counsel?

God has deliberately chosen to use ideas the world considers foolish and of little worth in order to shame those people considered by the world as wise and great. He has chosen a plan despised by the world, counted as nothing at all, and used it to bring down to nothing those the world considers great, so that no one anywhere can ever brag in the presence of God.

Just as you can hear the wind but can't tell where it comes from or where it will go next, so it is with the Spirit. We do not know on whom he will next bestow this life from heaven. □ Reborn! —not a physical rebirth resulting from human passion or plan—but from the will of God.

I promised . . . that my Spirit would remain among you; so don't be afraid. □ The battle is not yours, but God's!

The Lord does not depend on weapons to fulfill his plans—he works without regard to human means!

Zech. 4:6. Is. 40:13. 1 Cor. 1:27–29. Jn. 3:8. Jn. 1:13. Hag. 2:5. 2 Chron. 20:15. 1 Sam. 17:47.

Always try to do good.

This suffering is all part of the work God has given you. Christ, who suffered for you, is your example. Follow in his steps: He never sinned, never told a lie, never answered back when insulted; when he suffered he did not threaten to get even; he left his case in the hands of God who always judges fairly. □ If you want to keep from becoming fainthearted and weary, think about his patience as sinful men did such terrible things to him.

Let us strip off anything that slows us down or holds us back, and especially those sins that wrap themselves so tightly around our feet and trip us up; and let us run with patience the particular race that God has set before us. Keep your eyes on Jesus, our leader and instructor. He was willing to die a shameful death on the cross because of the joy he knew would be his afterwards; and now he sits in the place of honor by the throne of God.

Let me say this one more thing: Fix your thoughts on what is true and good and right. Think about things that are pure and lovely, and dwell on the fine, good things in others. Think about all you can praise God for and be glad about.

1 Thess. 5:15. 1 Pet. 2:21–23. Hebr. 12:3. Hebr. 12:1, 2. Phil. 4:8.

The paths of the Lord are true and right, and good men walk along them. But sinners trying it will fail.

He is very precious to you who believe; and to those who reject him . . . he is the Stone that some will stumble over, and the Rock that will make them fall. They will stumble because they will not listen to God's Word, nor obey it, and so this punishment must follow—that they will fall. □ God protects the upright but destroys the wicked.

If ever you were willing to listen, listen now! □ Listen, if you are wise, to what I am saying. Think about the lovingkindness of the Lord! □ If your eye is pure, there will be sunshine in your soul. □ If any of you really determines to do God's will, then you will certainly know whether my teaching is from God or is merely my own. □ For to him who has will more be given . . . and he will have great plenty.

Anyone whose Father is God listens gladly to the words of God. Since you don't, it proves you aren't his children. □ You won't come to me so that I can give you this life eternal! □ My sheep recognize my voice, and I know them, and they follow me.

Hos. 14:9. 1 Pet. 2:7, 8. Prov. 10:29. Mt. 11:15. Ps. 107:43. Mt. 6:22. Jn. 7:17. Mt. 13:12. Jn. 8:47. Jn. 5:40. Jn. 10:27.

*There is wonderful joy ahead, even though
the going is rough for a while down here.*

Dear friends, don't be bewildered or surprised
when you go through the fiery trials ahead. Instead, be really glad—because these trials will
make you partners with Christ in his suffering,
and afterwards you will have the wonderful joy
of sharing his glory. ☐ Have you quite forgotten
the encouraging words God spoke to you, his
child? He said, "My son, don't be angry when
the Lord punishes you. Don't be discouraged
when he has to show you where you are wrong."
☐ Being punished isn't enjoyable while it is happening—it hurts! But afterwards we can see the
result, a quiet growth in grace and character.

This High Priest of ours understands our weaknesses, since he had the same temptations we do,
though he never once gave way to them and
sinned. ☐ For since he himself has now been
through suffering and temptation, he knows what
it is like when we suffer and are tempted, and he
is wonderfully able to help us. ☐ No temptation
is irresistible. You can trust God to keep the temptation from becoming so strong that you can't
stand up against it, for he has promised this and
will do what he says. He will show you how to
escape temptation's power so that you can bear
up patiently against it.

*1 Pet. 1:6. 1 Pet. 4:12, 13. Hebr. 12:5. Hebr. 12:11. Hebr. 4:15.
Hebr. 2:18. 1 Cor. 10:13.*

Oh, that . . . men would praise the Lord for his lovingkindness, and for all of his wonderful deeds!

Oh, put God to the test and see how kind he is! See for yourself the way his mercies shower down on all who trust in him. □ Oh, how great is your goodness to those who publicly declare that you will rescue them. For you have stored up great blessings for those who trust and reverence you.

His unchanging plan has always been to adopt us into his own family by sending Jesus Christ to die for us. And he did this because he wanted to! Now all praise to God for his wonderful kindness to us and his favor that he has poured out upon us, because we belong to his dearly loved Son.

How wonderful and beautiful all shall be! The abundance of grain and wine will make the young men and girls flourish; they will be radiant with health and happiness. □ He is good to everyone, and his compassion is intertwined with everything he does. All living things shall thank you, Lord, and your people will bless you. They will talk together about the glory of your kingdom and mention examples of your power. They will tell about your miracles and about the majesty and glory of your reign.

Ps. 107:8. Ps. 34:8. Ps. 31:19. Eph. 1:5, 6. Zech. 9:17. Ps. 145:9–12.

Lead me; teach me.

When the Holy Spirit, who is truth, comes, he shall guide you into all truth, for he will not be presenting his own ideas, but will be passing on to you what he has heard. □ The Holy Spirit has come upon you, and you know the truth.

Check these witches' words against the Word of God. If their messages are different than mine, it is because I have not sent them; for they have no light or truth in them. □ The whole Bible was given to us by inspiration from God and is useful to teach us what is true and to make us realize what is wrong in our lives; it straightens us out and helps us do what is right. It is God's way of making us well prepared at every point, fully equipped to do good to everyone.

I will instruct you (says the Lord) and guide you along the best pathway for your life; I will advise you and watch your progress. □ If your eye is pure, there will be sunshine in your soul. □ If any of you really determines to do God's will, then you will certainly know whether my teaching is from God or is merely my own. □ God will walk there with you; even the most stupid cannot miss the way.

Ps. 25:5. Jn. 16:13. 1 Jn. 2:20. Is. 8:20. 2 Tim. 3:16, 17. Ps. 32:8. Mt. 6:22. Jn. 7:17. Is. 35:8.

We know how happy they are now because they stayed true.

We can rejoice, too, when we run into problems and trials for we know that they are good for us—they help us learn to be patient. And patience develops strength of character in us and helps us trust God more each time we use it until finally our hope and faith are strong and steady. Then, when that happens, we are able to hold our heads high no matter what happens and know that all is well, for we know how dearly God loves us.

Being punished isn't enjoyable while it is happening—it hurts! But afterwards we can see the result, a quiet growth in grace and character. □ When your patience is finally in full bloom, then you will be ready for anything, strong in character, full and complete.

I am glad to boast about how weak I am; I am glad to be a living demonstration of Christ's power, instead of showing off my own power and abilities. Since I know it is all for Christ's good, I am quite happy about "the thorn," and about insults and hardships, persecutions and difficulties; for when I am weak, then I am strong—the less I have, the more I depend on him.

Jas. 5:11. Rom. 5:3–5. Hebr. 12:11. Jas. 1:4. 2 Cor. 12:9, 10.

*Always please the Lord and honor him, so
that you will always be doing good, kind
things for others, while all the time you are
learning to know God better and better.*

Dear brothers, I plead with you to give your
bodies to God. Let them be a living sacrifice, holy
—the kind he can accept. When you think of what
he has done for you, is this too much to ask? Don't
copy the behavior and customs of this world, but
be a new and different person with a fresh newness in all you do and think. Then you will learn
from your own experience how his ways will really
satisfy you. □ Just as you used to be slaves to all
kinds of sin, so now you must let yourselves be
slaves to all that is right and holy. □ What counts
is whether we really have been changed into new
and different people. May God's mercy and peace
be upon all of you who live by this principle and
upon those everywhere who are really God's own.

My true disciples produce bountiful harvests.
This brings great glory to my Father. □ You didn't
choose me! I chose you! I appointed you to go and
produce lovely fruit always, so that no matter what
you ask for from the Father, using my name, he
will give it to you.

Col. 1:10.   Rom. 12:1, 2.   Rom. 6:19.   Gal. 6:15, 16.   Jn. 15:8.   Jn.
15:16.

I got up to look for him but couldn't find him.

Return to the Lord, your God, for you have been crushed by your sins. Bring your petition. Come to the Lord and say, "O Lord, take away our sins; be gracious to us and receive us, and we will offer you the sacrifice of praise."

Remember, when someone wants to do wrong it is never God who is tempting him, for God never wants to do wrong and never tempts anyone else to do it. Temptation is the pull of man's own evil thoughts and wishes. These evil thoughts lead to evil actions and afterwards to the death penalty from God. So don't be misled, dear brothers. But whatever is good and perfect comes to us from God, the Creator of all light, and he shines forever without change or shadow.

Don't be impatient. Wait for the Lord, and he will come and save you! Be brave, stouthearted and courageous. Yes, wait and he will help you. □ It is good both to hope and wait quietly for the salvation of the Lord. □ Don't you think that God will surely give justice to his people who plead with him day and night?

I stand silently before the Lord, waiting for him to rescue me. For salvation comes from him alone.

Song 3:1. Hos. 14:1, 2. Jas. 1:13–17. Ps. 27:14. Lam. 3:26. Lk. 18:7. Ps. 62:1.

God sometimes uses sorrow in our lives to help us turn away from sin and seek eternal life.

Peter remembered what Jesus had said, "Before the cock crows, you will deny me three times." And he went away, crying bitterly. □ If we confess our sins to him, he can be depended on to forgive us and to cleanse us from every wrong. □ The blood of Jesus his Son cleanses us from every sin.

I perish, for problems far too big for me to solve are piled higher than my head. Meanwhile my sins, too many to count, have all caught up with me and I am ashamed to look up. My heart quails within me. Please, Lord, rescue me! Quick! Come and help me!

You have been crushed by your sins. □ Come back to God. Live by the principles of love and justice, and always be expecting much from him, your God. □ Rest in the Lord; wait patiently for him to act.

It is a broken spirit you want—remorse and penitence. A broken and a contrite heart, O God, you will not ignore. □ He heals the brokenhearted, binding up their wounds. □ He has told you what he wants, and this is all it is: *to be fair and just and merciful, and to walk humbly with your God.*

2 Cor. 7:10. Mt. 26:75. 1 Jn. 1:9. 1 Jn. 1:7. Ps. 40:12, 13. Hos. 14:1. Hos. 12:6. Ps. 37:7. Ps. 51:17. Ps. 147:3. Mic. 6:8.

These trials are only to test your faith, to see whether or not it is strong and pure.

The world ignores us, but we are known to God; we live close to death, but here we are, still very much alive. We have been injured but kept from death. Our hearts ache, but at the same time we have the joy of the Lord. We are poor, but we give rich spiritual gifts to others. We own nothing, and yet we enjoy everything.

We are pressed on every side by troubles, but not crushed and broken. We are perplexed because we don't know why things happen as they do, but we don't give up and quit. We are hunted down, but God never abandons us. We get knocked down, but we get up again and keep going.

Though our bodies are dying, our inner strength in the Lord is growing every day. These troubles and sufferings of ours are, after all, quite small and won't last very long. Yet this short time of distress will result in God's richest blessing upon us forever and ever!

So we do not look at what we can see right now, the troubles all around us, but we look forward to the joys in heaven which we have not yet seen. The troubles will soon be over, but the joys to come will last forever.

1 Pet. 1:7.   2 Cor. 6:9, 10.   2 Cor. 4:8, 9, 16–18.

Love each other as much as I love you.

Be full of love for others, following the example of Christ who loved you and gave himself to God as a sacrifice to take away your sins. And God was pleased, for Christ's love for you was like sweet perfume to him. ☐ The message to us from the beginning has been that we should love one another. ☐ As far as God is concerned there is a sweet, wholesome fragrance in our lives. It is the fragrance of Christ within us.

You have a new life. It was not passed on to you from your parents, for the life they gave you will fade away. This new one will last forever, for it comes from Christ, God's ever-living Message to man. ☐ Make them pure and holy through teaching them your words of truth. ☐ Unless one is born of water and the Spirit, he cannot enter the Kingdom of God. ☐ He saved us—not because we were good enough to be saved, but because of his kindness and pity—by washing away our sins and giving us the new joy of the indwelling Holy Spirit. ☐ Your promises . . . refresh and revive me!

May God who gives patience, steadiness, and encouragement help you to live in complete harmony with each other—each with the attitude of Christ toward the other.

Jn. 15:12. Eph. 5:2. 1 Jn. 3:11. 2 Cor. 2:15. 1 Pet. 1:23. Jn. 17:17. Jn. 3:5. Tit. 3:5. Ps. 119:49, 50. Rom. 15:5.

When the Holy Spirit controls our lives he will produce . . . self-control.

To win the contest you must deny yourselves many things that would keep you from doing your best. An athlete goes to all this trouble just to win a blue ribbon or a silver cup, but we do it for a heavenly reward that never disappears. So I run straight to the goal with purpose in every step. I fight to win. I'm not just shadow-boxing or playing around. Like an athlete I punish my body, treating it roughly, training it to do what it should, not what it wants to. Otherwise I fear that after enlisting others for the race, I myself might be declared unfit and ordered to stand aside.

Don't drink too much wine, for many evils lie along that path; be filled instead with the Holy Spirit, and controlled by him.

If anyone wants to be a follower of mine, let him deny himself and take up his cross and follow me.

Be on your guard, not asleep like the others. Watch for his return and stay sober. Night is the time for sleep and the time when people get drunk. But let us who live in the light keep sober. □ God wants us to turn from godless living and sinful pleasures and to live good, God-fearing lives day after day.

Gal. 5:22, 23. 1 Cor. 9:25–27. Eph. 5:18. Mt. 16:24. 1 Thess. 5:6–8. Tit. 2:12.

God . . . always does just what he says,
and he is the one who invited you into this
wonderful friendship with his Son, even
Christ our Lord.

We can look forward to the salvation God has
promised us. There is no longer any room for
doubt, and we can tell others that salvation is
ours, for there is no question that he will do what
he says. ☐ You are God's temple, the home of the
living God, and God has said of you, "I will live
in them and walk among them, and I will be their
God and they shall be my people." ☐ Share the
fellowship and the joys we have with the Father
and with Jesus Christ his Son. ☐ Be really glad—
because these trials will make you partners with
Christ in his suffering, and afterwards you will
have the wonderful joy of sharing his glory in
that coming day when it will be displayed.

I pray that Christ will be more and more at
home in your hearts, living within you as you
trust in him. May your roots go down deep into
the soil of God's marvelous love; and may you
be able to feel and understand, as all God's children should, how long, how wide, how deep, and
how high his love really is; and to experience this
love for yourselves, though it is so great that you
will never see the end of it or fully know or understand it. And so at last you will be filled up
with God himself.

1 Cor. 1:9. Hebr. 10:23. 2 Cor. 6:16. 1 Jn. 1:3. 1 Pet. 4:13. Eph.
3:17–19.

*Make them pure and holy through teaching
them your words of truth.*

He has already tended you by pruning you
back for greater strength and usefulness by means
of the commands I gave you. □ Remember what
Christ taught and let his words enrich your lives
and make you wise.

How can a young man stay pure? By reading
your Word and following its rules. I have tried
my best to find you—don't let me wander off
from your instructions.

For wisdom and truth will enter the very center
of your being, filling your life with joy. You will
be given the sense to stay away from evil men.

I have stayed in God's paths, following his
steps. I have not turned aside. I have not refused
his commandments but have enjoyed them more
than my daily food. □ Nothing is perfect except
your words. Oh, how I love them. I think about
them all day long. They make me wiser than my
enemies, because they are my constant guide.
Yes, wiser than my teachers, for I am ever thinking of your rules. □ You are truly my disciples if
you live as I tell you to, and you will know the
truth, and the truth will set you free.

*Jn. 17:17. Jn. 15:3. Col 3:16. Ps. 119:9, 10. Prov. 2:10, 11. Job
23:11, 12. Ps. 119:96–99. Jn. 8:31, 32.*

How deep are your thoughts!

We have kept on praying and asking God to help you understand what he wants you to do; asking him to make you wise about spiritual things. ☐ And I pray that Christ will be more and more at home in your hearts, living within you as you trust in him. May your roots go down deep into the soil of God's marvelous love; and may you be able to feel and understand, as all God's children should, how long, how wide, how deep, and how high his love really is; and to experience this love for yourselves, though it is so great that you will never see the end of it or fully know or understand it. And so at last you will be filled up with God himself.

How great are his wisdom and knowledge and riches! How impossible it is for us to understand his decisions and his methods! ☐ This plan of mine is not what you would work out, neither are my thoughts the same as yours! For just as the heavens are higher than the earth, so are my ways higher than yours, and my thoughts than yours. ☐ O Lord my God, many and many a time you have done great miracles for us, and we are ever in your thoughts. Who else can do such glorious things? No one else can be compared with you.

Ps. 92:5. Col. 1:9. Eph. 3:17–19. Rom. 11:33. Is. 55:8, 9. Ps. 40:5.

A man will always reap just the kind of crop he sows!

Experience teaches that it is those who sow sin and trouble who harvest the same. □ They have sown the wind and they will reap the whirlwind. □ If he sows to please his own wrong desires, he will be planting seeds of evil and he will surely reap a harvest of spiritual decay and death.

The good man's reward lasts forever. □ If he plants the good things of the Spirit, he will reap the everlasting life which the Holy Spirit gives him. And let us not get tired of doing what is right, for after a while we will reap a harvest of blessing if we don't get discouraged and give up. That's why whenever we can we should always be kind to everyone, and especially to our Christian brothers.

It is possible to give away and become richer! It is also possible to hold on too tightly and lose everything. Yes, the liberal man shall be rich! By watering others, he waters himself. □ If you give little, you will get little. A farmer who plants just a few seeds will get only a small crop, but if he plants much, he will reap much.

Gal. 6:7. Job 4:8. Hos. 8:7. Gal. 6:8. Prov. 11:18. Gal. 6:8–10. Prov. 11:24, 25. 2 Cor. 9:6.

*He has punished Israel but a little, exiling
her far from her own land as though blown
away in a storm from the east.*

It is better to fall into the hand of the Lord
(for his mercy is great) than into the hands of
men. □ "I am with you and I will save you," says
the Lord ". . . I will not exterminate you; I will
punish you, yes—you will not go unpunished." □
He never bears a grudge, nor remains angry forever. He has not punished us as we deserve for all
our sins. For he knows we are but dust. □ I will
spare them as a man spares an obedient and duti-
ful son.

No temptation is irresistible. You can trust
God to keep the temptation from becoming so
strong that you can't stand up against it, for he
has promised this and will do what he says. He
will show you how to escape temptation's power
so that you can bear up patiently against it. □
Satan has asked to have you, to sift you like
wheat, but I have pleaded in prayer for you that
your faith should not completely fail.

To the poor, O Lord, you are a refuge from
the storm, a shadow from the heat, a shelter
from merciless men who are like a driving rain
that melts down an earthen wall.

*Is. 27:8. 2 Sam. 24:14. Jer. 30:11. Ps. 103:9, 10, 14. Mal. 3:17.
1 Cor. 10:13. Lk. 22:31, 32. Is. 25:4.*

When I sit in darkness, the Lord himself will be my Light.

When you go through deep waters and great trouble, I will be with you. When you go through rivers of difficulty, you will not drown! When you walk through the fire of oppression, you will not be burned up—the flames will not consume you. For I am the Lord your God, your Savior, the Holy One of Israel. ☐ He will bring blind Israel along a path they have not seen before. He will make the darkness bright before them and smooth and straighten out the road ahead. He will not forsake them. ☐ Who among you fears the Lord and obeys his Servant? If such men walk in darkness, without one ray of light, let them trust the Lord, let them rely upon their God.

Even when walking through the dark valley of death I will not be afraid, for you are close beside me, guarding, guiding all the way. ☐ When I am afraid, I will put my confidence in you. Yes, I will trust the promises of God. And since I am trusting him, what can mere man do to me? ☐ The Lord is my light and my salvation; whom shall I fear?

Mic. 7:8. Is. 43:2, 3. Is. 42:16. Is. 50:10. Ps. 23:4. Ps. 56:3, 4. Ps. 27:1.

*Learning to pray in the power and strength
of the Holy Spirit.*

God is Spirit, and we must have his help to
worship as we should. ☐ All of us, whether Jews
or Gentiles, may come to God the Father with
the Holy Spirit's help because of what Christ has
done for us.

My Father! If it is possible, let this cup be
taken away from me. But I want your will, not
mine.

The Holy Spirit helps us with our daily problems and in our praying. For we don't even
know what we should pray for, nor how to pray
as we should; but the Holy Spirit prays for us
with such feeling that it cannot be expressed in
words. And the Father who knows all hearts
knows, of course, what the Spirit is saying as he
pleads for us in harmony with God's own will. ☐
And we are sure of this, that he will listen to us
whenever we ask him for anything in line with
his will. ☐ When the Holy Spirit, who is truth,
comes, he shall guide you into all truth.

Pray all the time. Ask God for anything in line
with the Holy Spirit's wishes. Plead with him, reminding him of your needs, and keep praying
earnestly for all Christians everywhere.

*Jude 20. Jn. 4:24. Eph. 2:18. Mt. 26:39. Rom. 8:26, 27. 1 Jn.
5:14. Jn. 16:13. Eph. 6:18.*

There is hope for a tree—if it's cut down it sprouts again, and grows tender, new branches.

He will not break the bruised reed. □ He restores my failing health.

God sometimes uses sorrow in our lives to help us turn away from sin and seek eternal life. We should never regret his sending it. But the sorrow of the man who is not a Christian is not the sorrow of true repentance and does not prevent eternal death. □ Being punished isn't enjoyable while it is happening—it hurts! But afterwards we can see the result, a quiet growth in grace and character.

I used to wander off until you punished me; now I closely follow all you say.

Do not rejoice against me, O my enemy, for though I fall, I will rise again! When I sit in darkness, the Lord himself will be my Light. I will be patient while the Lord punishes me, for I have sinned against him; then he will defend me from my enemies, and punish them for all the evil they have done to me. God will bring me out of my darkness into the light, and I will see his goodness.

Job 14:7. Is. 42:3. Ps. 23:3. 2 Cor. 7:10. Hebr. 12:11. Ps. 119:67. Mic. 7:8, 9.

My Kingdom is not of the world.

Christ gave himself to God for our sins as one sacrifice for all time, and then sat down in the place of highest honor at God's right hand, waiting for his enemies to be laid under his feet. □ In the future you will see me, the Messiah, sitting at the right hand of God and returning on the clouds of heaven.

Christ will be King until he has defeated all his enemies.

We thank God for all of this! It is he who makes us victorious through Jesus Christ our Lord! □ It is that same mighty power that raised Christ from the dead and seated him in the place of honor at God's right hand in heaven, far, far above any other king or ruler or dictator or leader. Yes, his honor is far more glorious than that of anyone else either in this world or in the world to come. And God has put all things under his feet and made him the supreme Head of the church—which is his body, filled with himself, the Author and Giver of everything everywhere. □ For in due season Christ will be revealed from heaven by the blessed and only Almighty God, the King of kings and Lord of lords.

Jn. 18:36. Hebr. 10:12, 13. Mt. 26:64. 1 Cor. 15:25. 1 Cor. 15:57. Eph. 1:19–23. 1 Tim. 6:15.

What are you doing here, Elijah?

He knows every detail of what is happening to me. □ O Lord, you have examined my heart and know everything about me. You know when I sit or stand. When far away you know my every thought. You chart the path ahead of me, and tell me where to stop and rest. Every moment, you know where I am. I can *never* be lost to your Spirit! I can *never* get away from my God! If I ride the morning winds to the farthest oceans, even there your hand will guide me, your strength will support me.

Elijah was as completely human as we are. □ Fear of man is a dangerous trap, but to trust in God means safety. □ If they fall it isn't fatal, for the Lord holds them with his hand. □ Don't you know that this good man, though you trip him up seven times, will each time rise again?

Let us not get tired of doing what is right, for after a while we will reap a harvest of blessing if we don't get discouraged and give up. □ The spirit indeed is willing, but how weak the body is! □ He is like a father to us, tender and sympathetic to those who reverence him. For he knows we are but dust.

1 Kgs. 19:9. Job 23:10. Ps. 139:1-3, 7, 9, 10. Jas. 5:17. Prov. 29:25. Ps. 37:24. Prov. 24:16. Gal. 6:9. Mt. 26:41. Ps. 103:13, 14.

*Now you are free from your old master, sin;
and you have becomes slaves to your new
master, righteousness.*

You cannot serve two masters: God and money. □ When you were slaves of sin you didn't bother much with goodness. And what was the result? Evidently not good, since you are ashamed now even to think about those things you used to do, for all of them end in eternal doom. But now you are free from the power of sin and are slaves of God, and his benefits to you include holiness and everlasting life.

Christ gives to those who trust in him everything they are trying to get by keeping his laws.

If these Greeks want to be my disciples, tell them to come and follow me, for my servants must be where I am. And if they follow me, the Father will honor them. □ Wear my yoke—for it fits perfectly—and let me teach you; for I am gentle and humble, and you shall find rest for your souls; for I give you only light burdens.

O Lord our God, once we worshiped other gods; but now we worship you alone. □ If you will only help me to want your will, then I will follow your laws even more closely.

Rom. 6:18. Mt. 6:24. Rom. 6:20–22. Rom. 10:4. Jn. 12:26. Mt. 11:29, 30. Is. 26:13. Ps. 119:32.

*Anyone who asks for mercy from the Lord
shall have it and shall be saved.*

Manasseh . . . rebuilt the hilltop shrines
which his father Hezekiah had destroyed. He
built altars for Baal and made a shameful Ash-
erah idol, just as Ahab the king of Israel had
done. Heathen altars to the sun god, moon god,
and the gods of the stars were placed even in the
Temple of the Lord—in the very city and building which the Lord had selected to honor his own
name. And he sacrificed one of his sons as a burnt
offering on a heathen altar. He practiced black
magic and used fortune-telling, and patronized
mediums and wizards. So the Lord was very
angry, for Manasseh was an evil man, in God's
opinion. □ Then at last he came to his senses and
cried out humbly to God for help. And the Lord
listened, and answered his plea by returning him
to Jerusalem and to his kingdom! At that point
Manasseh finally realized that the Lord was
really God!

"Come, let's talk this over," says the Lord; "no
matter how deep the stain of your sins, I can
take it out and make you as clean as freshly
fallen snow. Even if you are stained as red as
crimson, I can make you white as wool." □ He
is not willing that any should perish.

Acts 2:21. 2 Kgs. 21:1, 3–6. 2 Chron. 33:12, 13. Is. 1:18. 2 Pet. 3:9.

If young toughs tell you, "Come and join us"—turn your back on them!

The woman was convinced . . . It would make her so wise! So she ate some of the fruit and gave some to her husband, and he ate it too. □ Don't you remember that when Achan, the son of Zerah, sinned against the Lord, the entire nation was punished in addition to the one man who had sinned?

Don't join mobs intent on evil.

Heaven can be entered only through the narrow gate! The highway to hell is broad, and its gate is wide enough for all the multitudes who choose its easy way.

We are not our own bosses to live or die as we ourselves might choose. □ Dear brothers, you have been given freedom: not freedom to do wrong, but freedom to love and serve each other. □ Be careful not to use your freedom to . . . cause some Christian brother to sin whose conscience is weaker than yours. And it is a sin against Christ to sin against your brother by encouraging him to do something he thinks is wrong.

We are the ones who strayed away like sheep! *We,* who left God's paths to follow our own. Yet God laid on *him* the guilt and sins of every one of us!

Prov. 1:10. Gen. 3:6. Josh. 22:20. Ex. 23:2. Mt. 7:13. Rom. 14:7. Gal. 5:13. 1 Cor. 8:9, 12. Is. 53:6.

Just as the body is dead when there is no spirit in it, so faith is dead if it is not the kind that results in good deeds.

Not all who sound religious are really godly people. They may refer to me as Lord, but still won't get to heaven. For the decisive question is whether they obey my Father in heaven.

Seek to live a clean and holy life, for one who is not holy will not see the Lord. □ You need more than faith; you must also work hard to be good, and even that is not enough. For then you must learn to know God better and discover what he wants you to do. Next, learn to put aside your own desires so that you will become patient and godly, gladly letting God have his way with you. This will make possible the next step, which is for you to enjoy other people and to like them, and finally you will grow to love them deeply. The more you go on in this way, the more you will grow strong spiritually and become fruitful and useful to our Lord Jesus Christ. But anyone who fails to go after these additions to faith is blind indeed, or at least very shortsighted, and has forgotten that God delivered him from the old life of sin so that now he can live a strong, good life for the Lord.

Salvation is not a reward for the good we have done, so none of us can take any credit for it.

Jas. 2:26. Mt. 7:21. Hebr. 12:14. 2 Pet. 1:5–10. Eph. 2:9.

Do you . . . believe?

What's the use of saying that you have faith and are Christians if you aren't proving it by helping others? Will *that* kind of faith save anyone? It isn't enough just to have faith. You must also do good to prove that you have it. Faith that doesn't show itself by good works is no faith at all—it is dead and useless.

While God was testing him, Abraham still trusted in God and his promises, and so he offered up his son Isaac, and was ready to slay him on the altar of sacrifice; yes, to slay even Isaac, through whom God has promised to give Abraham a whole nation of descendants! He believed that if Isaac died God would bring him back to life again. □ Our father Abraham was declared good because of what he *did,* when he was willing to obey God, even if it meant offering his son Isaac to die on the altar. So you see, a man is saved by what he does, as well as by what he believes.

The way to identify a tree or a person is by the kind of fruit produced. Not all who sound religious are really godly people. They may refer to me as Lord, but still won't get to heaven. For the decisive question is whether they obey my Father in heaven. □ You know these things— now do them! That is the path of blessing.

Jn. 16:31. Jas. 2:14, 17. Hebr. 11:17–19. Jas. 2:21, 24. Mt. 7:20, 21. Jn. 13:17.

May the Lord of peace himself give you his peace no matter what happens. The Lord be with you all.

May you have grace and peace from God who is, and was, and is to come! □ God's peace . . . far more wonderful than the human mind can understand. His peace will keep your thoughts and your hearts quiet and at rest as you trust in Christ Jesus.

Jesus himself was suddenly standing there among them, and greeted them. □ I am leaving you with a gift—peace of mind and heart! And the peace I give isn't fragile like the peace the world gives. So don't be troubled or afraid.

The Comforter—the Holy Spirit, the source of all truth. □ When the Holy Spirit controls our lives he will produce this kind of fruit in us: love, joy, peace. □ His Holy Spirit speaks to us deep in our hearts, and tells us that we really are God's children.

"I myself will go with you and give you success." For Moses had said, "If you aren't going with us, don't let us move a step from this place. If you don't go with us, who will ever know that I and my people have found favor with you?"

2 Thess. 3:16. Rev. 1:4. Phil. 4:7. Lk. 24:36. Jn. 14:27. Jn 15:26. Gal. 5:22. Rom. 8:16. Ex. 33:14–16.

We can rejoice, too, when we run into problems and trials for we know that they are good for us.

If being a Christian is of value to us only now in this life, we are the most miserable of creatures.

Dear friends, don't be bewildered or surprised when you go through the fiery trials ahead, for this is no strange, unusual thing that is going to happen to you. Instead, be really glad—because these trials will make you partners with Christ in his suffering, and afterwards you will have the wonderful joy of sharing his glory in that coming day when it will be displayed. ☐ Our hearts ache, but at the same time we have the joy of the Lord.

Always be full of joy in the Lord; I say it again, rejoice! ☐ They left the Council chamber rejoicing that God had counted them worthy to suffer dishonor for his name.

I pray . . . that God who gives you hope will keep you happy and full of peace as you believe in him.

Even though the fig trees are all destroyed, and there is neither blossom left nor fruit, and though the olive crops all fail, and the fields lie barren; even if the flocks die in the fields and the cattle barns are empty, yet I will rejoice in the Lord; I will be happy in the God of my salvation.

Rom. 5:3. 1 Cor. 15:19. 1 Pet. 4:12, 13. 2 Cor. 6:10. Phil. 4:4. Acts 5:41. Rom. 15:13. Hab. 3:17, 18.

My eyes are ever looking to the Lord for help.

Is anything too hard for God? □ Commit everything you do to the Lord. Trust him to help you do it and he will. □ Don't worry about anything; instead, pray about everything; tell God your needs and don't forget to thank him for his answers. □ Let him have all your worries and cares, for he is always thinking about you and watching everything that concerns you. □ Be delighted with the Lord. Then he will give you all your heart's desires.

When Moses and Aaron and Samuel, his prophets, cried to him for help, he answered them. He spoke to them from the pillar of cloud and they followed his instructions.

I will answer them before they even call to me. While they are still talking to me about their needs, I will go ahead and answer their prayers! □ The earnest prayer of a righteous man has great power and wonderful results.

I love the Lord because he hears my prayers and answers them. Because he bends down and listens, I will pray as long as I breathe!

Ps. 25:15. Gen. 18:14. Ps. 37:5. Phil. 4:6. 1 Pet. 5:7. Ps. 37:4. Ps. 99:6, 7. Is. 65:24. Jas. 5:16. Ps. 116:1, 2.

They don't know where to find wisdom.

If you want to know what God wants you to do, ask him, and he will gladly tell you, for he is always ready to give a bountiful supply of wisdom to all who ask him; he will not resent it. But when you ask him, be sure that you really expect him to tell you, for a doubtful mind will be as unsettled as a wave of the sea that is driven and tossed by the wind. □ Trust the Lord completely; don't ever trust yourself. In everything you do, put God first, and he will direct you and crown your efforts with success. □ He alone is God, and full of wisdom. □ Don't be conceited, sure of your own wisdom.

"O Lord God," I said, "I can't do that! I'm far too young! I'm only a youth!" "Don't say that," he replied, "for you will go wherever I send you and speak whatever I tell you to. And don't be afraid of the people, for I, the Lord, will be with you and see you through."

Go directly to the Father and ask him, and he will give you what you ask for because you use my name. You haven't tried this before, [but begin now]. Ask, using my name, and you will receive, and your cup of joy will overflow. □ You can get anything—*anything* you ask for in prayer —if you believe.

Job 28:12. Jas. 1:5, 6. Prov. 3:5, 6. 1 Tim. 1:17. Prov. 3:7. Jer. 1:6–8. Jn. 16:23, 24. Mt. 21:22.

The punishment you gave me was the best thing that could have happened to me, for it taught me to pay attention to your laws.

Even though Jesus was God's Son, he had to learn from experience what it was like to obey, when obeying meant suffering. □ If we are to share his glory, we must also share his suffering. Yet what we suffer now is nothing compared to the glory he will give us later. □ Is your life full of difficulties and temptations? Then be happy, for when the way is rough, your patience has a chance to grow. So let it grow, and don't try to squirm out of your problems.

He knows every detail of what is happening to me; and when he has examined me, he will pronounce me completely innocent—as pure as solid gold! I have stayed in God's paths, following his steps. I have not turned aside.

Do you remember how the Lord led you through the wilderness for all those forty years, humbling you and testing you to find out how you would respond, and whether or not you would really obey him? So you should realize that, as a man punishes his son, the Lord punishes you to help you. Obey the laws of the Lord your God. Walk in his ways and fear him.

Ps. 119:71. Hebr. 5:8. Rom. 8:17, 18. Jas. 1:2–4. Job 23:10, 11. Deut. 8:2, 5, 6.

No one shall succeed by strength alone.

David shouted in reply, "You come to me with a sword and a spear, but I come to you in the name of the Lord of the armies of heaven and of Israel—the very God whom you have defied." David . . . reaching into his shepherd's bag, took out a stone, hurled it from his sling, and hit the Philistine in the forehead. The stone sank in, and the man fell on his face to the ground. So David conquered the Philistine giant with a sling and a stone.

The best-equipped army cannot save a king— for great strength is not enough to save anyone. But the eyes of the Lord are watching over those who fear him, who rely upon his steady love. □ Riches and honor come from you alone, and you are the Ruler of all mankind; your hand controls power and might, and it is at your discretion that men are made great and given strength.

I am glad to boast about how weak I am; I am glad to be a living demonstration of Christ's power, instead of showing off my own power and abilities. For when I am weak, then I am strong —the less I have, the more I depend on him.

1 Sam. 2:9. 1 Sam. 17:45, 49, 50. Ps. 33:16, 18. 1 Chron. 29:12. 2 Cor. 12:9, 10.

The spirit indeed is willing, but how weak the body is!

O Lord, we love to do your will! Our hearts' desire is to glorify your name. All night long I search for you; earnestly I seek for God.

I know I am rotten through and through so far as my old sinful nature is concerned. No matter which way I turn I can't make myself do right. I want to but I can't. I love to do God's will so far as my new nature is concerned; but there is something else deep within me, in my lower nature, that is at war with my mind and wins the fight and makes me a slave to the sin that is still within me. □ For we naturally love to do evil things that are just the opposite from the things that the Holy Spirit tells us to do; and the good things we want to do when the Spirit has his way with us are just the opposite of our natural desires. These two forces within us are constantly fighting each other to win control over us, and our wishes are never free from their pressures.

I can do everything God asks me to with the help of Christ who gives me the strength and power. □ Our only power and success comes from God. □ I am with you; that is all you need.

Mt. 26:41. Is. 26:8, 9. Rom. 7:18, 22, 23. Gal. 5:17. Phil. 4:13. 2 Cor. 3:5. 2 Cor. 12:9.

God took the sinless Christ and poured into him our sins. Then, in exchange, he poured God's goodness into us!

God laid on *him* the guilt and sins of every one of us! □ He personally carried the load of our sins in his own body when he died on the cross, so that we can be finished with sin and live a good life from now on. For his wounds have healed ours! □ Adam caused many to be sinners because he *disobeyed* God, and Christ caused many to be made acceptable to God because he *obeyed*.

When the time came for the kindness and love of God our Savior to appear, then he saved us— not because we were good enough to be saved, but because of his kindness and pity—by washing away our sins and giving us the new joy of the indwelling Holy Spirit whom he poured out upon us with wonderful fullness—and all because of what Jesus Christ our Savior did so that he could declare us good in God's eyes—all because of his great kindness; and now we can share in the wealth of the eternal life he gives us, and we are eagerly looking forward to receiving it. □ So there is now no condemnation awaiting those who belong to Christ Jesus.

The Lord Our Righteousness.

2 Cor. 5:21. Is. 53:6. 1 Pet. 2:24. Rom. 5:19. Tit. 3:4–7. Rom 8:1. Jer. 23:6.

The dust returns to the earth as it was.

Our earthly bodies . . . die and decay. The bodies we have now embarrass us for they become sick and die. Yes, they are weak, dying bodies . . . human bodies. □ Adam was made from the dust of the earth.

You were made from the ground, and to the ground you will return. □ He destroys those who are healthy, wealthy, fat, and prosperous; God also destroys those in deep and grinding poverty who have never known anything good. Both alike are buried in the same dust, both eaten by the same worms.

Heart, body and soul are filled with joy. □ I know that after this body has decayed, this body shall see God! □ The Lord Jesus Christ . . . will take these dying bodies of ours and change them into glorious bodies like his own, using the same mighty power that he will use to conquer all else everywhere.

Lord, help me to realize how brief my time on earth will be. Help me to know that I am here for but a moment more. □ Teach us to number our days and recognize how few they are; help us to spend them as we should.

Eccl. 12:7. 1 Cor. 15:42–44. 1 Cor. 15:47. Gen. 3:19. Job 21:23–26. Ps. 16:9. Job 19:26. Phil. 3:20, 21. Ps. 39:4. Ps. 90:12.

God is more pleased when we are just and fair than when we give him gifts.

He has told you what he wants, and this is all it is: *to be fair and just and merciful, and to walk humbly with your God.* □ Has the Lord as much pleasure in your burnt offerings and sacrifices as in your obedience? Obedience is far better than sacrifice. He is much more interested in your listening to him than in your offering the fat of rams to him. □ It is far more important to love him with all my heart and understanding and strength, and to love others as myself, than to offer all kinds of sacrifices on the altar of the Temple.

Oh, come back to God. Live by the principles of love and justice, and always be expecting much from him, your God. □ Mary sat on the floor, listening to Jesus as he talked. "There is really only one thing worth being concerned about. Mary has discovered it—and I won't take it away from her!"

God is at work within you, helping you want to obey him, and then helping you do what he wants. May he . . . produce in you through the power of Christ all that is pleasing to him. To him be glory forever and ever. Amen.

Prov. 21:3. Mic. 6:8. 1 Sam. 15:22. Mk. 12:33. Hos. 12:6. Lk. 10:39, 42. Phil. 2:13. Hebr. 13:21.

The spirit returns to God who gave it.

The Lord God formed a man's body from the dust of the ground and breathed into it the breath of life. And man became a living person. □ It is not mere age that makes men wise. Rather, it is the spirit in a man, the breath of the Almighty which makes him intelligent.

We look forward with confidence to our heavenly bodies, realizing that every moment we spend in these earthly bodies is time spent away from our eternal home in heaven with Jesus. □ I long to go and be with Christ. How much happier for *me* than being here! □ And now, dear brothers, I want you to know what happens to a Christian when he dies so that when it happens, you will not be full of sorrow, as those are who have no hope. For since we believe that Jesus died and then came back to life again, we can also believe that when Jesus returns, God will bring back with him all the Christians who have died.

There are many homes up there where my Father lives, and I am going to prepare them for your coming. When everything is ready, then I will come and get you, so that you can always be with me where I am.

Eccl. 12:7. Gen. 2:7. Job 32:8, 9. 2 Cor. 5:6. Phil. 1:23. 1 Thess. 4:13, 14. Jn. 14:2, 3.

No one can kidnap them from me.

I know the one in whom I trust, and I am sure that he is able to safely guard all that I have given him until the day of his return. ☐ The Lord will always deliver me from all evil and will bring me into his heavenly kingdom. ☐ Overwhelming victory is ours through Christ who loved us enough to die for us. For I am convinced that nothing can ever separate us from his love. Death can't, and life can't. The angels won't, and all the powers of hell itself cannot keep God's love away. Our fears for today, our worries about tomorrow, or where we are—high above the sky, or in the deepest ocean—nothing will ever be able to separate us from the love of God demonstrated by our Lord Jesus Christ when he died for us. ☐ Your real life is in heaven with Christ and God.

God has chosen poor people to be rich in faith, and the Kingdom of Heaven is theirs, for that is the gift God has promised to all those who love him.

May our Lord Jesus Christ himself and God our Father, who has loved us and given us everlasting comfort and hope which we don't deserve, comfort your hearts with all comfort, and help you in every good thing you say and do.

Jn. 10:29. 2 Tim. 1:12. 2 Tim. 4:18. Rom. 8:37–39. Col. 3:3. Jas. 2:5. 2 Thess. 2:16, 17.

*Don't do anything that will cause criticism
against yourself even though you know that
what you do is right.*

Keep away from every kind of evil. □ God
knows we are honest, but I want everyone else to
know it too. □ It is God's will that your good
lives should silence those who foolishly condemn
the Gospel without knowing what it can do for
them, having never experienced its power.

Don't let me hear of your suffering for murdering or stealing or making trouble or being a busybody and prying into other people's affairs. But it
is no shame to suffer for being a Christian. Praise
God for the privilege of being in Christ's family
and being called by his wonderful name!

For, dear brothers, you have been given freedom: not freedom to do wrong, but freedom to
love and serve each other. □ The important thing
for us as Christians is not what we eat or drink
but stirring up goodness and peace and joy from
the Holy Spirit. □ But be careful . . . lest you
cause some Christian brother to sin whose conscience is weaker than yours. □ But if any of you
causes one of these little ones who trusts in me to
lose his faith, it would be better for you to have
a rock tied to your neck and be thrown into the
sea. □ When you refused to help the least of these
my brothers you were refusing help to me.

*Rom. 14:16. 1 Thess. 5:22. 2 Cor. 8:21. 1 Pet. 2:15. 1 Pet. 4:15,
16. Gal. 5:13. Rom. 14:17. 1 Cor. 8:9. Mt. 18:6. Mt. 25:45.*

*Awake, O sleeper, and rise up from the
dead; and Christ shall give you light.*

Wake up, for the coming of the Lord is nearer
now than when we first believed. □ So be on your
guard, not asleep like the others. Watch for his
return and stay sober. Night is the time for sleep
and the time when people get drunk. But let us
who live in the light keep sober, protected by the
armor of faith and love, and wearing as our
helmet the happy hope of salvation.

Let your light shine for all the nations to see!
For the glory of the Lord is streaming from you.
Darkness as black as night shall cover all the
peoples of the earth, but the glory of the Lord
will shine from you.

You can look forward soberly and intelligently
to more of God's kindness to you when Jesus
Christ returns. □ Be prepared—all dressed and
ready—for your Lord's return from the wedding
feast. Then you will be ready to open the door
and let him in the moment he arrives and knocks.
□ God will shed his own glorious light upon you.
He will heal you; your godliness will lead you
forward, and goodness will be a shield before you,
and the glory of the Lord will protect you from
behind.

*Eph. 5:14. Rom. 13:11. 1 Thess. 5:6–8. Is. 60:1, 2. 1 Pet. 1:13.
Lk. 12:35, 36. Is. 58:8.*

Be strong with the strength Christ Jesus gives you.

Filled with his mighty, glorious strength so that you can keep going no matter what happens—always full of the joy of the Lord. □ Just as you trusted Christ to save you, trust him, too, for each day's problems; live in vital union with him. Let your roots grow down into him and draw up nourishment from him. See that you go on growing in the Lord, and become strong and vigorous in the truth you were taught. Let your lives overflow with joy and thanksgiving for all he has done. □ God has planted them like strong and graceful oaks for his own glory. □ What a foundation you stand on now: the apostles and the prophets; and the cornerstone of the building is Jesus Christ himself!

And now I entrust you to God and his care and to his wonderful words which are able to build your faith and give you all the inheritance of those who are set apart for himself. □ May you always be doing those good, kind things which show that you are a child of God, for this will bring much praise and glory to the Lord.

Fight on for God. □ Fearlessly, no matter what your enemies may do.

2 *Tim.* 2:1. *Col.* 1:11. *Col.* 2:6, 7. *Is.* 61:3. *Eph.* 2:20. *Acts* 20:32. *Phil.* 1:11. 1 *Tim.* 6:12. *Phil.* 1:28.

He rewards each one of us according to the work we do for him.

No one can ever lay any other real foundation than that one we already have—Jesus Christ. Every workman who has built on the foundation with the right materials, and whose work still stands, will get his pay. But if the house he has built burns up, he will have a great loss. He himself will be saved, but like a man escaping through a wall of flames. □ We must all stand before Christ to be judged and have our lives laid bare— before him. Each of us will receive whatever he deserves for the good or bad things he has done in his earthly body.

When you do a kindness to someone, do it secretly—don't tell your left hand what your right hand is doing. And your Father who knows all secrets will reward you. □ There will be glory and honor and peace from God for all who obey him.

Not because . . . we can do anything of lasting value by ourselves. Our only power and success comes from God. □ Lord, grant us peace; for all we have and are has come from you.

Ps. 62:12. 1 Cor. 3:11, 14, 15. 2 Cor. 5:10. Mt. 6:3, 4. Rom. 2:10.
2 Cor. 3:5. Is. 26:12.

Try hard to live without sinning; and be at peace with everyone so that he will be pleased with you when he returns.

Now we are no longer slaves, but God's own sons. And since we are his sons, everything he has belongs to us, for that is the way God planned.

So look upon your old sin nature as dead and unresponsive to sin, and instead be alive to God, alert to him, through Jesus Christ our Lord. Do not let sin control your puny body any longer; do not give in to its sinful desires. Do not let any part of your bodies become tools of wickedness, to be used for sinning; but give yourselves completely to God—every part of you—for you are back from death and you want to be tools in the hands of God, to be used for his good purposes. □ Obey God because you are his children; don't slip back into your old ways—doing evil because you knew no better. But be holy now in everything you do, just as the Lord is holy, who invited you to be his child. □ If you stay away from sin you will be like . . . purest gold . . . Christ himself can use you for his highest purposes.

So, my dear brothers, since future victory is sure, be strong and steady, always abounding in the Lord's work, for you know that nothing you do for the Lord is ever wasted.

2 Pet. 3:14. Gal. 4:7. Rom. 6:11–13. 1 Pet. 1:14, 15. 2 Tim. 2:21. 1 Cor. 15:58.

God's deepest secrets.

I no longer call you slaves, for a master doesn't confide in his slaves; now you are my friends, proved by the fact that I have told you everything the Father told me.

And God has actually given us his Spirit (not the world's spirit) to tell us about the wonderful free gifts of grace and blessing that God has given us.

When I think of the wisdom and scope of his plan I fall down on my knees and pray to the Father of all the great family of God—some of them already in heaven and some down here on earth—that out of his glorious, unlimited resources he will give you the mighty inner strengthening of his Holy Spirit. And I pray that Christ will be more and more at home in your hearts, living within you as you trust in him. May your roots go down deep into the soil of God's marvelous love; and may you be able to feel and understand, as all God's children should, how long, how wide, how deep, and how high his love really is; and to experience this love for yourselves, though it is so great that you will never see the end of it or fully know or understand it. And so at last you will be filled up with God himself.

1 Cor. 2:10. Jn. 15:15. 1 Cor. 2:12. Eph. 3:14–19.

Revive us to trust in you.

Only the Holy Spirit gives eternal life. □ And in the same way—by our faith—the Holy Spirit helps us with our daily problems and in our praying. For we don't even know what we should pray for, nor how to pray as we should; but the Holy Spirit prays for us with such feeling that it cannot be expressed in words. And the Father who knows all hearts knows, of course, what the Spirit is saying as he pleads for us in harmony with God's own will. □ Pray all the time. Ask God for anything in line with the Holy Spirit's wishes. Plead with him, reminding him of your needs.

I will never lay aside your laws, for you have used them to restore my joy and health. □ The old way, trying to be saved by keeping the Ten Commandments, ends in death; in the new way, the Holy Spirit gives them life. □ If you stay in me and obey my commands, you may ask any request you like, and it will be granted! □ And we are sure of this, that he will listen to us whenever we ask him for anything in line with his will.

Ps. 80:18. Jn. 6:63. Rom. 8:26, 27. Eph. 6:18. Ps. 119:93. Jn. 6:63. 2 Cor. 3:6. Jn. 15:7. 1 Jn. 5:14.

Let us come boldly to the very throne of God and stay there to receive his mercy and to find grace to help us in our times of need.

Don't worry about anything; instead, pray about everything; tell God your needs and don't forget to thank him for his answers. If you do this you will experience God's peace, which is far more wonderful than the human mind can understand. His peace will keep your thoughts and your hearts quiet and at rest as you trust in Christ Jesus. □ And so we should not be like cringing, fearful slaves, but we should behave like God's very own children, adopted into the bosom of his family, and calling to him, "Father, Father."

You can ask him for *anything,* using my name, and I will do it. □ And so, dear brothers, now we may walk right into the very Holy of Holies where God is, because of the blood of Jesus. Let us go right in, to God himself, with true hearts fully trusting him to receive us, because we have been sprinkled with Christ's blood to make us clean, and because our bodies have been washed with pure water. □ That is why we can say without any doubt or fear, "The Lord is my Helper and I am not afraid of anything that mere man can do to me."

Hebr. 4:16. Phil. 4:6, 7. Rom. 8:15. Jn. 14:14. Hebr. 10:19, 22. Hebr. 13:6.

When darkness overtakes him, light will come bursting in.

Who among you fears the Lord and obeys his Servant? If such men walk in darkness, without one ray of light, let them trust the Lord, let them rely upon their God. □ If they fall it isn't fatal, for the Lord holds them with his hand. □ Their advice is a beam of light directed into the dark corners of your mind to warn you of danger and give you a good life.

Do not rejoice against me, O my enemy, for though I fall, I will rise again! When I sit in darkness, the Lord himself will be my Light. I will be patient while the Lord punishes me, for I have sinned against him; then he will defend me from my enemies, and punish them for all the evil they have done to me. God will bring me out of my darkness into the light, and I will see his goodness.

If your eye is pure, there will be sunshine in your soul. But if your eye is clouded with evil thoughts and desires, you are in deep spiritual darkness. And oh, how deep that darkness can be!

Ps. 112:4. Is. 50:10. Ps. 37:24. Prov. 6:23. Mic. 7:8, 9. Mt. 6:22, 23.

That couldn't happen if the Lord made windows in the sky!

Have faith in God. □ You can never please God without faith. □ With God, everything is possible.

Was I too weak to save you? Is that why the house is silent and empty when I come home? Have I no longer power to deliver?

This plan of mine is not what you would work out, neither are my thoughts the same as yours! For just as the heavens are higher than the earth, so are my ways higher than yours, and my thought than yours. □ I will open up the windows of heaven for you and pour out a blessing so great you won't have room enough to take it in!

The Lord isn't too weak to save you. And he isn't getting deaf! He can hear you when you call! □ "O Lord," he cried out to God, "no one else can help us! Here we are, powerless against this mighty army. Oh, help us, Lord our God! For we trust in you alone to rescue us."

We felt we were doomed to die and saw how powerless we were to help ourselves; but that was good, for then we put everything into the hands of God, who alone could save us, for he can even raise the dead.

2 Kgs. 7:2. Mk. 11:22. Hebr. 11:6. Mt. 19:26. Is. 50:2. Is. 55:8, 9. Mal. 3:10. Is. 59:1. 2 Chron. 14:11. 2 Cor. 1:9.

Your days of mourning all will end.

Here on earth you will have many trials and sorrows. □ For we know that even the things of nature, like animals and plants, suffer in sickness and death as they await this great event. And even we Christians, although we have the Holy Spirit within us as a foretaste of future glory, also groan to be released from pain and suffering. We, too, wait anxiously for that day when God will give us our full rights as his children, including the new bodies he has promised us—bodies that will never be sick again and will never die. □ These earthly bodies make us groan and sigh.

"These are the ones coming out of the Great Tribulation," he said; "they washed their robes and whitened them by the blood of the Lamb. That is why they are here before the throne of God, serving him day and night in his temple. The one sitting on the throne will shelter them; they will never be hungry again, nor thirsty, and they will be fully protected from the scorching noontime heat. For the Lamb standing in front of the throne will feed them and be their Shepherd and lead them to the springs of the Water of Life. And God will wipe their tears away."

Is. 60:20. Jn. 16:33. Rom. 8:22, 23. 2 Cor. 5:4. Rev. 7:14–17.

*Teacher, don't you even care that we are
all about to drown?*

He is good to everyone, and his compassion is
intertwined with everything he does.

"All wild animals and birds and fish will be
afraid of you," God told him; "for I have placed
them in your power, and they are yours to use for
food, in addition to grain and vegetables." □ As
long as the earth remains, there will be spring-
time and harvest, cold and heat, winter and summer, day and night.

The Lord is good. When trouble comes, he is
the place to go! And he knows everyone who
trusts in him! □ Then God answered the lad's
cries, and the Angel of God called to Hagar from
the sky, "Hagar, what's wrong? Don't be afraid!
For God has heard the lad's cries as he is lying
there." Then God opened her eyes and she saw
a well; so she refilled the canteen and gave the lad
a drink.

So don't worry at all about having enough food
and clothing. Why be like the heathen? For they
take pride in all these things and are deeply concerned about them. But your heavenly Father
already knows perfectly well that you need them.
□ Trust . . . in the living God who always richly
gives us all we need for our enjoyment.

*Mk. 4:38. Ps. 145:9. Gen. 9:2, 3. Gen. 8:22. Nah. 1:7. Gen. 21:17,
19. Mt. 6:31, 32. 1 Tim. 6:17.*

Your strong faith.

This is the will of God, that you believe in the one he has sent.

Faith that doesn't show itself by good works is no faith at all—it is dead and useless. □ All we need is faith working through love. □ If he sows to please his own wrong desires, he will be planting seeds of evil and he will surely reap a harvest of spiritual decay and death; but if he plants the good things of the Spirit, he will reap the everlasting life which the Holy Spirit gives him. □ It is God himself who has made us what we are and given us new lives from Christ Jesus; and long ages ago he planned that we should spend these lives in helping others. □ He died under God's judgment against our sins, so that he could rescue us from constant falling into sin and make us his very own people, with cleansed hearts and real enthusiasm for doing kind things for others.

God will make you the kind of children he wants to have—will make you as good as you wish you could be!—rewarding your faith with his power. □ God is at work within you, helping you want to obey him, and then helping you do what he wants.

1 Thess. 1:3. Jn. 6:29. Jas. 2:17. Gal. 5:6. Gal. 6:8. Eph. 2:10. Tit. 2:14. 2 Thess. 1:11. Phil. 2:13.

What is it that God has said? That he has given us eternal life, and that this life is in his Son.

The Father has life in himself, and has granted his Son to have life in himself. He will even raise from the dead anyone he wants to, just as the Father does.

I am the one who raises the dead and gives them life again. Anyone who believes in me, even though he dies like anyone else, shall live again. He is given eternal life for believing in me and shall never perish. □ I am the Good Shepherd. The Good Shepherd lays down his life for the sheep. The Father loves me because I lay down my life that I may have it back again. No one can kill me without my consent—I lay down my life voluntarily. For I have the right and power to lay it down when I want to and also the right and power to take it again. For the Father has given me this right. □ I am the Way—yes, and the Truth and the Life. No one can get to the Father except by means of me. □ So whoever has God's Son has life; whoever does not have his Son, does not have life. □ You should have as little real desire for this world as a dead person does. Your real life is in heaven with Christ and God. And when Christ who is our real life comes back again, you will shine with him and share in all his glories.

1 Jn. 5:11. Jn. 5:26, 21. Jn. 11:25, 26. Jn. 10:11, 17, 18. Jn. 14:6. 1 Jn. 5:12. Col. 3:3, 4.

God did as he had promised, and Sarah became pregnant and gave Abraham a baby son.

Trust him all the time. Pour out your longings before him, for he can help. □ David took strength from the Lord. □ God will surely come and get you, and bring you out of this land of Egypt and take you back to the land he promised to the descendents of Abraham, Isaac and Jacob. □ I have seen the anguish of my people in Egypt and have heard their cries. I have come down to deliver them. Come, I will send you to Egypt. And by means of many remarkable miracles he led them out of Egypt and through the Red Sea, and back and forth through the wilderness for forty years. □ Every good thing the Lord had promised them came true.

There is no question that he will do what he says. □ God is not a man, that he should lie; he doesn't change his mind like humans do. Has he ever promised, without doing what he said? □ God also bound himself with an oath, so that those he promised to help would be perfectly sure and never need to wonder whether he might change his plans. □ Heaven and earth will disappear, but my words remain forever. □ The grass withers, the flowers fade, but the Word of our God shall stand forever.

Gen. 21:1. Ps. 62:8. 1 Sam. 30:6. Gen. 50:24. Acts 7:34, 36. Josh. 21:45. Hebr. 10:23. Num. 23:19. Hebr. 6:17. Mt. 24:35. Is. 40:8.

He will save his people from their sins.

You know that he became a man so that he could take away our sins. □ That we can be finished with sin and live a good life. □ He is able to save completely all who come to God through him.

He was wounded and bruised for *our* sins. He was chastised that we might have peace; he was lashed—and we were healed! *We* are the ones who strayed away like sheep! We, who left God's paths to follow our own. Yet God laid on *him* the guilt and sins of every one of us! He was oppressed and he was afflicted, yet he never said a word. From prison and trial they led him away to his death. □ It was written long ago that the Messiah must suffer . . . that this message of salvation should be taken from Jerusalem to all the nations: There is forgiveness of sins for all who turn to me. □ He came . . . to put away the power of sin forever by dying for us.

With mighty power, God exalted him to be a Prince and Savior . . . for repentance. □ In this man Jesus, there is forgiveness for your sins! Everyone who trusts in him is freed from all guilt and declared righteous—something the Jewish law could never do. □ Your sins have been forgiven in the name of Jesus our Savior.

Mt. 1:21. 1 Jn. 3:5. 1 Pet. 2:24. Hebr. 7:25. Is. 53:5–8. Lk. 24:46, 47. Hebr. 9:26. Acts 5:31. Acts 13:38, 39. 1 Jn. 2:12.

*The Philistine commanders demanded,
"What are these Israelis doing here?"*

Be happy if you are cursed and insulted for being a Christian, for when that happens the Spirit of God will come upon you with great glory.

Don't do anything that will cause criticism against yourself even though you know that what you do is right. □ Be careful how you behave among your unsaved neighbors; for then, even if they are suspicious of you and talk against you, they will end up praising God for your good works when Christ returns.

Don't be teamed with those who do not love the Lord, for what do the people of God have in common with the people of sin? How can light live with darkness? And what union can there be between God's temple and idols? For you are God's temple, the home of the living God, and God has said of you, "I will live in them and walk among them, and I will be their God and they shall be my people."

You have been chosen by God himself . . . that you may show to others how God called you out of the darkness into his wonderful light.

1 Sam. 29:3. 1 Pet. 4:14. Rom. 14:16. 1 Pet. 2:12. 2 Cor. 6:14, 16. 1 Pet. 2:9.

He calls his own sheep by name and leads them out.

God's truth stands firm like a great rock, and nothing can shake it. It is a foundation stone with these words written on it: "The Lord knows those who are really his." □ At the Judgment many will tell me, "Lord, Lord, we told others about you and used your name to cast out demons and to do many other great miracles." But I will reply, "You have never been mine. Go away, for your deeds are evil." □ For the Lord watches over all the plans and paths of godly men, but the paths of the godless lead to doom.

I have tattooed your name upon my palm. □ Seal me in your heart with permanent betrothal, for love is strong as death and jealousy is as cruel as Sheol. □ The Lord is good. When trouble comes, he is the place to go! And he knows everyone who trusts in him!

There are many homes up there where my Father lives, and I am going to prepare them for your coming. When everything is ready, then I will come and get you, so that you can always be with me where I am.

Jn. 10:3. 2 Tim. 2:19. Mt. 7:22, 23. Ps. 1:6. Is. 49:16. Song 8:6. Nah. 1:7. Jn. 14:2, 3.

Free from all sin and guilt on that day when he returns.

You who were once so far away from God . . . were his enemies and hated him and were separated from him by your evil thoughts and actions, yet now he has brought you back as his friends. He has done this through the death on the cross of his own human body, and now as a result Christ has brought you into the very presence of God, and you are standing there before him with nothing left against you—nothing left that he could even chide you for; the only condition is that you fully believe the Truth, standing in it steadfast and firm, strong in the Lord, convinced of the Good News that Jesus died for you, and never shifting from trusting him to save you. □ Live clean, innocent lives as children of God in a dark world full of people who are crooked and stubborn. Shine out among them like beacon lights.

And now—all glory to him who alone is God, who saves us through Jesus Christ our Lord; yes, splendor and majesty, all power and authority are his from the beginning; his they are and his they evermore shall be. And he is able to keep you from slipping and falling away, and to bring you, sinless and perfect, into his glorious presence with mighty shouts of everlasting joy. Amen.

1 Cor. 1:8. Col. 1:21–23. Phil. 2:15. Jude 24, 25.

He will protect his godly ones.

If we say we are his friends, but go on living in spiritual darkness and sin, we are lying. But if we are living in the light of God's presence, just as Christ does, then we have wonderful fellowship and joy with each other, and the blood of Jesus his Son cleanses us from every sin. □ Let us strip off anything that slows us down or holds us back, and especially those sins that wrap themselves so tightly around our feet and trip us up.

I would have you learn this great fact: that a life of doing right is the wisest life there is. If you live that kind of life, you'll not limp or stumble as you run. Don't do as the wicked do. Avoid their haunts—turn away, go somewhere else. Look straight ahead; don't even turn your head to look. Watch your step. Stick to the path and be safe. Don't sidetrack; pull back your foot from danger.

The Lord will always deliver me from all evil and will bring me into his heavenly kingdom. To God be the glory forever and ever. Amen.

1 Sam. 2:9. 1 Jn. 1:6, 7. Hebr. 12:1. Prov. 4:11, 12, 14, 15, 25–27. 2 Tim. 4:18.

*Try to find out and do whatever the Lord
wants you to.*

God wants you to be holy and pure. ☐ Quit
quarreling with God! Agree with him and you
will have peace at last! His favor will surround
you if you will only admit that you were wrong.
☐ And this is the way to have eternal life—by
knowing you, the only true God, and Jesus Christ,
the one you sent to earth! ☐ And we know that
Christ, God's Son, has come to help us understand and find the true God. And now we are in
God because we are in Jesus Christ his Son, who
is the only true God; and he is eternal Life.

Ever since we first heard about you we have
kept on praying and asking God to help you
understand what he wants you to do; asking him
to make you wise about spiritual things. ☐ God,
the glorious Father of our Lord Jesus Christ . . .
give you wisdom to see clearly and really understand who Christ is and all that he has done for
you. I pray that your hearts will be flooded with
light so that you can see something of the future
he has called you to share. I want you to realize
that God has been made rich because we who are
Christ's have been given to him! I pray that you
will begin to understand how incredibly great his
power is to help those who believe him.

*Eph. 5:17. 1 Thess. 4:3. Job 22:21. Jn. 17:3. 1 Jn. 5:20. Col. 1:9.
Eph. 1:17–19.*

His royal title: Wonderful.

And Christ became a human being and lived here on earth among us and was full of loving forgiveness and truth. And some of us have seen his glory—the glory of the only Son of the heavenly Father. □ Your promises are backed by all the honor of your name.

He shall be called Emmanuel meaning God with us. □ Jesus: he will save his people from their sins.

Everyone will honor the Son, just as they honor the Father. □ God raised him up to the heights of heaven and gave him a name which is above every other name. □ Far, far above any other king or ruler or dictator or leader. Yes, his honor is far more glorious than that of anyone else either in this world or in the world to come. And God has put all things under his feet. □ A name was written on his forehead, and only he knew its meaning . . . King of Kings and Lord of Lords.

We cannot imagine the power of the Almighty. □ If there is any other, what is his name?

Is. 9:6. Jn. 1:14. Ps. 138:2. Mt. 1:23. Mt. 1:21. Jn. 5:23. Phil. 2:9. Eph. 1:21, 22. Rev. 19:12, 16. Job 37:23. Prov. 30:4.

Counselor.

And the Spirit of the Lord shall rest upon him, the Spirit of wisdom, understanding, counsel and might; the Spirit of knowledge and of the fear of the Lord. His delight will be obedience to the Lord.

Can't you hear the voice of wisdom? She is standing at the city gates and at every fork in the road, and at the door of every house. "Listen, men!" she calls. "How foolish and naive you are! Let me give you understanding. O foolish ones, let me show you common sense! Listen to me! For I have important information for you. Everything I say is right and true. I, Wisdom, give good advice and common sense. Because of my strength, kings reign in power."

The Lord of Hosts is a wonderful teacher and gives the farmer wisdom. □ If you want to know what God wants you to do, ask him, and he will gladly tell you, for he is always ready to give a bountiful supply of wisdom to all who ask him; he will not resent it. □ Trust the Lord completely; don't ever trust yourself. In everything you do, put God first, and he will direct you and crown your efforts with success.

Is. 9:6. Is. 11:2, 3. Prov. 8:1–7, 14. Is. 28:29. Jas. 1:5. Prov. 3:5, 6.

The Mighty God.

You are the fairest of all; your words are filled with grace; God himself is blessing you forever. Arm yourself, O Mighty One, so glorious, so majestic! And in your majesty go on to victory, defending truth, humility and justice. Go forth to awe-inspiring deeds! Your throne, O God, endures forever. Justice is your royal scepter. □ Who is this . . . with his magnificent garments of crimson? Who is this in kingly robes, marching in the greatness of his strength? "It is I, the Lord, announcing your salvation; I, the Lord, the one who is mighty to save."

See, God has come to save me! I will trust and not be afraid, for the Lord is my strength and song; he is my salvation. □ But thanks be to God! For through what Christ has done, he has triumphed over us.

God's Son shines out with God's glory, and all that God's Son is and does marks him as God. He is the one who died to cleanse us and clear our record of all sin, and then sat down in highest honor beside the great God of heaven. □ He is able to keep you from slipping and falling away, and to bring you, sinless and perfect, into his glorious presence with mighty shouts of everlasting joy. Amen.

Is. 9:6. Ps. 45:2–4, 6. Is. 63:1. Is. 12:2. 2 Cor. 2:14. Hebr. 1:3. Jude 25.

The Everlasting Father.

O Israel, listen: Jehovah is our God, Jehovah alone.

I and the Father are one. The Father is in me, and I in the Father. □ You don't know who I am, so you don't know who my Father is. If you knew me, then you would know him too. □ Philip said, "Sir, show us the Father and we will be satisfied." Jesus replied, "Don't you even yet know who I am, Philip, even after all this time I have been with you? Anyone who has seen me has seen the Father! So why are you asking to see him?" □ Here am I and the children God gave me. □ When he sees all that is accomplished by the anguish of his soul, he shall be satisfied. □ "I am the A and the Z, the Beginning and the Ending of all things," says God, who is the Lord, the All Powerful One who is, and was, and is coming again! □ I was in existence before Abraham was ever born! □ The sovereign God . . . I Am has sent me!

Of his Son he says, "Your kingdom, O God, will last forever and ever." □ He was before all else began and it is his power that holds everything together. □ In Christ there is all of God in a human body.

Is. 9:6. Deut. 6:4. Jn. 10:30, 38. Jn. 8:19. Jn. 14:8, 9. Hebr. 2:13. Is. 53:11. Rev. 1:8. Jn. 8:58. Ex. 3:14. Hebr. 1:8. Col. 1:17. Col. 2:9.

The Prince of Peace.

Help him to give justice to your people, even to the poor. May the mountains and hills flourish in prosperity because of his good reign. Help him to defend the poor and needy and to crush their oppressors. May the poor and needy revere you constantly, as long as sun and moon continue in the skies! Yes, forever! □ Glory to God . . . and peace on earth for all those pleasing him.

Because the mercy of our God is very tender . . . heaven's dawn is about to break upon us, to give light to those who sit in darkness and death's shadow, and to guide us to the path of peace. □ Peace with God through Jesus, the Messiah, who is Lord of all creation.

I have told you all this so that you will have peace of heart and mind. Here on earth you will have many trials and sorrows; but cheer up, for I have overcome the world. □ I am leaving you with a gift—peace of mind and heart! And the peace I give isn't fragile like the peace the world gives. So don't be troubled or afraid. □ God's peace . . . far more wonderful than the human mind can understand. His peace will keep your thoughts and your hearts quiet and at rest as you trust in Christ Jesus.

Is. 9:6. Ps. 72:2–5. Lk. 2:14. Lk. 1:78, 79. Acts 10:36. Jn. 16:33. Jn. 14:27. Phil. 4:7.

*Thank God for his Son—his Gift too won-
derful for words.*

Shout with joy before the Lord, O earth! Obey
him gladly; come before him, singing with joy.
Go through his open gates with great thanksgiving; enter his courts with praise. Give thanks to
him and bless his name. □ For unto us a Child
is born; unto us. a Son is given; and the govern-
ment shall be upon his shoulder. These will be his
royal titles: Wonderful, Counselor, the Mighty
God, the Everlasting Father, the Prince of Peace.

God loved the world so much. □ He did not
spare even his own Son for us but gave him up
for us all. □ There was only one left—his only
son. He finally sent him. □ Anyone who believes
in him shall . . . have eternal life. □ He has
given you the whole world to use, and life and
even death are your servants. He has given you
all of the present and all of the future. All are
yours, and you belong to Christ, and Christ is
God's.

Oh, that these men would praise the Lord for
his lovingkindness and for all of his wonderful
deeds! □ I bless the holy name of God with all
my heart.

Oh, how I praise the Lord. How I rejoice in
God my Savior!

*2 Cor. 9:15. Ps. 100:1, 2, 4. Is. 9:6. Jn. 3:16. Rom. 8:32. Mk. 12:6.
Jn. 3:16. 1 Cor. 3:22, 23. Ps. 107:21. Ps. 103:1. Lk. 1:46, 47.*

*Be strong and steady, always abounding in
the Lord's work.*

You know that nothing you do for the Lord is
ever wasted. □ Just as you trusted Christ to save
you, trust him, too, for each day's problems; live
in vital union with him. Let your roots grow down
into him and draw up nourishment from him. See
that you go on growing in the Lord, and become
strong and vigorous in the truth you were taught.
Let your lives overflow with joy and thanksgiving
for all he has done. □ Those enduring to the end
shall be saved.

Your faith . . . it is strong.

All of us must quickly carry out the tasks assigned us by the one who sent me, for there is
little time left before the night falls and all work
comes to an end.

If he sows to please his own wrong desires, he
will be planting seeds of evil and he will surely
reap a harvest of spiritual decay and death; but
if he plants the good things of the Spirit, he will
reap the everlasting life which the Holy Spirit
gives him. And let us not get tired of doing what
is right, for after a while we will reap a harvest
of blessing if we don't get discouraged and give
up.

*1 Cor. 15:58. 1 Cor. 15:58. Col. 2:6, 7. Mt. 24:13. 2 Cor. 1:24.
Jn. 9:4. Gal. 6:8, 9.*

*He is able to save completely all who come
to God through him.*

I am the Way—yes, and the Truth and the Life.
No one can get to the Father except by means of
me. □ There is salvation in no one else! Under
all heaven there is no other name for men to call
upon to save them.

My sheep recognize my voice, and I know
them, and they follow me. I give them eternal life
and they shall never perish. No one shall snatch
them away from me, for my Father has given
them to me, and he is more powerful than anyone else, so no one can kidnap them from me. □
God who began the good work within you will
keep right on helping you grow in his grace until
his task within you is finally finished on that day
when Jesus Christ returns. □ Is anything too hard
for God?

And now—all glory to him who alone is God,
who saves us through Jesus Christ our Lord; yes,
splendor and majesty, all power and authority are
his from the beginning; his they are and his they
evermore shall be. And he is able to keep you
from slipping and falling away, and to bring you,
sinless and perfect, into his glorious presence with
mighty shouts of everlasting joy. Amen.

*Hebr. 7:25. Jn. 14:6. Acts 4:12. Jn. 10:27, 28. Phil. 1:6. Gen.
18:14. Jude 24, 25.*

Christ himself is our way of peace.

For God was in Christ, restoring the world to himself, no longer counting men's sins against them but blotting them out. This is the wonderful message he has given us to tell others. For God took the sinless Christ and poured into him our sins. Then, in exchange, he poured God's goodness into us! □ It was through what his Son did that God cleared a path for everything to come to him—all things in heaven and on earth—for Christ's death on the cross has made peace with God for all by his blood. And now as a result Christ has brought you into the very presence of God, and you are standing there before him with nothing left against you—nothing left that he could even chide you for. □ He forgave all your sins, and blotted out the charges proved against you, the list of his commandments which you had not obeyed. He took this list of sins and destroyed it by nailing it to Christ's cross.

I am leaving you with a gift—peace of mind and heart! And the peace I give isn't fragile like the peace the world gives. So don't be troubled or afraid.

Eph. 2:14. 2 Cor. 5:19, 21. Col. 1:20, 22. Col. 2:13, 14. Jn. 14:27.

Your sins are forgiven!

I will forgive and forget their sins. □ Only God can forgive sins.

I, yes, I alone am he who blots away your sins for my own sake and will never think of them again. □ What happiness for those whose guilt has been forgiven! What joys when sins are covered over! What relief for those who have confessed their sins and God has cleared their record. □ Where is another God like you, who pardons the sins of the survivors among his people?

God has forgiven you because you belong to Christ. □ The blood of Jesus his Son cleanses us from every sin. If we say that we have no sin, we are only fooling ourselves, and refusing to accept the truth. But if we confess our sins to him, he can be depended on to forgive us and to cleanse us from every wrong.

He has removed our sins as far away from us as the east is from the west. □ Sin need never again be your master, for now you are no longer tied to the law where sin enslaves you, but you are free under God's favor and mercy.

Mk. 2:5. Jer. 31:34. Mk. 2:7. Is. 43:25. Ps. 32:1, 2. Mic. 7:18. Eph. 4:32. 1 Jn. 1:7–9. Ps. 103:12. Rom. 6:14.

You know how he has cared for you again and again here in the wilderness, just as a father cares for his child!

I brought you to myself as though on eagle's wings. □ In his love and pity he redeemed them and lifted them up and carried them through all the years. □ He spreads his wings over them, even as an eagle overspreads her young. She carries them upon her wings—as does the Lord his people!

I will be your God through all your lifetime, yes, even when your hair is white with age. I made you and I will care for you. I will carry you along and be your Savior. □ For this great God is our God forever and ever. He will be our guide until we die. □ The steps of good men are directed by the Lord. He delights in each step they take. If they fall it isn't fatal, for the Lord holds them with his hands.

Give your burdens to the Lord. He will carry them. He will not permit the godly to slip or fall. □ Don't worry about *things*—food, drink, and clothes. Your heavenly Father already knows perfectly well that you need them.

Deut. 1:31. Ex. 19:4. Is. 63:9. Deut. 32:11, 12. Is. 46:4. Ps. 48:14. Ps. 37:23, 24. Ps. 55:22. Mt. 6:25, 32.

There are still many nations to be conquered.

I haven't learned all I should even yet, but I keep working toward that day when I will finally be all that Christ saved me for and wants me to be.

You are to be perfect, even as your Father in heaven is perfect. □ You need more than faith; you must also work hard to be good, and even that is not enough. For then you must learn to know God better and discover what he wants you to do. Next, learn to put aside your own desires so that you will become patient and godly, gladly letting God have his way with you. This will make possible the next step, which is for you to enjoy other people and to like them, and finally you will grow to love them deeply.

My prayer for you is that you will overflow more and more with love for others, and at the same time keep on growing in spiritual knowledge and insight.

No mere man has ever seen, heard or even imagined what wonderful things God has ready for those who love the Lord.

There is a full complete rest *still waiting* for the people of God. □ Your eyes will see the King in his beauty, and the highlands of heaven far away.

Josh. 13:1. Phil. 3:12. Mt. 5:48. 2 Pet. 1:5–7. Phil. 1:9. 1 Cor. 2:9. Hebr. 4:9. Is. 33:17.

Now that you have finished *The One Year Book of Bible Readings,* you may want to use *The One Year Book of Personal Prayer* to direct your devotions in the coming year. *The One Year Bible* is also ideal for personal devotions, and it is available in many translations, including *The Living Bible, The New American Standard Bible,* the King James Version, the New King James Version, the New International Version, and the New Revised Standard Version. All these One Year books and Bibles are available at your local Christian bookstore.